W9-ARV-450

Baltimore with Children

Mike Strzelecki

Camino Books, Inc.

Philadelphia

Copyright © 2004 by Mike Strzelecki
All Rights Reserved

No part of this book may be reproduced in any form or by any electronic or
mechanical means including information storage and retrieval systems without permission in writing from the publisher, except by a reviewer who may
quote brief passages in a review.

Manufactured in the United States of America

1 2 3 4 5 07 06 05 04

Library of Congress Cataloging-in-Publication Data

Strzelecki, Mike, 1963-
    Baltimore with children / Mike Strzelecki.
        p. cm.
    ISBN 0-940159-76-7 (paperbound : alk. paper)
    1. Baltimore Region (Md.)—Guidebooks. 2.
Children—Travel—Maryland—Baltimore Region. 3. Family
recreation—Maryland—Baltimore Region—Guidebooks. I. Title.

    F189.B13S84 2004
    917.52'604044—dc22   2004001388

Cover and interior design: Jerilyn Bockorick

This book is available at a special discount on bulk purchases for promotional,
business, and educational use.

Publisher
Camino Books
P. O. Box 59026
Philadelphia, PA 19102

www.caminobooks.com

This book is dedicated to Zi Li and Graham,
charter members of the Strzelecki Explorers Club.

Contents

Camping 28

City Parks 40

County and State Parks 51

DC Attractions 71

Acknowledgments

Ed Jutkowitz, my editor and publisher, gets the biggest pat on the back for recognizing the value in publishing a guidebook series for parents, and for making Baltimore part of that series. Thanks, Ed!

My wife Kelly, again and again, has shown her tolerance in allowing me to skip off and research yet another attraction for this book. Her unwavering support does not go unnoticed, and is greatly appreciated. And Zi Li and Graham get extra-big bear-hugs for making the research trips fun and for imposing their own toddler perspectives on the subject matter.

Finally, the advice and commentary of friends honed this book to its final product. Big kisses go out to Geoff Baker and Ann Hackeling, Cathy and David Fu, Rich and Debbie McGuire, Sarah Montgomery and Daryl Walsh, Amy Schacht and Paul Whong, Jackie and Rob Scott, Judy and Michael Wall, Bob and Michele Wetzelberger, and Lynda and Paul Willing.

Introduction

We, as parents, spend our entire existence educating and enlightening our children, instilling in them values and morals, and (hopefully) molding them into upstanding adults. We often forget that the parent/child relationship is symbiotic. In return, we receive pleasures and satisfactions of unquantifiable magnitude. Likewise, we often derive from our children a renewed and re-energized sense of inquisitiveness, wanderlust, and exploration—this time experienced through the prism of youth and innocence. That's where *Baltimore With Children* comes in. The book is designed to guide families through such periods of discovery—when your child's thirst for fun and adventure extends beyond the four walls of your living room. The guide discusses over 250 attractions in the Baltimore area agreeable to both parent and child.

Baltimore With Children is not a definitive work on the subject. It's merely a guide to what I consider to be the best options for fun in particular categories of attractions (i.e., best museums, best nature centers, best places to ride a bike, camp, or swim). I chose attractions based on personal experience and research, and on countless interviews with other parents. Attractions covered span the entire Baltimore metropolitan area, plus some outlying areas. For each attraction I include commentary with personal observations and recommendations, directions, visitor information such as hours and admission (if any), and contact information. The hours and admissions included were those in effect at the time I researched each attraction, and may have changed. Treat them as approximations or call ahead to verify. Lastly, for the sake of space, I did not address disabled access or pet restrictions. Families for whom these are special concerns should phone ahead.

Thanks for sharing Baltimore with your family and for using this book as your road map.

Agritainment

Maryland farms are going belly-up at a rate of about 200 each year. They're being pinched out of business by low crop prices, a hair-trigger economy, and overzealous developers. A growing number of small farms are turning to "agritainment" for salvation. Farmers are opening their operations to the general public. Pick-your-own farms, petting zoos, Christmas tree farms, and wineries are all examples of Maryland agritainment venues. Along with crops, farmers harvest fun and smiles. Here's an assortment of agritainment farms near Baltimore.

Baugher's

For five decades, the Baugher family has been growing fresh fruits and vegetables for Carroll County residents, baking fresh-from-the-oven pies and serving up an abundance of grandma-caliber home cooking. Based in Westminster, Baugher's has a pick-your-own orchard west of town, and a restaurant and farmers' market a few miles away. It makes for a nice country-living escape from the city.

Kids will most relish a visit to their orchard and farm, located on Baugher Road, where they can pick their own fruit. Strawberry lovers will want to visit in early June, while those craving sweet cherries and black raspberries should wait until later in the month. Sour cherries ripen early in July. In fall, apples and peaches are ripe for picking. Specific times when fruit ripens vary with weather conditions, so call first to verify availability.

Baugher's offers nice, kid-friendly touches at its farm. Fruit pickers are carted to the field in a wagon. Picnic tables and play areas are spread around, and a small petting zoo, open from June through October, provides a pleasant diversion. Pumpkin-picking and hayrides are also offered on fall weekends.

Sweet-toothed parents will gravitate to the bakery and farm market, where no less than three dozen kinds of fruit pies are crafted. Pies made from fresher ingredients could not possibly be found. Cakes, brownies, muffins, and other pastries are also on the menu. Next door is the orchard market where produce and farm foods can be bought.

Baugher's also runs a busy fruit market and restaurant closer to town. It's a great place to buy the full array of locally grown fruits and vegetables, but it also offers lots of plants, gardening tools, some handcrafted gifts, decorative items, and a wide selection of jarred foods like apple butter and jams. The restaurant next door is very small-townish, and is busy enough that a rambunctious child will not so much as raise an eyebrow. The menu is large and the food inexpensive. The menu reads like one from 30 years ago, with items like chicken livers, breaded veal, and hamburger steak. Remember to nightcap each meal with a slice of homemade pie—a bargain at $1.50.

Locations and Directions: The restaurant and fruit market are located at 289 West Main Street, in Westminster. From Baltimore, take Interstate 795 west, and where it terminates, follow Route 140 west to Westminster. Just past Westminster, turn left onto Route 31. The restaurant and fruit market are down the hill on the right. The farm and orchard are located at 1236 Baugher Road. To get there, continue straight on Route 140 for two miles past the restaurant and market store, and turn right onto Baugher Road. The facilities are immediately to the right.

Hours: The orchard and farm market are open daily from June to December 24, from 8 a.m. to 6 p.m., with reduced hours in December. The restaurant is open daily from 7:30 a.m. to 9 p.m. The fruit market next to the restaurant is open daily from 8 a.m. to 9 p.m.

Website and Phone: www.baughers.com; (410) 848-5541.

Clark's Elioak Farm

For 20 years, former state senator James Clark, Jr., has been dairying, raising sweet corn, and selling produce on his 540-acre farm on the Columbia/Ellicott City border. He recently made the move to agritourism, converting a portion of his operation into a petting farm and agricultural education center. This demure, but well-maintained, attraction draws swarms of kids from spring through fall. The most popular stopping point is the petting zoo, which is well stocked with lots of goats, pigs, turkeys, rabbits, sheep, an emu, and even a battalion of llamas. The Clarks also offer a pumpkin patch, hayrides, a hay maze, pony rides, and plenty of space for running around. Special seasonal programs include scarecrow-making and face-painting. Folk concerts are occasionally held. A modest farm store on the premises sells produce, crafts, art, and private-label goods like jams and honey. The farm is splendidly beautiful, and is a breath of fresh air amid the suburban sprawl of Columbia and Ellicott City.

Location and Directions: At 10380 Clarksville Pike (Route 108), in Ellicott City. From Baltimore, take Interstate 70 west. In Ellicott City, take Route 29 south. In about five miles, take Route 108 west. Continue for two miles to the farm, which is on the right.

Hours and Admission: The farm is open from spring through fall. Hours vary according to day and season. Admission is $3 per person (with children under 1 free). A pony ride is $2 and a hayride is $1.50.

Website and Phone: www.clarklandfarm.com; (410) 730-4049.

Horizon Organic Farm and Education Center

Organic foods are more and more on the public conscience these days. Horizon Organic Dairy is the largest organic dairy-farming operation in the country, with a 3,800-acre spread in Idaho and a smaller farm near Baltimore, in Gambrills. You may recall Horizon-brand products from your grocery; their logo features a cheery black and white cow bounding across the face of the earth, wielding a yellow banner.

The primary purpose of Horizon's Gambrills operation is to educate the public on the importance of organic agriculture, but a visit also provides an enjoyable way for families to pass an afternoon. Regular guided walk-in tours of the organic farm are offered on weekends from 10 a.m. to 4 p.m., and on weekdays by appointment (groups of 10 or more). Tours last about one hour. Participants get to browse through barns and check out a day in the life of a hormone- and antibiotic-free cow. With good timing, you may get to see one of the bovines being milked.

Tours include a visit to the Discovery Barn, where interactive exhibits teach guests all about organic farming and local environmental issues. Follow the path a drop of milk takes from swollen udder to bowl of Captain Crunch. Learn about pasteurization. Find out which garden bugs are good, and which are evil pests. Kids can crawl through a tunnel to see first-hand the difference between healthy organic soil and chemically depleted soil. Tours include a hayride across farm grounds.

Following the tour, feel free to wander certain parts of the 875-acre farm. There is a picnic pavilion for lunch. Pack your own or visit the snack bar, which offers lots of healthy snacks like salads and organic beef hot dogs. It should come as no surprise that the ice cream is particularly tasty. In summer, the dairy farm has Family Farm Fest Saturdays featuring music and kid-centered activities. In late summer, kids can negotiate a cornfield maze. A nice market on the premises sells lots of organic foods, gardening paraphernalia, some recycled wares, and a sizable allotment of goods based on the theme of the Holstein cow. The farm also gives regular classes on such relevant topics as organic gardening, composting, and cooking with organic foods.

Horizon's farm occupies the grounds of the former dairy farm run by, and operated for, the U.S. Naval Academy. In 1911, a large number of academy midshipmen, including the captain of the football team, were stricken with typhoid fever from drinking tainted milk. The academy decided to operate their own dairy farm instead of entrusting their milk supply to others. They operated the farm until 2000, at which time it was turned over to Horizon as an education center. Bill the Goat, the Naval Academy mascot, still resides here and can be visited on the tour.

Location and Directions: At 100 Dairy Lane, in Gambrills. From Baltimore, take Interstate 97 south. Take Exit 7, Route 3, south (not Business Route 3). Stay left, continuing on Route 3. At the first light, turn right onto Route 175, heading west. Continue for one mile, and turn left onto Dairy Lane.

Hours and Admission: Tuesdays through Saturdays from 10 a.m. to 5 p.m., and Sundays from noon to 5 p.m. Closed on Mondays. Admission to the farm is free, which offers access to the market and 4-H Club animal barn. Guided tours, which include a stop at the Discovery Barn, cost $7 for adults 13-61, $5.50 for seniors 62 and up, $4.50 for kids 2-12, and are free for infants under 2.

Website and Phone: www.horizonorganic.com/farm/index.html; (410) 923-7600.

Maryland State Symbols

Bird—Baltimore Oriole
Boat—Skipjack
Cat—Calico
Crustacean—Maryland Blue Crab
Dinosaur—Astrodon johnstoni
Dog—Chesapeake Bay Retriever
Drink—Milk
Fish—Rockfish (Striped Bass)
Flower—Black-Eyed Susan
Folk Dance—Square Dance
Insect—Baltimore Checkerspot Butterfly
Reptile—Diamondback Terrapin
Song—"Maryland, My Maryland"
Sport—Jousting
Tree—White Oak

Larriland Farm

Baltimore-area residents are fortunate to live in close proximity to one of the nation's leading agritainment operations. Larriland Farm is situated in the patchwork farmland of western Howard County. It's a 285-acre expanse of apple and peach orchards, berry patches, vegetable fields, flower gardens, ponds, and other attractions—all open for public enjoyment. Few attractions are as perfectly suited for both parent and child.

Late spring and early summer berry-picking is fun and not very crowded, but autumn is the best time to visit Larriland Farm. The apple orchards are hung thick with the voluptuous fruit and the surrounding hillsides are ablaze in yellows, oranges, and russets. (If it is peaches you desire, late summer is the time to visit.) The farm boasts 18 acres of apples, featuring about 20 varieties. Apple-picking season begins in late August when the Galas ripen, and extends through early November when the tasty Pink Ladies dot the trees (a variety the farm owner calls her "hidden jewel"). In between, unusual crowd-pleasing varieties like Mutsu, Braeburn, and Suncrisps come of age. Taste-test several varieties, paying particular

▲ Spring blueberry picking at Larriland Farm

attention to those not readily available in retail stores. Pick generously and with an open mind; think applesauce and fritters and pie.
Vegetables like broccoli, beets, tomatoes, and spinach are also available for picking.

After gathering produce, work your way to the lower barn
area, where visitors congregate to taste hot-from-the-pan, stick-to-
the-ribs apple fritters—the best in the area. Wash them down with a
glass of freshly pressed cider.

Before leaving, the kids will want to join the swarm of other
children buzzing about the barn attractions. There are penned-up
cows and pigs to observe, a hay-bale maze to negotiate, hayrides to
explore the farm's far-flung territories, and a haunted house walk-
through for toddlers. Don't forget to drop by the pumpkin patch to
pluck your own special jack-o-lantern-to-be. Before leaving, parents may want to check out the farm store in the weatherbeaten red
barn, where cider, baked goods, and other produce may be purchased. Larriland Farm also offers cut-your-own Christmas trees
leading up to the holiday season.

A visit to Larriland Farm tends to gobble up much of the day,
but the experience presents a unique way to expose children to the
rural lifestyle. And rest assured that you are supporting a forward-
thinking organization that values environmental ethics and land
stewardship; Larriland Farm won the Senator James Clark Jr. Land
Stewardship Award for its environment-friendly land management
practices.

▲ Hauling apples and kids at Larriland Farm

Location and Directions: At 2415 Woodbine Road, in Woodbine. From Baltimore, take Interstate 70 west. Take Exit 73, Route 94, and turn left, heading south. Continue on Route 94 for about three miles. Larriland Farm is on the left.

Hours: The farm is open from late May through early November, and then again on weekends around Christmas. Specific hours vary widely depending on the season. Call or check their website for details.

Website and Phone: www.pickyourown.com; (410) 442-2605.

Sharp's at Waterford Farm

Waterford Farm, tucked in a bucolic nook of southwestern Howard County, near Brookville, offers agritainment with a different slant. While most farms shoot for the festive, amusement park atmosphere to attract families, this farm seems more interested in providing an educational experience. Activities focus on learning about farms and nature, and Sharp's offers acres and acres of pretty farmland, ponds, and meadows on which to absorb the experience.

Most activities at the farm are geared toward groups like scout troops and school classes. Their most popular ticket is the general farm tour, which provides unique insight into farm life and the environment. Specific tours can be arranged that hone in on such topics as butterflies, birds, or pond life. Each tour must have at least 15 participants, and the subject matter can be tailored to the age group. Group fishing, campfire programs, and hayrides are also available.

For individual families, the farm is open on weekends from late September through October. The farm is probably most noted for its huge pumpkin patch, where visitors are hauled by tractor to the field to pluck their own autumn orb. They also offer pick-your-own herbs and flowers in the greenhouse. A corn maze, small farm museum, and petting zoo, where kids can feed the slobbering beasts, round out a nice fall Saturday afternoon.

Location and Directions: At 4003 Jennings Chapel Road. From Baltimore, take Interstate 70 west for about 17 miles. Take Exit 76, Route 97, and continue south, toward Olney, for just over six miles. Turn right onto Jennings Chapel Road and continue for just over one mile. Look for the Waterford Farm sign to the right.

Website and Phone: www.sharpfarm.com; (301) 854-6275.

Weber's Farm

For most of the year, Weber's Farm market stands solitary amidst suburban sprawl—a mild-mannered roadside stand hawking traditional farm goods like produce, jams and jellies, hand-dipped ice cream, fudge, homemade pies, and crafts. But come fall, it peels off its gingham apron and lacy bonnet, and transforms itself into a local epicenter for fall family entertainment.

The party commences around September 1, when apple-picking begins. Gala, jonathan, cortlandt, golden delicious, and red delicious fill the trees until the last ones are plucked. Kids can visit the menagerie of goats, sheep, turkeys, rabbits, and other small critters that call the farm home. Hayrides around the farm are offered for $1 per person, and in October, a buck will also get you a walk through the Boo Barn. Pumpkinland, a series of pumpkins painted and decorated to resemble Mother Goose characters, is another enjoyable children's activity that runs through October.

Older kids will have a blast making their own scarecrow in a series of October weekend workshops. The $15 fee is reduced if you bring your own shirt and pants for the straw guy. There's also a maze made of hay, lots of food stands, and fresh-pressed apple cider. The farm runs other special events throughout the year, such as a fire prevention weekend and a peach recipe contest. For an added dash of fun, visit during the Johnny Appleseed festival, usually held over the course of an entire weekend in late September, when music and extra kids' games are offered. Check their website for a calendar of specific events.

The farm is situated close to the city, just one mile from the northernmost arc of the beltway. Farming operations have occurred on the premises since 1908, although Pine Grove Middle School was built on much of the original farm land.

Location and Directions: At 2526 Proctor Lane. From Baltimore, take the Interstate 695 beltway to the north of the city. Take Exit 30B, Perring Parkway, heading north. Continue on Perring Parkway for about one-half mile until it dead-ends. Turn left onto Waltham Woods Road. At the first stop sign, turn right onto Proctor Lane. Weber's Farm is on the left.

Hours: From April 12 to October 30, the farm is open daily from 9 a.m. to 8 p.m., with reduced hours on holidays. From October 31 to November 30, it's open daily from 9 a.m. to 6 p.m., with reduced hours on Thanksgiving. From December 1 to December 24, it's open daily from 9 a.m. to 8 p.m., with reduced hours on Christmas Eve. The farm is closed from December 25 to April 11.

Website and Phone: www.webersfarm.com; (410) 668-4488.

Bicycling

Congested streets often make bicycle riding in and around Baltimore dangerous and frustrating, especially when children are involved. Luckily, the Baltimore area offers plenty of "rails-to-trails" facilities, and other opportunities for bicycling on traffic-free pathways. Here is a selection of Baltimore's safest and most enjoyable places to push pedal. Please note that these are all multi-use trails, which means bikers will be sharing the pathways with runners, hikers, in-line skaters, and a trickle of skateboarders.

For parents seeking more information on bicycling opportunities in the Baltimore area, contact the Baltimore Bicycling Club. Information can be found at their website at www.baltobikeclub. org. A list of bicycling clubs in the state of Maryland can be found at www.bicycle-rides.com/ClubLinksMD.asp.

Baltimore and Annapolis Trail

The Baltimore and Annapolis (B&A) Trail is a 13.3-mile-long straight shot between Glen Burnie and Annapolis. The trail is a project of the Rails-to-Trails Conservancy, and follows the course of a former passenger and cargo railway that bounced between the two cities until 1968. The trail is paved, flat, and about ten feet wide. Many rails-to-trails run through areas that are quiet and remote. This trail is more urban, following Route 2 much of the way, often pinching between strip shopping centers and circling a shopping mall. This aspect may appeal to some, since access to shops and restaurants is frequent. Since about half of Anne Arundel County's population lives within a mile of the B&A Trail, it tends to be very busy.

Access to the B&A Trail is plentiful. There is a parking lot at the northern terminus, on Dorsey Road, just off Route 3, in Glen

Burnie. Marley Station Mall provides another access point. The trail runs through downtown Glen Burnie. At the Jumpers Hole Road crossing, about four miles south of the northern terminus, are picnic tables and a food store. The trail's midway point is at the Earleigh Heights Ranger Station, at mile seven, which offers water, a restroom, a telephone, picnic tables, and parking. The lovely Victorian building was once a post office, general store, and railroad station.

Nine miles south of Glen Burnie is the restored Severna Park Railroad Station, which was built in 1919 and is open for public inspection. Several strip malls encroach on the trail as it passes through Severna Park. Along its southern section, the B&A Trail passes through mostly leafy residential developments in Arnold, before terminating near the Severn River. This stretch is very pretty with lots of flowering plants lining the pathway. Intrepid bikers can continue on to Annapolis by crossing the Severn River, though traffic is a concern on these roads. Mileage markers are planted along most of the trail, showing half-mile increments. One negative aspect of this trail is that there are numerous road crossings, some which may require a dismount.

A spur from the northern terminus of the B&A Trail interconnects with the BWI Trail, a recently developed bike trail that loops around the Baltimore Washington International Airport.

BWI Trail

The BWI Trail is a recently constructed 14.5-mile trail network that includes an 11-mile loop around the Baltimore-Washington International (BWI) Airport. The trail is paved and has some hilly sections. The trail is popular among commuters, but is lightly used by recreationists. It includes some surprisingly pretty stretches, running through wetlands at several locations, and through a glade of pine trees near Dorsey Road. Kids will love biking this trail, as it provides clear views of the BWI airport runways with planes taking off and landing.

The most popular place to access the BWI Trail is at the Thomas A. Dixon Aircraft Observation Area, located on Dorsey Road along the south face of the airport. This lot fills quickly on nice days, but other parking options are located nearby. Another popular access point is Andover Park, situated along the northern leg of the trail. Andover Park is located on Andover Road, east of West Nursery Road.

When biking the BWI Trail, bring your own drink and snacks, since there are few guaranteed places to purchase refreshments along the way. The Amtrak train station has some vending machines, and on warm days, a snowball truck sometimes sets up camp in the parking lot of the Dixon observation area.

The BWI Trail is a fine choice for those without cars, since it is accessible by mass transit, including the light rail, which runs from downtown Baltimore, and Amtrak trains. A short spur of the trail leads to the B&A Trail, which is discussed above.

Centennial Park

Centennial Park, part of the Howard County Department of Recreation and Parks system, is the favorite respite spot of county residents. The park envelops the 54-acre Centennial Lake, which is picturesque and home to a world of birds. Around the lake is a 2.4-mile paved pathway, called the Lake Loop, which is popular with biking families. The path is wide and safe. It has some flat stretches perfect for novices pushing their first pedal, and a selection of hills for kids seeking an added thrill. Getting lost along the loop is virtually impossible, since the path hugs the lake shore. And parents appreciate the fact that along the loop are restrooms and a concession stand featuring hot dogs and hamburgers as well as the usual snack foods.

Centennial Park is certainly popular with bikers, but offers much more. Fishermen often line the lake shores and canoes and kayaks ply the waters. Picnic pavilions, sports facilities (including basketball and tennis courts), and playing areas are sprinkled about. A few short hiking trails bisect small wooded lots. The park is also a favorite destination of birders. Centennial Lake has won several awards for how it was built, integral with, and sensitive to, the natural environment. For more details on Centennial Park, see the County Parks chapter.

Centennial Park is located in northeastern Howard County. The main parking area is along Route 108, about one mile west of Route 29. Information on Centennial Park can be found on its website at www.co.ho.md.us/RAP/RAP_HoCoParksCentennial.htm.

Chesapeake and Ohio Canal Towpath

The Chesapeake and Ohio (C&O) Canal towpath is a national treasure. It follows the course of the Potomac River for 184 miles between Cumberland, Maryland, and Washington, D.C. It passes through some of our country's most poignant history, including Antietam National Battlefield and Harpers Ferry National Historical Park. The eastern terminus of the towpath is in the fine-china neighborhood of Georgetown, one of the country's most spectacular. The canal was built in the early 19th-century to link the Chesapeake Bay with the state of Ohio, but was almost immediately rendered obsolete thanks to the advent of railroads.

Biking is a popular way to explore the towpath. The experience can be rich and rewarding, and worth the hour drive from Baltimore. Bikers may encounter rarely seen wildlife like beaver and fox. Hundreds of bird species live around or pass through the towpath corridor. The mighty Potomac River is almost always in view. The towpath provides access to spectacular parks and throwback towns. The towpath surface varies from dust to sand to crushed stone, with no sections paved. Bikers should come prepared to fix flat tires.

Riding the entire length of the towpath over several days is a popular challenge. Campsites, inns, and bed-and-breakfasts along the way make the chore realizable. Towns and stores pop up periodically, offering refreshment breaks.

Access is too plentiful along the towpath to fully delineate here. Some of the more popular access points closest to Baltimore are at the venerable Old Anglers Inn (circa 1860); on MacArthur Boulevard in Potomac; the C&O Canal Historical Park, near Great Falls; Swains Lock, near trail mile 16.6; and White's Ferry, in southern Montgomery County. White's Ferry is the site of the only remaining ferry crossing of the Potomac River, and has a general store and deli right on the towpath. The towpath through Georgetown is very picturesque, but parking can be difficult to come by.

General information on the C&O Canal can be found at www.candocanal.org, which is the website of the C&O Canal Association. Loads of information about biking the canal, including several trip accounts, can be found at www.fred.net/kathy/canal/co-bikeinfo.html. Serious users of the canal should refer to *The C&O Canal Companion*, by Mike High, which is the definitive guide to recreating along the towpath.

Columbia Trail System

You may or may not like the pre-planned suburban community of Columbia, but most recreationists would agree that its trail system is superb: 83 miles of paved biking (and walking) trails thread throughout the city, tying together the various village centers. The trails are well maintained and feature few major road crossings, making them ideal for children. The loop around Lake Elkhorn, measuring in at slightly less than two miles, is a popular destination and offers relatively flat and scenic peddling. Don't miss the beaver dams just upstream from the lake's inlet. Lake Kittamaqundi, at the town center, is another fun place to ride to, and has lots of restaurants and shopping opportunities nearby. A lesser-known, but pretty, stretch of trail is from the Oakland Mills Road tunnel to the diminutive Jackson Pond, in the village of Long Reach. Intrepid bikers should head downhill to Savage Park for a more scenic and challenging ride. Several tot lots and picnic tables line the trails, making for nice break stops. Before setting off, call the Columbia Association at (410) 715-3000 to obtain a map of the trail system.

Downs Memorial Park

Downs Park is an ideal destination for bikers drawn to big water as well as woodland. The park is part of Bodkin Neck, and juts out into the Chesapeake Bay, offering sweeping views clear across to Rock Hall on the Eastern Shore.

Downs Park, administered by Anne Arundel County, offers a range of biking opportunities, with most routes being flat, paved, and shaded. A trail map, available at the park office, is recommended here. The most popular trail to bike is the 3.6-mile Perimeter Trail which outlines the park's 231 acres. Bay waves lap up to a quarter-mile stretch of this trail. The Perimeter Trail also passes a small pond crammed full of turtles and fish, and cuts through large tracts of deciduous woodland. Along the way, bikers are offered interpretive signs explaining the park's history—from its ownership by Charles Carroll (the only Catholic signer of the Declaration of Independence), to its use as a fruit and vegetable farm, to its service as a summer retreat for the wealthy Thom family.

Another popular trail in Downs Park is the 1.8-mile Senior Exercise Trail. The unpaved 0.6-mile nature trail is ideal for walking. Bikers at Downs Park should not miss the osprey nest just off the observation pier near the park office.

Downs Park is located near Gibson Island. From Baltimore, take Route 100 east, which merges with Route 177. Follow signs to the park.

Ellicott City #9 Trolley Trail

The #9 trolley trail is a paved hiking and biking trail that is short, little known, and lightly used. It meanders for 1.5 miles through thick woodland between Catonsville and Ellicott City. It traces the path of the former trolley service that connected the two villages until the 1960s. A three-mile out-and-back bike ride along this trail, starting in Catonsville, presents a nice family biking venue, with historic Ellicott City—and its many restaurants and coffee shops—beckoning at the turnaround.

Biking the #9 trolley trail provides more than a bike ride through lush woodland. It offers historical insight as well. To the right, before the first road crossing (Oella Avenue), is the stone Mt. Gilboa A.M.E. Church, established by descendants of freed slaves. It's thought to be the oldest African American church in the Baltimore area, dating to 1859. Just past the second road crossing (a private driveway), the trail hems the boundary of Benjamin Banneker Historical Park, homestead of the First Black Man of Science, who built the first clock in the new world, made many astronomical discoveries, helped survey the District of Columbia, and published an acclaimed international almanac.

Just before the turnaround, the trail squeezes through an impressive 60-foot-high rock cut, revealing the formidable task of running trains through such rugged terrain. Teetering atop the cut is Alhambra, a stunning Greek Revival mansion built in 1859 for John Ellicott, a member of the town's founding family.

One negative of the #9 trolley trail is that it is downhill the entire length from Catonsville to Ellicott City, making it uphill (albeit, gradual) the entire way back.

The #9 trolley trail can be reached by taking Edmondson Avenue west from the Interstate 695 beltway for three miles, until it dead-ends at Stonewall Road to the left and Chalfonte Drive to the right. On-street parking is usually available near this intersection. Access is also available at the Ellicott City end of the trail, in a parking lot on Oella Avenue, near its intersection with Frederick Road.

Fort McHenry National Monument

What is probably the shortest bike trail in the area happens to pack the biggest punch. Fort McHenry National Monument, which includes a lovely sprawl of parkland, stretches across the outermost reach of the Locust Point peninsula, pushing out into the Patapsco River at its mouth with the Chesapeake Bay. It's one of the city's most scenic lairs, offering wide-lens views of the harbor, the Key Bridge, countless vintage piers and warehouses, and a handful of waterfront communities. Looping the park along the waterfront is a paved biking path that registers just shy of one mile. For most of its course it runs alongside a seawall, offering harbor vantages seen nowhere else in the city. To further the experience, boats of all shapes and sizes (from sea kayaks to container ships) cruise just feet from the biking trail, offering kids a heightened thrill. A warning: don't venture here if your child is an erratic biker, since the bike trail comes dangerously close to some steep drop-offs into the harbor.

Fort McHenry National Monument is situated at the eastern terminus of Fort Avenue, in Locust Point. For more information on the facility, see the City Parks chapter.

Grist Mill Trail

Patapsco Valley State Park offers the most complex trail network in the Baltimore area for hiking and mountain-biking. Most of the trails are rugged and challenging. Often overlooked is the tame, but

◄ The Grist Mill Trail offers
lovely vantages of the
Patapsco River

very attractive and bicycle-friendly, Grist Mill Trail, which runs stone-flat and paved for the 1.5 miles along the north bank of the Patapsco River. The Grist Mill Trail offers a peaceful ride through terrain that is rich in wildlife and beauty and steeped in history.

The Grist Mill Trail begins in the Avalon area, once a thriving mill town with school, stores, and about 30 mill houses. A monstrous flood in 1886 destroyed the town, leaving few remains (look for dam remnants near the trailhead). The trail terminates at the 300-foot-long swinging bridge, in the Orange Grove area, another mill-town-turned-ghost-town. Bikers have the option of backtracking to the parking lot along the Grist Mill Trail, or crossing the swinging bridge and returning along the lightly traveled River Road, which hugs the south bank of the river. Returning via River Road, which has some hills, will take the bike ride to about four miles.

Access to the Avalon area of Patapsco Valley State Park is via Route 1 in Elkridge. Inside the park, turn right at the T-intersection to the Grist Mill trailhead. Parking is usually available near the fishing pond.

Gwynns Falls Trail

Gwynns Falls Trail is what happens when community groups, government agencies, and conservation groups play together nicely. Unveiled in 1999 as a result of intense community cooperation, the trail slices through Leakin Park in west Baltimore, tracing the flow of the tumbling Gwynns Falls, which once drove many mills along its course. The trail is mostly paved, with some crushed stone. Currently, four miles of the Gwynns Falls Trail are open for public use. Eventually it will extend for 14 miles into South Baltimore, near Middle Branch Park. The completed trail will link 20 Baltimore neighborhoods. Amenities along the trail include sports fields, a picnic pavilion, restrooms, a playground, and wildlife observation decks.

Access to Gwynns Falls Trail is best via the Winans Meadow trailhead or Leon Day Park. Both are situated along Franklintown Road, which can be accessed from Security Boulevard.

Lake Montebello

City dwellers not wanting to drive far to ride a bike can always turn to Lake Montebello. Located east of the Waverly section of northeast Baltimore, the lake is circumscribed by the one-and-a-quarter-mile drive that has a lane designated solely for running and biking. It is a lightly traveled road and very flat. Some may find the urban setting of Lake Montebello appealing. Herring Run Park borders a large chunk of Lake Montebello.

Lake Montebello is situated between Hillen and Harford Roads, just a little north of where those two streets intersect. It is accessible via 33rd Street, just past the former Memorial Stadium.

Loch Raven Reservoir

The Loch Raven Reservoir area is popular among weekend bikers, as several of the surrounding thoroughfares are closed to traffic at that time. Closure times are from 10 a.m. to 5 p.m. on both Saturday and Sunday. The scenery along the roads is fabulous, with the roads brushing up against the reservoir at many locations. The hills, however, could present a challenge to novice pedal pushers. The 4,500-acre reservoir collects water from Gunpowder Falls, and was built in 1881 to provide drinking water to Baltimore city and county residents.

Loch Raven Reservoir is best reached by taking Dulaney Valley Road north from the Interstate 695 beltway for a couple of miles. A popular meeting spot there is at the former Peerce's Plantation restaurant, along Dulaney Valley Road.

Northern Central Railroad Trail and York County Heritage Trail

The Northern Central Trail is Baltimore's favorite place to bike. The trail is in close proximity to the city, located just outside the northern arc of the beltway. It is flat and well-maintained. The trail is conducive to social riding, being wide enough to ride two or even three abreast. The pathway is forgiving, laid with a finely pulverized —almost dusty—limestone. Much of the trail runs beside the bubbling Gunpowder Falls and Little Falls, and is hemmed with lovely trees, providing pleasing summertime shade. And to the north, the trail traverses some of the state's most bucolic scenery. In short: it has it all.

The Northern Central Trail follows the right-of-way of the former Northern Central Railroad that once tied Baltimore to York, Pennsylvania. The trail begins in Cockeysville, Maryland, and runs for 19.7 miles to the Pennsylvania border. It continues on from there another 21 miles into York under a different name—the York County Heritage Trail. Though mostly flat, the trail undulates gradually as it approaches the Pennsylvania border.

The Northern Central Railroad and York County Heritage trails collectively carry an impressive history. Train service on the Northern Central Railroad ran between York and Baltimore between 1838 and 1972. Trains carried commerce and passengers, and even Union soldiers during the Civil War. The train service helped establish several picturesque hamlets along the route, including Sparks, Monkton, and New Freedom, Pennsylvania. Abraham Lincoln traveled the Northern Central Railroad en route to Gettysburg to deliver his famous address. Following his assassination, his body was transported on this railway to Harrisburg, Pennsylvania. Train service on the Northern Central Railroad petered out after World War II, and Hurricane Agnes dealt the coup de grace in 1972, wiping out many of its bridges. The rail line became a linear recreational park in 1984.

Be warned that some stretches of the Northern Central Trail, particularly to the south, burst at the seams with recreationists on fair-weather weekends. It's advisable to explore the equally attractive northern section of the trail on these occasions, and even venture up to the York County Heritage Trail in Pennsylvania. The York County Heritage Trail passes through the Howard Tunnel, the oldest standing railroad tunnel in the United States. It also runs through a rail yard of restored locomotives in New Freedom, Pennsylvania.

Access to the Northern Central Trail is generous. Parking is offered at the trail's southern terminus, on Ashland Road, which is just off York Road. Overflow parking is available along Paper Mill Road. Another popular point of origin is in Monkton, where the trail intersects Monkton Road. There is an interesting restored railroad station there, and facilities for food and rest. Bike rentals are also available. Access is possible in such towns as Phoenix, Sparks, White Hall, Parkton, and Bentley Springs, and along Freeland Road near the Pennsylvania border. Refer to a Maryland road map for access directions.

The Northern Central Railroad Trail is administered by the Maryland Department of Natural Resources. Contact them for more information. Directions to the trail are provided by their website at www.dnr.state.md.us/greenways/ncrt_trail.html.

Quiet Waters Park

Quiet Waters Park is snuggled between the South River and Harness Creek, just south of Annapolis. It's as appealing as its name insinuates. The 336-acre park bears a calm and relaxing demeanor. It is spacious, quiet, and pretty—and chock full of interesting fauna and lush flora. It is a prime spot for viewing raptors, songbirds, and waterfowl, and an occasional bald eagle soars overhead. Keep an eye peeled for deer and fox.

Bikers will be attracted to the park's six miles of paved trail, configured mainly in a loop. The trail hugs Harness Creek along one section, and at the far reach, a short spur leads to a lookout over the South River. Along the way, bikers traverse wetlands, meadowland, and some more developed park grounds. Quiet Waters Park offers an assortment of amenities, including concessions, a visitors' center, a seasonal ice rink, picnic pavilions, a multi-level playground, boat rentals, and an art gallery. The park has more of an artsy flair than most, and plays host to an annual arts festival. Interesting sculptures are spread throughout the park.

Until a few decades ago, the grounds of Quiet Waters Park were mostly forest and farmland. In 1986, the land was to be converted to a 250-unit housing development. Anne Arundel County intervened, buying the land and putting it under the jurisdiction of its Department of Recreation and Parks. It is now one of the most popular respite spots in Annapolis.

Quiet Waters Park is located just south of Annapolis. The entrance is near the intersection of Forest and Hillsmere Drives. A $4 per car entrance fee is usually charged at the gate. For more information on Quiet Waters Park, check out its website at web.aacpl. net/rp/parks/quietwaters/index.htm.

Boat Rentals

Despite being situated smack-dab on the Chesapeake Bay, not all of Baltimore's boat rental facilities serve that waterbody. Many can be found on the scenic lakes, ponds, and rivers freckling the surrounding countryside. Here's where Baltimore residents go to spend a day on sun-dappled water.

Centennial Lake

Centennial Lake is part of Centennial Park, and spreads for over 50 acres across a low-lying valley in central Howard County. The lake surface is usually calm, making it well suited for paddling. On nice days, the lake will be packed with boaters of all sorts, so this is not a place for those seeking solitude. On the other hand, Centennial Park was built to be integral with the surrounding environment, and the lake is quite pretty. It's surrounded mostly with trees and some recreational facilities. The lake is also a major nesting spot for waterfowl, and a stopover spot for migrating birds. A hint: stay clear of the tiny island situated just offshore from the boat rental facility, as it is seasonally lorded over by aggressive nesting geese.

Paddle boats, canoes, rowboats, and electric motorboats are available for rent. Paddle boats run $4 per half hour for two-seaters, and $6 per half hour for four-seaters. Canoes cost $5 per hour to rent, and have a maximum capacity of three riders. On weekdays, canoes can be rented all day for $10. Rowboats rent for $5 per hour, and have a maximum capacity of two riders. On weekdays, rowboats can be rented all day for $10. Boats with electric motors attached are available to rent for $25 for a half day of four hours or less, or $40 for a full day. These boats are popular with fishermen.

Each boat listed above must have a rider who is 16 years of age or older. A $10 deposit and driver's license are required to rent a boat.

Location and Directions: Centennial Park is located on Route 108, in Columbia, Maryland. From Baltimore, take Interstate 70 west. In Ellicott City, take Route 29 south. In about five miles, take Route 108 (Clarksville Pike) west. Boat rentals are available in the South Area, which is located about one mile up Route 108, to the right.

Hours: Boat rentals are available daily from May through August when weather is agreeable. Rentals start at 9 a.m. on weekends, and at 11 a.m. on weekdays. Boats must be returned one hour before dusk.

Website and Phone: www.co.ho.md.us/RAP/RAP_HoCoParks Centennial.htm; (410) 313-7303.

Gunpowder Falls State Park— Hammerman Area

No canoes or paddle boats here. This is where adrenalin junkies go for big-water boating using high-performance equipment. Ultimate Watersports runs a shop from the Hammerman Area of Gunpowder Falls State Park, and rents out windsurfers, kayaks, and Hobie Cat catamarans. Boating is done on the Gunpowder River, which is wide open and can serve up some nasty waves, so be prepared.

The rental season begins in May. Standard windsurfers rent for $20 per hour and $60 per day. Performance windsurfers go for $25 per hour and $75 per day. Ultimate Watersports offers both sea kayaks and sit-on-tops. One-person kayaks rent for $15 per hour and $40 per day (two-person kayaks rent for slightly more). Kayaks can also be taken offsite and rented for the entire weekend. Hobie Cat catamarans are offered in either 13-foot or 16-foot lengths, and go for $45 for the first hour and $15 for each additional hour, or for $130 for the entire day.

Special skills may be required to handle vessels of such rigor. Ultimate Watersports offers introductory lessons from certified instructors for all three activities. Beginner sea kayak lessons are given on Saturdays from April through September, and sunset kayak tours are offered in the evening. Eco kayak tours are offered on Sundays. Windsurfing lessons are offered on Saturdays and Sundays, and sailing lessons are given seven days a week. Lessons range in price from $35 for a two-hour introductory kayaking class, to $145 for six hours of windsurfing instruction. Kayak tours run from $45 to $65 per person, and last about two hours. Some tours have age restrictions in place.

Location and Directions: The Ultimate Watersports boat rental facility is located in the Hammerman Area of Gunpowder Falls State Park. From downtown, take Interstate 95 north. Take Exit 67-A, Route 43, and follow it east to Route 40. Take 40 east, and continue to the first light. Turn right onto Ebenezer Road and continue for about 4.5 miles, to the entrance to the Hammerman Area of Gunpowder Falls State Park. Follow the park access road to the waterfront, where parking is available.

Hours and Admission to Park: The Hammerman Area is open year-round. Summer hours are 8 a.m. to sunset. At other times, hours are 10 a.m. to sunset. Entrance to the park is $2 per person, though seniors 62 or older and children in car seats are free.

Website and Phone: www.ultimatewatersports.com; (410) 666-9463.

Gunpowder Falls Tubing

Deer Creek and the Patapsco River are fine local tubing rivers, but when the summer heat turns white-hot, seasoned tubers head to Gunpowder Falls. The Gunpowder is a well-shaded, blue-ribbon trout stream that tumbles and glides through pristine tracts of northern Baltimore County. The waters of the Gunpowder bubble from the depths of Prettyboy Reservoir, and run a bone-chilling 50 degrees or so year-round, providing for a refreshing tubing trip.

Tubing is possible anywhere along Gunpowder Falls, but those targeting the upstream stretches may contend with irate fly fishermen. I recommend heading to Monkton Station where access is easy and tubes are available for rent ($8 per day from Monkton Bike Rental). Tubers on this stretch of the Gunpowder slip through attractive and well-shaded woodland. The river runs about 30 to 50 feet wide and is gin-clear under normal conditions. Current here is slow-paced and rapids are little more than playful ripples (you can expect some rump-bumping). There may be obstacles like rocks and fallen logs to navigate around. Keep your eyes peeled for wildlife like blue heron and deer. Keen observers may see a trout flee, as Gunpowder Falls is one of the East Coast's most plentiful trout streams. Studies have shown that some reaches have as many as 4,000 trout per mile—more than any other waterway in the state.

Near dusk, watch for beaver congregating beneath the Monkton Road bridge.

Most tubers hike upstream from Monkton Station on the Northern Central Railroad Trail to the put-in. The length of float varies depending on how far upstream one cares to hike. In general, a one-quarter-mile walk will result in a half-hour float, and a one-half-mile walk will result in a one-hour float. Float time varies greatly depending on water level. Tubers may also float downstream from Monkton Station and return on the trail.

Location and Directions: From Baltimore, take Interstate 83 north. Take Exit 27, Mt. Carmel Road, east (right at the ramp top). Continue for about one-quarter mile, turn right onto York Road, and make a quick left onto Monkton Road. Monkton Bike Rental is located about three miles down Monkton Road on the left, just after crossing over Gunpowder Falls.

Hours: Monkton Bike Rental optimistically rents tubes year-round. Hours are daily from 10 a.m. to 7 p.m., though they often stay open later on weekends.

Inner Harbor Paddle Boats

A century ago, the piers along Pratt Street were lined with fancy passenger steamships and majestic wooden cargo ships laden with Baltimore harbor seafood and Eastern Shore vegetables bound for ports around the world. Today, the piers are the domain of paddle boats and electric boats available for rent. Though more modest in

▲ Paddle boats are a fun way to explore the Inner Harbor

stature than their predecessors, renting one provides a unique and fun perspective on the Inner Harbor.

The paddle boat concession is located just west of the World Trade Center. Rental prices for 30 minutes are $7 per boat for one person, $8 for two people, $9 for three people, and $10 for four people. Be forewarned that parties of three or four may end up chugging around the harbor in a boat resembling a big green dragon with red mane.

The Trident Electric Boat concession is located just east of the World Trade Center. Rental prices for 30 minutes are $12 for two people and $18 for three. Take note that electric boats are not as fast as they sound; I've passed them in a paddle boat.

Location and Directions: The paddle and electric boat docks are located along the north fringe of the Inner Harbor, near the World Trade Center. From Interstate 95, take Exit 53, Interstate 395, and follow signs to downtown Baltimore and the Inner Harbor.

Loch Raven Fishing Center

The Loch Raven Fishing Center is one of Baltimore's most popular locales to rent a boat. The water is protected and generally flat, there are many interesting nooks and inlets to explore, and the rates are surprisingly reasonable. The pristine, 2,400-acre reservoir has mostly undeveloped shoreline, so the day should be peaceful. But, as the name implies, patrons will be competing with fishermen for the boats. Not to worry, the center offers many for rent. Two types of motor boats are available: basic, 14-foot jonboats ($25 per day) and premium jonboats that include two swivel seats ($50 per day). These boats are powered by electric motors, since gas-powered ones are not allowed on the reservoir. Pacifists may be more drawn to the canoes ($14 per day) and rowboats ($14 per day). Aesthetes will enjoy the premium canoes that feature wooden gunwales and seats ($20 per day). All rentals include oars and life preservers. A concession stand serves up snacks and drinks.

While at the fishing center, why not do as the Romans do and wet a line. The reservoir is crammed with largemouth bass, smallmouth bass, yellow perch, and bluegill. Lucky anglers may even tie into a northern pike. Maryland fishing licenses are available at the concession stand, as are tackle and bait. Fishing center personnel will gladly offer advice to novice anglers. Be forewarned that the reservoir level depletes in drought conditions.

Location and Directions: At 12101 Dulaney Valley Road, in Timonium. From the Interstate 695 beltway, take Exit 27, Dulaney Valley Road, north. Continue on Dulaney Valley Road through several stop lights. The entrance to the Loch Raven Fishing Center is about one mile past Seminary Avenue, on the right. It is well marked.

Hours and Admission: The fishing center is open daily from the first Friday in April to Labor Day. From Labor Day to October 31, the center is open on Mondays, Wednesdays, Fridays, Saturdays, and Sundays. From November 1 to November 30, the center is open on Saturdays and Sundays. The center is closed from December 1 to the first Friday in April. Hours are from 6 a.m. to closing time, which varies depending on season and weather. Rental admissions are provided above.

Website and Phone: www.co.ba.md.us/agencies/recreation/fishingcenter; (410) 887-7692.

Piney Run Reservoir

Piney Run Reservoir is the showpiece of Piney Run Park, Carroll County's best place to commune with nature. The 300-acre lake was formed when Piney Run was dammed in 1974 for water resources management. Boating on Piney Run Reservoir is scenic, with the lake surrounded by pretty woodland and bucolic farmland. Surrounding hills generally protect the lake from winds, making for nice flat-water paddling.

Piney Run Park offers rowboats, canoes, paddle boats, and kayaks for rent. Seasonal rowboat rental begins on April 1, and the cost is $6 per hour. Canoes and kayaks are available for rent starting May 1, and cost the same as rowboats. Paddle boats also become available for rent beginning May 1, and cost $5 per hour. On non-holiday Mondays through Fridays, an all-day rate of $20 is available for the canoes, kayaks, and rowboats. No full-day discount is offered on holidays or weekends. Renting a boat requires a valid driver's license and a $10 deposit. Boats are rented on a first-come, first-served basis. No advance reservations are allowed. A playground is located next to the rental building, and restrooms are just a short skip away.

Piney Run Park also offers a lumbering but fun pontoon boat for rent. The *Ava Irene* seats 24 people, and is popular for birthday parties or nature discovery trips. The cost is $25 per hour, of which about 45 minutes is spent on the water. The park offers special children-oriented cruises on the *Ava Irene*, such as a Mickey Mouse ride and a stuffed animal ride.

Location and Directions: At 30 Martz Road, near Sykesville. To get there, take Interstate 70 west from Baltimore, and then Route 32 north. In Eldersburg, turn left onto Route 26 and continue for 2.1 miles. Turn left onto White Rock Road (there is a park sign there) and continue for 1.9 miles. Turn left onto Martz Road and continue to the park entrance.

Hours and Admission: Most park facilities are open daily from April 1 through October 31, from 6 a.m. to sunset. Admission to the park is $4 per car for Carroll County residents and $5 per car for all other visitors. Seniors 62 and older are free. Add $3 if you bring your own boat.

Phone: (410) 795-5165.

Camping

Camping is the most intimate way to introduce a child to the pleasures of being outdoors. Many private and public campgrounds are located within a reasonable drive from Baltimore. As a general rule, public sites (those administered by a government agency) tend to favor tent-camping, are located in wilderness areas, and offer few bells and whistles. Private sites, on the other hand, cater more to recreational vehicles and often include side-attractions like swimming pools or game rooms. Listed here are eight popular public campsites in the area and a private one that offers a unique sleeping experience. A more comprehensive list of Maryland campgrounds can be found at the Maryland Association of Campgrounds' website at www.kiz.com/campnet/html/cluborgs/mac/mac.htm.

Cunningham Falls State Park—Houck Area

Cunningham Falls State Park is a relatively rough-and-tumble wilderness area situated in reasonable proximity to Baltimore. The park is among the state's most scenic, featuring an attractive lake cradled by steep, leafy mountains. Its most popular campground is located in the Houck Area, situated on a rise above, and away from, the lake. It serves as the perfect base camp for outdoor-oriented families who want to explore the surrounding mountains.

Campers here have easy access to myriad hiking trails in the state park and adjoining Catoctin Mountain Park, which range from gentle rambles to rugged climbs. They can fish for trout in the blue-ribbon waters of Hunting Creek, swim in the lake, or paddle a canoe. Catoctin Mountain Park has an interesting visitors' center that's worth a stop.

The 140 campsites in the Houck Area are spread across five loops. Each site comes with a generous gravel-dust sleeping pad, picnic table, and fire pit. Each loop has a bathhouse with showers and flush toilets. Certain sites are also suitable for recreational vehicles. Electrical hook-ups are available on the Addison Run Loop and Deer Spring Branch Loop. Camping runs from mid-April through mid-October. The charge is $20 per night ($25 with electric hook-up). A large camp store offers supplies, food, and souvenirs. A power line runs through sections of the camp, so if you find this bothersome, take it into account when making reservations.

Catoctin Creek Loop has four cabins for rent, and Deer Spring Branch Loop has five cabins. Each cabin is 12-feet square with a nice front porch. Cabins have lighting and electrical outlets. Each sleeps four, with a double bed and a set of bunk beds. Cooking must be done outside. Cabins do not have heat or air conditioning, so on hot days bring a fan. Cabins rent for $40 per night.

The one detraction of the campground is that a car or long walk is needed to access most attractions. It's not the kind of place where you can unleash the kids by a stream or lake and just have them occasionally check in. A trail from camp leads to the lake, however, and another to Cunningham Falls, the region's highest.

Camping is also available in the Manor Area of Cunningham Falls State Park, which offers 31 sites within walking distance of a preserved colonial iron-smelting operation. Heartier souls can take advantage of winter camping here. Camping fees are similar to those of the Houck Area.

Location and Directions: In the Houck Area of Cunningham Falls State Park. From Baltimore, take Interstate 70 west. In Frederick, take Route 15 north. In Thurmont, take Route 77 west and continue for about three miles. Turn left onto Catoctin Hollow Road and follow signs for the campground.

Website and Phone: www.dnr.state.md.us/publiclands/western/cunninghamfalls.html; (301) 271-7574. For reservations, call 1-888-432-2267.

Elk Neck State Park

How you perceive camping at Elk Neck State Park depends on your general disposition. An optimist will see one of the state's premier campgrounds that's set in a pretty locale, has activities aplenty, and offers magnificent, postcard-perfect views of the bay and surrounding rivers. A glass-half-empty person will see a crowded camp-ground where one has a snowball's chance of getting a prime site on most summer weekends. I recommend that you give this camp a shot; the rewards are numerous.

The 278 campsites are spread around the park, making it among the largest in the state. Despite its size, the expansiveness of the campground nicely diffuses the crowds. Fun activities abound here. A swimming beach is very popular in warm-weather months, and is covered in the Swimming Holes chapter. Hiking trails weave throughout the park; I suggest taking the gentle walking path that leads past nice vistas to the Turkey Point Lighthouse. Boats can be rented, but paddlers will have to contend with a flotilla of power-boats. The campground features a sizeable playground and lots of ball fields. A tire park is situated near the swimming beach.

Family camping begins in late March, though the North East Loop is open year-round. Camping is $18 per night for tents, $23 for electric hook-ups, and $25 for full hook-ups. Nine full-service cabins that sleep up to four are also available for rent from early May through mid-October. Cost is $50 per night on weekends ($40 on weekdays). Camping cabins are open from late March through early November, and go for $35 per night.

Location and Directions: Elk Neck State Park is located on the Elk Neck peninsula, in Cecil County. From Baltimore, take Interstate 95 north. Take Exit 100, Route 272, south. Continue for about 10 miles past the town of North East, following signs to the state park.

Website and Phone: www.dnr.state.md.us/publiclands/central/elkneck.html; (410) 287-5333. For reservations, call 1-888-432-2267.

Gambrill State Park

Gambrill State Park is located just a few miles west of Frederick, and encompasses two recreational developments. The High Knob Area is a rugged mountaintop tract of woodland tied together with rocky trails that lead to several nice lookouts. This area includes the beautifully sit-uated Tea Room Lodge, which can be rented for day events. The Rock Run Area is located at the foot of the mountain, near the park's main entrance, and has a nicely groomed picnic area, restrooms, and a fish-ing pond full of largemouth bass and channel catfish.

To the back of the Rock Run Area is a campground, which of-fers 35 campsites and four cabins. Camping is available from the end of May through the end of October. Tent sites cost $17 per night ($22 with electric hook-up). Sites come with picnic tables and fire rings, and are generally quiet and pretty. Some sites along the top of the hill are more private, being shielded by a grove of pine trees. For kids, there's a swing set and large field for ball-playing or frisbee-throwing. Restrooms and showers are also available.

Each of the four cabins in the campground rents for $35 per night on weekdays, and $70 per night on weekends and holidays. Each cabin offers about 150 square feet of living space and comes with a front porch. Each sleeps four, with a double bed and set of bunk beds. The cabins have no heat or air conditioning. Cabin renters must bring their own bedding, and cooking must be done outside. Gambrill State Park accepts reservations for the campsites and cabins.

Most visitors to Gambrill State Park come to hike or bike its significant trail system. The trails are located in the High Knob Area, and are generally rugged and steep. The 1.1-mile, red-blazed Red Maple Trail connects the campground with the High Knob Area, and is generally easy walking. Parents wishing to avoid mountain bikes and steep climbs should stick to the white-blazed White Oak Trail, which traces a one-mile circuit through pretty woodland. This trail is off-limits to bikes. The White Oak trailhead is at the parking area along Gambrill Park Road, between the two developments. The blue-blazed Catoctin Trail, which originates at the same trailhead, is a good choice for seasoned hikers looking for a challenge that also offers rewarding scenery. A large map at the trailhead parking lot shows all hiking opportunities available in the park.

Location and Directions: Gambrill State Park is located a few miles west of Frederick, just off Route 40. From Baltimore, take Interstate 70 west. In Frederick, take Route 15 north. Continue for one mile and take Route 40 west. Continue for about three miles. At the Dan-Dee Country Inn, turn right onto Gambrill Park Road. The park's main entrance and campground are about one mile up, on the left.

Website and Phone: www.dnr.state.md.us/publiclands/western/ gambrill.html; (301) 271-7574. For reservations, call 1-888-432-2267.

Greenbrier State Park

Outdoorsy types who venture west from Baltimore usually stop at the Catoctin Mountains or the eastern face of South Mountain, where recreational opportunities abound. Those reaching a bit farther will be rewarded with a state park of supreme beauty and fun. Greenbrier State Park is an expansive spread of mountainous terrain punctuated by a 50-acre lake, situated on the Appalachian Trail, near Hagerstown. Greenbrier offers great day-use facilities, but being about 90 minutes from Baltimore, you may want to pack your tent and sleeping bags and make a night of it.

Greenbrier State Park has one of the area's largest campgrounds. The 165 sites are spread across four loops, each bearing the name of a tree. The Ash, Birch, and Cedar Loops each offer between 20 and 30 sites and a bathhouse with showers. The Dogwood Loop has 60 sites and two bathhouses. Each site comes with a picnic table and fire ring. The campground is quiet and well hidden, and no one site seems better than the others. Camping runs from late March through early November, and sites run $20 per night ($25 with electric hook-up). Reservations are accepted.

The jewel of Greenbrier State Park is the cool-water lake offering over 1,000 feet of sandy beach. Water depths in the swimming area are up to six feet, but shallow areas allow wading for toddlers. A lifeguard is on duty from Memorial Day through Labor Day and a bathhouse and concession stand are available. Day-use costs for using the beach are $3 per person on weekends and holidays during the summer months, and $2 per person on other weekends. Cost during the week is $2 per car. Boats are available for rent. The Visitor Center offers interesting and outdoorsy displays and exhibits, and hosts numerous nature programs.

Hikers in Greenbrier State Park have a nice list of trails to choose from. A particularly child-friendly path is the Green Trail, which loops for just under one mile from the Visitor Center. Another nice trail is the orange-blazed Camp Loop, which connects the campground to the west face of the lake. Kids as well as adults will love the rambling trail that circles the lake. More rugged trails weave around the hills to the west of the lake, but be careful in fall, since these trails pass through hunting grounds.

Location and Directions: Greenbrier State Park is located about 10 miles west of Hagerstown, along Route 40. From Baltimore, take Interstate 70 west. In Myersville, just past Frederick, take the Route 17 cut-off to Route 40. Turn left onto Route 40 and continue over South Mountain. The park entrance is located on Route 40 along the downhill stretch of the mountain.

Website and Phone: www.dnr.state.md.us/publiclands/western/greenbrier.html; (301) 791-4767. For reservations, call 1-888-432-2267.

Hart-Miller Island State Park

Recreational power-boaters should consider a camping trip to Hart-Miller Island State Park. The island, located in the Chesapeake

Bay about one mile off the mouth of Middle River, can only be accessed by water craft. Along the island's western face is a 3,000-foot sweep of lovely beach for swimming and wading. Just behind the beach, among a stand of pine and oak trees, are 22 campsites. Each site is comfortably sandy, and comes with a large picnic table and fire ring. Camping is available from early May through late September, on a first-come, first-served basis. Sites are $6 per evening. There is a visitors' center on the premises and concessions are sold from boats.

Hart-Miller Island is a unique topographic feature. It was originally two individual islands—one named Hart and the other Miller. In the 1970s , the Maryland Port Administration built a six-mile-long dike around the two islands and filled it in with sediment dredged from Baltimore's shipping channels, effectively creating one large island spanning over 1,000 acres. Currently the state park comprises about 244 acres of the island, with the remainder still being used for dredge disposal. An observation tower allows visitors to inspect the disposal operation. Dredged sediment will continue being piped to the island until 2009.

Naturalists find making the run to Hart-Miller Island worthwhile. Birders come to see one of the country's great congregations of waterfowl, shorebirds, gulls, and terns, which find the dredged sediment rich in snacks. Over 277 bird species have been spotted on the island. Fox, deer, and raccoon also lurk about the state park. A series of short hiking trails can be used to explore inland areas.

A word of warning about Hart-Miller Island: the difficulty in accessibility does not necessarily translate to seclusion. Things get pretty chaotic there on summer weekends. Up to 800 boats visit on nice days. Scores of boats moor off the beach, creating quite a lively party scene with lots of swimmers and revelers. Also, come armed with heavy-duty mosquito repellant, as this island attracts the little devils in droves.

Website and Phone: www.dnr.state.md.us/publiclands/central/ hartmiller.html; (410) 592-2897.

Maple Tree Campground

And now for something completely different. At Maple Tree Campground, visitors can stay the night in what are advertised as tree houses and tree cottages (in actuality, they are huts in thick and steep woodland raised off the ground by stilts). Kids love this twist

Eight Tips for Fun Family Camping

1. Empower the kids. Let them help pack, set up the tent, collect firewood, etc. Don't just show camping to them, let them experience it.
2. Choose child-friendly sites with lots to do for kids (a field to run through or a brook to wade in), but few opportunities for harm (rapids, cliffs, etc.).
3. Use quality equipment. Spending the night in a flooded tent or shivering in wet wool will not endear children to the activity.
4. Pack a treasure box laden with simple toys: dominos, puzzles, playing cards, jacks, candies, etc. Mix outdoor activities with more familiar games.
5. Bring a disposable camera and let the kids document their fun.
6. Find one activity your kids love and make it a camping tradition. Our family ends each day with a "spooky walk" through the woods, with each child wielding a flashlight.
7. Pack a first-aid kit and take extraordinary safety precautions around camp.
8. Pack your nature guidebooks and help the kids identify trees, salamanders, flowers, and birds.

on camping, but parents should be warned that the level of sleeping comfort does not drift far from that of a tent.

Maple Tree Campground offers three arboreal sleeping options. Guests may stay in a year-round tree cottage, of which four are available for rent. Tree cottages are insulated for four-season comfort, and come with beds, benches, and a wood-burning stove for cooking and heat. Each sleeps six. Tree cottages rent for $45 per night for up to four people, and $8 per person per night beyond that number. Guests also may rent one of nine tree houses, which have a tiny deck and perch about seven feet off the ground. The tree houses vary in size, with larger ones able to accommodate ten campers. Tree houses rent for $32 per night for up to four people, and $8 per person per night beyond that.

Maple Tree Campground also offers traditional tent camping. Fourteen wooded tent sites are also available for $8 per person per night, and a large number of field tent sites are available for $7 per person per night. The campground offers bathrooms, showers, a camp store, and a picnic pavilion. A 50-percent discount on all tree cottages, tree houses, and tent sites is given on Wednesdays.

Maple Tree Campground makes for a good hiking base camp, being situated adjacent to the Appalachian Trail. It's also close to Antietam National Battlefield, Crystal Grottos, Harper's Ferry National Historical Park, and other attractions. A stone's throw away is the very enjoyable Gapland State Park which offers lots of hiking and picnicking opportunities, not to mention a towering monument to war journalism and a tiny but interesting Civil War museum.

Location and Directions: At 20716 Townsend Road, in Gapland, Maryland. From Baltimore, take Interstate 70 west. Take Exit 52, Route 340, west and continue for about 15 miles. Take Route 67 north toward Boonsboro, and continue for about five miles. Turn right onto Gapland Road, and continue for about 1.5 miles. Turn left onto Townsend Road and follow signs to the campground.

Website and Phone: www.thetreehousecamp.com; (301) 432-5585.

Owens Creek Campground—
Catoctin Mountain Park

This campground, tucked deep in the far reaches of Catoctin Mountain Park, may be the area's quietest and most pleasant place to pitch a tent. There are no bells and whistles to distract visitors, just nature in its simple and most sublime form. This is a campground for the purist—those who need a patch of woods, perhaps a babbling brook, and a slice of their own wilderness to pass the night. It's also a great place to dust off those ecology guidebooks and learn about the abundant flora and fauna around camp.

Owens Creek Campground offers 51 wooded sites, with only a handful for recreational vehicles. Each site is equipped with a picnic table, fire ring, and tent pad (some pads are not level, so check before unloading the car). Two bathhouses have showers and flush toilets. All sites here are generally adequate, but the best ones are at the far end from the entrance, on the lower level, along the creek. Sites are $14 per night on a first-come, first-served basis. There is no camp office here, so payment is done on the honor system, though rangers will come around to check. The camp is generally open from mid-April through mid-November.

Around the campground is much for kids to do. A historic sawmill display not only educates, but also provides children with ample opportunity for climbing and playing. A boardwalk leads to Owens Creek, which harbors an abundant supply of salamanders, crayfish, dace, trout, and other slimy critters. Bring your aquarium nets and guidebooks. A short interpretive nature trail should not be missed, and ties into a longer horse trail system (I suggest getting a trail map from the visitors' center if you plan to go beyond the interpretive trail). The 26-mile-long Catoctin Trail, blazed in blue, runs through camp, but may be too rugged and rocky for smaller kids.

A few miles from the campground is Hunting Creek, popular for being Jimmy Carter's favorite trout stream (fly-fishing only is permitted through this stretch), and Cunningham Falls State Park, which offers a swimming lake and picturesque waterfall. The town of Thurmont, three miles away, offers eateries and convenience stores. Also nearby is the very beautiful Owens Creek Picnic Area for day-trippers. The picnic grove has an interesting half-mile interpretive nature trail that passes through turn-of-the-century homestead remains. A more challenging and visually rewarding hike to Wolf Rock and Chimney Rock is described in the Hikes chapter.

Owens Creek Campground is located beside Camp David, the highly classified presidential retreat that you will not find on park maps (and that you should not search for or ask about). Helicopters and fighter jets occasionally fly low overhead, so don't be startled.

Location and Directions: Owens Creek Campground is located in Catoctin Mountain Park. From Baltimore, take Interstate 70 west. In Frederick, take Route 15 north. In Thurmont, take Route 77 west and continue for about three miles. Turn right onto Park Central Road and follow signs to the campground.

Website and Phone: www.nps.gov/cato/pphtml/camping.html; (301) 663-9388.

Patapsco Valley State Park—Hollofield Area

This close-by campsite is one where you can take your kids on Friday after work and still be back in time for Saturday-morning chores. The campground is located off Route 40, near Ellicott City, but don't let the close proximity to Baltimore dissuade you from trying it. The setting is surprisingly quiet and scenic, set deep in a thick woodland away from the urban din.

The campground has 73 sites perched high above the Patapsco River. Most sites are set around a loop and each offers a large gravel tent pad, picnic table, and fire pit. The sites appear to be generously spaced out, but that may be an illusion brought about by the unusually dense woodland. In the bull's-eye of the loop is a modest camp store and bathhouse. Twelve campsites are set apart from the main camping area for visitors with pets. There is a small playground—mostly swings—between the two camping areas. Sites cost $18 per night ($23 with electric hook-up).

Campers may access a day-use facility, located about one mile away, which has playing fields, picnic tables, and a playground. There is a decent playground with swings and climbing apparatus, though most of the equipment is of the old-school, metal-bar variety. The day-use portion of the park costs $2 per person on weekends, and holidays (free for kids in car seats or seniors 62 or over).

The Hollofield Area also has a few trails you may want to try. Most interesting is the Union Dam Trail, which leads from the parking lot near the playground, down a steep decline, to the remnants of Union Dam on the Patapsco River. The dam once diverted water into a millrace that ran 1.5 miles to a former textile mill in Oella; it's said to have been the longest millrace in the country. The dam was breached during Hurricane Agnes in 1972. Another short trail leads to a fantastic lookout of the river valley, and the mile-and-a-half Ole Ranger Trail explores the surrounding woodland.

Location and Directions: The Hollofield Area of Patapsco Valley State Park is located off Route 40, between Ellicott City and Catonsville. From Baltimore, take the beltway to Exit 15B, Route 40. Continue west on Route 40 for about three miles, and follow signs to the state park.

Website and Phone: www.dnr.state.md.us/publiclands/central/patapscohollofield.html; (410) 461-5005. For reservations, call 1-888-432-2267.

Susquehanna State Park

Baltimore camping afficionados tend to head west to the Catoctin Mountains or skip over to the Eastern Shore for a night in the wild. For a change of pace, head north. Susquehanna State Park spans the south bank of the Susquehanna River in the bucolic hills of northern Harford County. The park includes a quiet and pleasant campground that provides access to a multitude of natural attractions and recreational opportunities.

The campground has 69 sites, six with electric hook-ups. The sites are spread equally among two loops, each with a bathhouse with showers and flush toilets. Sites come with the requisite picnic table and fire ring, and some are nicely secluded in thick foliage. Six of the sites are inhabited by cabins available for rent. A new and large playground on the premises features lots of slides and a short climbing tube. The campground is open from late April through early October. Cost for a site is $16 per night ($21 with electric hook-up). Cabins rent for $35 per night. Reservations are recommended. A two-day minimum stay is required on most weekends in summer.

Outdoor recreationists will find lots to do here. An impressive trail system takes hikers and bikers to the farthestmost reaches of the park, though I would recommend exploring the waterfront trails that offer powerful vistas of the Susquehanna River. Trail maps are available at the park office, which is the administrative and maintenance building. A three-mile ramble through the park is presented in the Hikes chapter. Picnic areas are located at several places in the park. Wet a line alongside the fishermen who line the river and Deer Creek, especially in spring when the shad are running.

Camping parents can use the opportunity to educate their children in local history and lore. Take them to the Rock Run Grist Mill, a restored waterfront grist mill with water wheel intact. Inside are displays telling about farming and milling in the 1800s. Milling demonstrations are given. Just upriver from the mill is the whitewashed Jersey Toll House, which once served a covered bridge that crossed the river at this point. Pedestals of the former bridge can still be seen in the river. On the hill overlooking the mill is Rock Run House, a stunning 1804 mansion once owned by John Carter, a partner in the mill operation. It's also open for tours.

The Steppingstone Museum, located in the south portion of the park, on Quaker Bottom Road, presents another educational side-trip opportunity. It features displays on farming and rural history, including arts and crafts from the period 1880 to 1920 It also offers special programs and demonstrations. The museum is open on weekends between May and the first Sunday in October, from 1 p.m. to 5 p.m. Admission is $2 for adults, and is free for children 12 and under.

Location and Directions: Three miles northwest of Havre de Grace, in Harford County. From Baltimore, take Interstate 95 north. Take Exit 89, Route 155, and head west. In about two miles, turn right onto Route 161, and go right again onto Rock Run Road. Follow signs to the campground.

Website and Phone: www.dnr.state.md.us/publiclands/central/ susquehanna.html; (410) 557-7994. For reservations, call 1-888-432-2267.

City Parks

Baltimore city dwellers have a secret that many suburban denizens do not share: Baltimore has some of the nation's finest urban parks. Some hunch spectacularly along the waterfront, others spread across the hills north of town, and a few are tucked into historic rowhouse communities. Here are a few worth checking out.

Canton Waterfront Park

Canton rivals Fells Point and Federal Hill as the city's most trendy neighborhood. Canton was once the quintessential blue-collar community, built on the sweat of Polish, Irish, German, and Ukrainian immigrants who settled here beginning centuries ago, toiling in the canning factories and on the shipping wharves. But the community has been gentrified. Tiny rowhouses now command six-figure price tags, factories have been converted to condominiums, and coffee shops and chic eateries stand where corner pubs once did.

Canton Waterfront Park is a small sliver of green space spread out along the waterfront, just off Boston Street. It's where peace-seeking Canton residents catch some fair-weather respite. Picnicking and fishing are popular activities here, and it's one of Baltimore's best spots to view tall ships and pleasure boats coming in and out of the Inner Harbor. The park also offers sweeping views of Fort McHenry. There is little shade, so bring sunscreen on sunny days. A parking lot is located on the premises. The park offers no concessions, though a slew of eateries can be found two blocks north on Canton Square.

The park area was once referred to as the "Baptizing Shores," used by local Baptist church congregations for their ceremonies. In 1893, it became the site of Baltimore's first public bathing beach (remember: no indoor plumbing back then). The cove area just off-shore was where, centuries ago, Baltimore clipper ships moored after returning from Brazil laden with coffee beans.

When at Canton Waterfront Park, be sure to check out the Korean Veterans Memorial, which is a tribute to Marylanders who lost their lives in that conflict. A map of Korea, incised on a rock floor, is surrounded by two low walls. One wall is inscribed with the names of all Maryland residents who died in the war, and the other describes various battles. A string of brick laid across the stone floor, connecting two flagpoles, represents the 38th parallel. The residential building just west of the park is Canton Cove Condominiums, a former tin-decorating plant where containers for such products as Coca-Cola and Lucky Strikes were produced. Just beyond that is Tindeco Wharf, once the largest tin lithography plant in the world, and now condominiums.

Location and Directions: In the 3000 block of Boston Street, in Canton. From downtown, take Pratt Street east. Just past Little Italy, turn right onto Broadway, and continue to Fells Point. Just before the Broadway Market, turn left onto Fleet Street and continue for about one-half mile. Veer right onto Boston Street, and continue through Canton. The waterfront park is on the right.

Cylburn Arboretum

Cylburn Arboretum is a 207-acre showplace for flora and fauna in northeast Baltimore. It's one city park that most folks have heard of, but few have visited. Being generally bereft of crowds, the arboretum is an ideal destination for families seeking a peaceful and pretty place to pass a day and learn about nature. Spring is an ideal time to visit, as the grounds burst into full color.

To fully understand Cylburn Arboretum, it helps to know its history. The grounds and stunning mansion (which still stands) were the former estate of Jesse Tyson, a wealthy industrialist and chromium magnate. Tyson began construction of the mansion in 1863, but it was delayed 25 years because of the Civil War. Tyson lived there in the summers with his mother and young bride. After his death, his widow remarried and decided to stick around the mansion. She hired the Olmsted brothers (of Manhattan's Central Park fame) to landscape the grounds, and she threw lavish parties in the well-trimmed gardens. Upon her death in 1942, she bequeathed the estate to the city—stunning landscape and all.

For a short spell, the mansion and grounds served as a home for neglected children, but soon found its true calling as a park. The mansion is among the most arresting in the city. It's of Second Empire design and constructed of gneiss from a nearby quarry. It has an attractive mansard roof with Italianate cupola. Lots of the interior design embellishments—molded plaster, carved wood features, inlaid floors, and tapestries—remain and are worth a look-see. The wrap-around porch offers sweet shade. Don't miss the wall mosaics in the entry foyer.

The mansion contains a modest but interesting nature center on the third floor (just flick on the light switch), and also offers a bird display curated by the Maryland Ornithological Society. About 100 watercolors of Maryland wildflowers are shown on the first floor. It also houses the administrative offices of the Cylburn Arboretum Association and the City Horticultural Division. An extensive horticultural library is open to the public by appointment.

The gardens are what attracts the lion's share of visitors. They are numerous, beautiful, and dispersed neatly around the grounds. Some gardens feature butterfly-attracting plants and roses. Others feature vegetables and herbs. My favorite displays are those that replicate rowhouse backyard gardens. A formal Victorian garden flourishes just east of the mansion.

A particularly interesting arrangement is the All-America Selections Display Garden, which grows and shows new flower varieties not yet on the market. A Garden of the Senses was set up for the visually impaired and wheelchair-bound; it was designed with flora offering sharp odors or interesting textures. A map of the various gardens can be obtained inside the mansion.

Scattered about are attractive trees like magnolias, conifers, and Japanese maples, and lots of shrubs. Most of the displays are identified by placards, but coming to the arboretum presents a fun opportunity to finally use that wildflower or tree guidebook withering away on your shelf. Six trails snake about the property, allowing visitors to make their own surreptitious discoveries. Parents should note that picnicking and ball-playing are not allowed on the grounds.

Location and Directions: At 4915 Greenspring Avenue. From Interstate 83, take the Northern Parkway exit heading west. Continue for about one-half mile and turn left onto Cylburn Avenue. Follow Cylburn Avenue for another one-half mile until it terminates at Greenspring Avenue. Turn left onto Greenspring Avenue and make a quick left onto the Cylburn Arboretum grounds.

Hours and Admission: Grounds are open daily from 6 a.m. to 9 p.m., except in winter when the gates close at dusk. The mansion is open on Mondays through Fridays from 7:30 a.m. to 3:30 p.m. The museum is open on Tuesdays and Thursdays from 1 p.m. to 3 p.m., or by arrangement. No admission is charged.

Website and Phone: www.cylburnassociation.org; (410) 367-2217.

Druid Hill Park

In a bygone era, Druid Hill Park was Baltimore's crown jewel public area, offering a leafy retreat for carriage rides and recreating. The mass appeal of this park has waned a bit, but it remains one of the city's largest and most fun gathering spots.

Druid Hill Park is best known as home of the Baltimore Zoo, which is discussed in the Zoos chapter, but it offers substantially more. To the north is a lightly used disc golf course. The nearby gold-brick building holds the Baltimore Zoo's reptile collection, and can be toured for $1, with children under 2 free. Reptile House hours are 10 a.m. to 4 p.m. daily.

Near the Gwynns Falls Parkway entrance is an eye-catching, 90-foot-tall glass structure belonging to the Baltimore Conservatory and Botanical Gardens. The Victorian Palm House, as it is called, is one of the most stunning structures in the city. Inside is a lush tropical paradise of plants, and on the surrounding grounds are smaller greenhouses and lots of gardens. Visitors may wander around to see flora from around the globe. It's a haven for flower lovers and garden aficionados. The Victorian Palm House is open on Thursdays through Sundays from 10 a.m. to 4 p.m., and admission is free.

Most visitors to the park head to the south, where many recreational facilities are located. The focal point here is Druid Hill Lake, which is surrounded by a running and biking path. The lake was formed in 1871 by construction of an earthen dam that, at the time, was the largest in the country. The embankment can be seen from Interstate 83. The lake remains a city water-supply reservoir. Parking is plentiful here.

Scattered around this area are numerous picnic pavilions and playing fields, including a volleyball court, soccer fields, and a basketball court. A public swimming pool sees lots of activity in summer. The Druid Hill Park Tennis Center is one of the area's most popular. Visitors exploring this area will also see interesting fountains and statues, including one of the original Braveheart, William Wallace, who was popularized by Mel Gibson. The lovely Druid Hill mansion, the former estate house of the grounds, now serves as administrative offices for the zoo.

Just beyond the lake is Safety City, a scale-model urban area operated by the city's Department of Public Works to teach children public safety. It includes roads, a pool, and mini skyscrapers, and is open from mid-April to mid-October by appointment only.

It's worth mentioning that the urban decay being experienced by some communities adjacent to Druid Hill Park has caused a decrease in park use. I've always found Druid Hill Park to be safe and fun in daylight hours, and would not hesitate to use its facilities. Use your own discretion.

Location and Directions: In west Baltimore. From downtown, take Interstate 83 north. Take the Druid Park Lake Drive, and follow it around the south face of the park. It will merge with McCulloh Street along the west face of the park. Several park entrances are along this stretch. The main entrance is where Gwynns Falls Parkway terminates at the park.

Federal Hill Park

Federal Hill Park is tiny. A good chunk of the park is too steep to walk on. The playground equipment is pretty basic, and draws maddening crowds on nice days. At times the park is too congested even for flinging a Frisbee. Then why do I call Federal Hill Park one of the best in the city, which everyone must visit at least once? It's because visitors are privy to one of the country's most arresting urbanscapes. The park perches high above downtown Baltimore, and commands jaw-dropping views of Baltimore harbor's many faces— from the glitzy to the gritty.

Federal Hill Park is situated on the south bank of the Inner Harbor, just beyond Rash Field. It's an unusual protrusion of land that appears man-made, but is really a natural formation of red clay. Residents of the adjacent Federal Hill neighborhood meet atop the hill to walk dogs and let their kids play. The atmosphere is loose and friendly. Kids will enjoy the swings and slides, but will also find fun in climbing over the Civil War-era cannons pointing over downtown (the cannons were trained on the city to deter aggression from southern sympathizers). Some space is available for ball-playing, and a fence has been installed to separate kids from dogs.

Federal Hill Park offers outstanding views in three directions. The east side looks out over the church spires and rowhouse roofs of the Federal Hill neighborhood. A walk down Montgomery Street, located at the base of the staircase, is highly recommended; it will reveal

▲ Downtown Baltimore as seen from Federal Hill Park

one of Baltimore's most coveted streets, where historical rowhouses have been restored to pristine quality. The view to the north is of the Inner Harbor and its many attractions. To the east is the port of Baltimore—the city's blue-collar district. Kids will love seeing the ships moving in and out of the harbor. The leveled property bordered by a marina across the channel is the former Allied Signal plant, once a chromium manufacturing facility. It was listed as one of the nation's most critical Superfund sites, but has been remediated back to health and is awaiting redevelopment. Across the water, the Domino Sugar sign, supposedly the largest neon sign in the world with the "D" standing 32 feet tall, stares down on the waterfront.

Federal Hill has a rich past. Its name comes from a raucous party that was held there in 1788 to celebrate Maryland's ratification of the federal constitution. A fort atop Federal Hill kept a watchful eye over the city during the Civil War. Upon its military discharge, the hill became a public park, at one point having a handsome Victorian-style observation tower protruding from its peak. Today it's quiet and low-key, though some tourists wander up from the harbor.

Parking at Federal Hill Park may be a problem. Free on-street parking is located in the residential area just south of the park, on Warren Avenue, but be mindful of signs providing parking restrictions. Meter parking (25 cents for 15 minutes) can be found along Key Highway, which runs adjacent to and north of the park. Bring lots of quarters. Long-term meter parking can be found along Covington Street, which runs adjacent to and east of the park. Uphill meters here are a bargain at 75 minutes for each quarter, with a 10-hour limit. If your tummy rumbles while playing at the park, Sam's Bagels, as well as several other cafes, are located on Light Street, a short and safe two blocks west and one block south of the park.

Location and Directions: Federal Hill Park is located along Key Highway, just south of the Inner Harbor. From Interstate 95, take Interstate 395 into the city, following signs for downtown. In front of Oriole Park at Camden Yards, turn right onto Conway Street and continue three blocks to the waterfront. Turn right onto Light Street and veer left onto Key Highway. The park is on the right.

Fort McHenry National Monument

Fort McHenry park is where South Baltimore residents flee to escape the summer swelter. The park impressively wraps around the headland of the Locust Point peninsula, and receives cool breezes whipping off the bay. There are ample grounds for picnicking, ball-playing, kite-flying, or just lazing around. A favorite activity is watching ships come in and out of the harbor—everything from tall ships to sailboats to luxurious cabin cruisers to behemoth container ships. The nearby historical fort sponges up tourists by the busload, but few visitors pay heed to the beautiful park section.

▲ Watching boats at Fort McHenry National Monument

▲ The wide-open spaces of Fort McHenry National Monument

A nice feature of the park is the paved walking and biking trail that traces the waterfront for just under one mile, offering nice views of the bay, the Key Bridge, and various port areas. The industrial community of Fairfield, where the world's first container ship was made, can be seen from the south face of the park. This stretch of park was the site of the city's first coed bathing beach, which opened in 1915; each day, thousands paid the nickel to take a cleansing dip here.

The industrial waterfront of Canton can be seen from the park's north face. Look for four silos emblazoned with Lehigh Cement. This is Lazaretto Point, where the city's smallpox quarantine station once stood. "Lazaretto" is Italian for "fever hospital" or "pesthouse." A black Coast Guard tower along this stretch of park guides ships into Baltimore's harbor by flashing a green beacon every two seconds.

Fort McHenry's historical significance should not be lost in its surrounding beauty. The fort is best known for its impregnable stand against the British in the War of 1812, enduring a 25-hour bombardment. It was during this war, and just off this shoreline, that Francis Scott Key penned the words to "The Star-Spangled Banner." He wrote them from a British truce ship where he was negotiating a prisoner exchange. Few people know that our national anthem is actually Key's lyrics set to the tune "To Anacreon in Heaven," a British drinking ditty.

Visitors to the park may want to check out the historical fort area. The Visitor Center offers some exhibits and a short film titled *The Defense of Fort McHenry*. Visitors can also walk through the actual fort to see the restored barracks and quarters, supplemented with interpretive signs. The cost to enter the historic area is $5 for those 17 or older, and free for those under 17. (There is no cost to enter the recreational area of the park.)

Two other historical peculiarities may be of interest to fort visitors. Just north of the park's entry gates is a brick building bearing the title Naval Reserve Center. This is where, beginning in 1916, immigrants entering the United States through Baltimore were processed. Few people realize that Locust Point was the second most prolific entry point in the nation for immigrants after Ellis Island. Also, in a building once located near the current entrance to the park, Simon Lake invented the modern submarine in 1897. Dubbed the *Argonaut*, it was 36 feet long and could stay underwater for 10 hours. Its maiden voyage was off the tip of Fort McHenry.

Location and Directions: In Locust Point, at the eastern terminus of Fort Avenue. From Interstate 95, take the Key Highway exit and follow signs to that road. Continue on Key Highway for about one-half mile. Just after a sharp left bend, turn left onto Lawrence Street, and continue for one block until it dead-ends. Turn left onto Fort Avenue and continue for about one mile to Fort McHenry.

Hours and Admission: The Visitor Center and fort are open daily from 8 a.m. to 4:45 p.m., with extended hours in summer. Admission is free to get into the park grounds, and $5 per person to get into the historical attractions (free for those under 17).

Website and Phone: www.nps.gov/fomc/index.htm; (410) 962-4290.

Gwynns Falls/Leakin Park

At over 1,200 acres, Gwynns Falls/Leakin Park is the third largest urban park in the country, behind Fairmount Park in Philadelphia and Central Park in New York City. For most of its existence, the park was little more than dense woodland offering few recreational opportunities, but noteworthy for unsavory activities. It has recently experienced a community-driven renaissance, and is now a fun and safe family destination spot.

Most recreational visitors to the park use the Gwynns Falls Trail, a four-mile hiking and biking trail that follows the course of the pretty Gwynns Falls. The trail opened in 1999, and is part of a plan to connect Gwynns Falls/Leakin Park with Middle Branch Park, in South Baltimore. When complete, the trail will be 14 miles long and serve 15 neighborhoods. The opening of the Gwynns Falls Trail brought other amenities to the park, including sports fields, a picnic pavilion, a basketball court, restrooms, a playground, and wildlife observation decks. The park is home to the Carrie Murray Nature Center, which is discussed in the Nature Centers chapter. It's also where kids go to ride the miniature steam trains, which are discussed in the Railroads chapter. The Chesapeake Bay Outward Bound Program operates a program from here, and scenes from *The Blair Witch Project* were filmed here.

The park is named for Richard Gwynn and J. Wilson Leakin. The former held exclusive trading rights with the Algonquin Indians in this area, and the latter, in 1942, donated a sizeable tract for development of the park.

Location and Directions: In West Baltimore. Several facilities are best accessed via Windsor Mill Road, which runs along the park's northern boundary. From the Interstate 695 beltway, take Exit 17, Security Boulevard, east. Continue on Security Boulevard for about two miles, and turn left onto Forest Park Avenue. Proceed for about one-half mile and turn right onto Windsor Mill Road. The Gwynns Falls Trail is best accessed via the Winans Meadow trailhead or Leon Day Park. Both are situated along Franklintown Road, which can be accessed from Security Boulevard.

Patterson Park

The 155-acre Patterson Park is the wellspring of several vibrant East Baltimore communities. The well-used park offers an ensemble of attractions, including an Olympic-sized swimming pool, ball fields, tennis and basketball courts, a recreation center, and, in winter, a bubble-covered ice rink for skating and hockey. Along the south border of the park is a tiny pond that is used for fishing and bird-watching. Mallard and wood ducks winter-over here and are fun to watch.

Patterson Park features an inordinate amount of open space, and is a great place to picnic or fly a kite. There are paved trails that weave around the park for biking or skating, but be mindful that the park spans a hillside and some pathways are rather steep.

The park's most recognizable attraction is the Patterson Park Observatory, better known as the Pagoda. This 60-foot-high octagonal structure was designed by Charles Latrobe and built in 1891. Recently refurbished, it offers panoramic views of the city and surrounding areas clear to the Chesapeake Bay. The five cannons lined up next to the Pagoda were successfully used to stave off a British invasion during the War of 1812. Just beyond the Pagoda is a stone fountain that stood at what was once the park's grand entrance during its halcyon days. The gatekeeper's house stands beside the fountain.

Patterson Park is the former estate of merchant William Patterson, and opened for public use in 1853. In the early 19th century, waterfront residents retreated here in droves to escape the scourge of yellow fever. During the Civil War, troops were stationed here, and many of those soldiers wounded at Gettysburg were brought here for care. Butchers Hill, the community of large rowhouses along the park's northern border, was so named because it is where the city butchers settled. The rowhouses are unusually spacious and ornate because the butchers got very wealthy selling meat to the Civil War soldiers stationed here. Communities of more diminutive rowhouses stretch south of the park, and are fun to walk through.

Location: In East Baltimore. From downtown, take Pratt Street east. About one mile past President Street, Pratt Street dead-ends at the park. Turn right onto Patterson Park Avenue and make a left onto Eastern Avenue. On-street parking is available along these two streets.

Sherwood Gardens

An annual pilgrimage to Sherwood Gardens is how many Baltimore families celebrate the coronation of spring. In April and May, this tiny seven-acre hideaway explodes with color, thanks to 100,000 tulips and thousands of azaleas—not to mention cherry, dogwood, and other spectacular blooms. The park is tucked away in a nook of the Guilford neighborhood, and is framed by some of Baltimore's most magnificent mansions. Sherwood Gardens may, quite frankly, be the most beautiful quiet spot in the city. There is plenty of grass for picnicking and benches for resting, but no playgrounds or recreational facilities. The gardens get thronged during the spring months on weekends. Parking is on-street. To make the day complete, stroll down Greenway to see what your house would look like had your grandfather been a railroad baron.

Location and Directions: Sherwood Gardens is located in the Guilford section of the city, and is bordered by Greenway, Stratford Road, Underwood Road, and Highfield Road. From Interstate 83, take Cold Spring Lane, heading east. Continue for two miles on Cold Spring Lane. Just past the reservoir, turn right onto Underwood Road, and after two blocks, turn right onto Stratford Road. The gardens are immediately to your left.

County and State Parks

Parks and playgrounds in and around Baltimore number in the hundreds. Most are tiny, postage stamp parks serving a particular neighborhood or community. A few, however, transcend the corner-lot notion and offer outstanding facilities or unusually beautiful scenery that make a visit worthwhile, even if it involves a drive. Here are a few area parks that have a wider appeal than most.

Centennial Park

Centennial Park is a well-planned and very well-used recreational facility in central Howard County. Its grounds are spacious, and the park offers a host of fun opportunities—hiking, running, picnicking, kite-flying, boating, bird-watching, and biking to name a few. It offers enough menu choices to tie up a family for the entire day.

Perhaps the most intensely used venue at Centennial Park is the paved walking/biking path that circles a 54-acre lake. The path is hilly and pretty, and leads to neat pockets of the park. The west fringe of the lake is a waterfowl nesting area, so keep your eyes peeled for unusual ducks and geese. The path passes through an arboretum area with lots of interpretive signs. On nice days the pathway can get a bit congested with runners, bikers, in-line skaters, and battalions of walkers. A circumnavigation of the lake is just shy of 2.5 miles.

Centennial Park is composed primarily of four recreational areas. The South Area attracts most visitors, and is situated just off Route 108. It holds a prodigious number of picnic tables and pavilions, and is a great place to access the walking path. A concession stand offers snacks and sandwiches. Nearby is a boat rental facility, where canoes, paddle boats, and rowboats can be rented by the hour or day (see the Boat Rental chapter for details). A private boat launch is located a few hundred feet down the shoreline from the rental facility. A permit is required for all private vessels. Located between the private boat launch area and the boat rental facility is a small patch of woodland with a few gentle hiking trails running through. This is a great place to introduce toddlers to hiking.

The West Area is situated high on the west bank of the lake, off Centennial Road. The area is mostly athletic venues such as soccer fields, basketball courts, tennis courts, a volleyball court, and other ballfields. A nice playground has many sliding boards and lots of climbing tunnels and runways. The North Area, located away from the lake off Old Annapolis Road, is mostly athletic venues, and has six outdoor racquetball (or handball) courts. A short paved walking path leads from this area to the lake.

The East Area is located near the base of the earthen dam that forms Centennial Lake, and is accessed from Woodland Road. Its focus is a large-group picnic pavilion, but it also has lots of playing fields, a tot lot, and tennis and basketball courts.

Planners of Centennial Park won three awards for how the design integrates so well with, and is sensitive to, the surrounding environment. The park continues to hold its beauty and wildlife in high esteem. Certain areas are off-limits to visitors to accommodate fish-spawning and bird-breeding. It's a favorite bird-watching spot for local birding clubs. The park offers lots of outdoor-related programs for kids, including nature walks.

Location and Directions: Centennial Park is located on Route 108 in Columbia. From Baltimore, take Interstate 70 west. In Ellicott City, take Route 29 south. In about five miles, take Route 108 (Clarksville Pike) west. The main park entrance is located about one mile up Route 108, to the right.

Hours: From April through November, the park is open daily from dawn to dusk. Winter hours are daily from 8 a.m. to 5 p.m.

Website and Phone: www.co.ho.md.us/RAP/RAP_HoCoParks Centennial.htm; (410) 313-4700.

Cromwell Valley Park

What's so appealing about this Baltimore County park is not what it offers, but what it doesn't offer. No playgrounds or swimming pools, no paved bike trails, no heavy development. Cromwell Valley Park is 367 acres of pristine farmland and woodland that provide a perfect opportunity to explore nature close to the city. Go there to hike, identify birds, sight other wildlife, or just traipse through the woods and meadows.

Cromwell Valley Park was created in the mid-1990s when the county purchased three adjacent farms. The Willow Grove Farm once belonged to Robert Merrick, a prominent Baltimore banker. The Sherwood Farm is a former peach and apple orchard. The Good Fellowship Farm is a commercial Christmas tree farm that still operates. The three farms are tied together by Minebank Run, a small cascading creek named for the mining operations that occurred here centuries ago. Lime kilns operated in this valley into the 1920s, with remnants remaining. The lime was made by burning marble quarried in nearby Cockeysville, and was used for whitewashing and for farming purposes.

Cromwell Valley Park supports over four miles of hiking trails. Follow the red trail for a long ramble to the park's far reaches and highest elevations. The red trail interconnects with the trail system around Loch Raven Reservoir. The orange trail is a nice and easy track that connects the Willow Grove Farm to the Sherwood Farm, following the course of Minebank Run. Keep an eye peeled for herons and kingfisher along this stretch. Be forewarned that not all trails are well marked, so pay attention as you explore and, should you get lost, just head downhill to return to the parking area.

The park hosts many family-oriented programs. Topics range from gardening to nature to Native American skills to animal story time. The park also hosts a Community Supported Agricultural Program, where farmers, many living on site, grow organic vegetables and sell them to the public through a cooperative arrangement. A gardening program for children happens every Saturday morning from March through October. Special events include hayrides, nature walks, campfires, and Easter egg hunts.

At the time of this writing, officials were considering turning the Merrick farmhouse into an interpretive center featuring displays on local flora and fauna and providing educational lessons on agricultural subjects such as sustainable organic farming.

Location and Directions: At 2002 Cromwell Bridge Road. From the Interstate 695 beltway, take Exit 29A, Cromwell Bridge Road, and head outside the beltway. Continue on Cromwell Bridge Road for about 1.5 miles, and take the second left into the park, which is clearly marked Willow Grove Farm (the first left in the park is at Sherwood Farm, which leads to the park office).

Hours: Daily from dawn to dusk.

Website and Phone: www.co.ba.md.us/agencies/recreation/
cromwell.html; (410) 887-2503.

Downs Park

This park is an ideal destination for families drawn to big water as
well as woodland. The park is part of Bodkin Neck, which juts into
the Chesapeake Bay, offering sweeping views clear across to Rock
Hall on the Eastern Shore. The majority of its 231 acres is natural
woodland, with most development situated along the waterfront.
Facilities include a nice visitors' center, an expansive playground,
restroom facilities, and a lovely spread of flowers and shrubs referred to as Mother's Garden. A viewing pier overlooking the bay
lets visitors see an osprey's nest close up. Ballfields are located in the
park's western quadrant.

The best reason to make the drive to Downs Park, however, is
the well-maintained trail system. The park offers five miles of trails,
most being flat, paved, and shaded, which are described in the Bicycling chapter. They are perfect for hiking, biking, or pushing a
stroller. A nice spot for lunch is at the picnic tables along Locust
Creek, and another is on the grassy area by the bay-front beach. The
park hosts a free concert series in summer.

Users of Downs Park's trail system may notice a series of interpretive signs that detail the park's interesting childhood. The
land was originally purchased by Charles Carroll, the only Catholic
signer of the Declaration of Independence. It was later used as a
farm to grow vegetables, tomatoes, peaches, and melons, which
were shipped to Baltimore via sailboat. Then, around the turn of
the last century, it became the summer retreat for the family of H.R.
Mayo Thom, a wealthy importer of Cuban tobacco who resided
during other months in Roland Park.

Location and Directions: At 8311 John Downs Loop, in Pasadena.
From Baltimore, take Interstate 97 south, and Route 100 east toward
Gibson Island. Route 100 will merge with Route 177 (Mountain
Road). Stay on Mountain Road for 3.5 miles to the park entrance.

Hours and Admission: Park hours are from 9 a.m. to dusk daily except Tuesdays, when it is closed. Park office hours are from 9 a.m. to 4
p.m. daily except Tuesdays. Entry fee is $4 per vehicle ($2 for disabled).

Website and Phone: web.aacpl.net/rp/parks/dp; (410) 222-6230.

Hannah More Park

Hannah More Park is 63 acres of playing fields and picnic pavilions, located just off Interstate 795, in Reisterstown. For parents, the main focus of the park is its fine play area, called the Sunshine Playground. It's one of the nicest in Baltimore's western suburbs. The playground includes three sets of play apparatus, each featuring slides and ramps. There are swing sets and one stand-alone slide that is unusually high and windy. A sandbox on the premises includes a sliding board and a play train to climb on. Lots of open space is available for ballplaying.

A nice feature of the Sunshine Playground is the paved pathways that weave around and link the various activity areas. They are painted with a double-yellow center line to resemble a road. Toddlers will love scooting around these pathways in their plastic cars or trikes, pretending they are buzzing down Interstate 95. It makes for a great place to learn how to ride bikes and scooters, or to try out those in-line skates. A restroom is situated on the premises, but the doors are sometimes locked.

The attractive building at the entrance to the park is the former home of the Hannah More Academy, which opened its doors in 1832 as an Episcopalian boarding school for women. It was named for Hannah More, an English author who altruistically started up lots of free schools in London for poor children. A newer version of the Hannah More School, which serves children who are emotionally disturbed or who have autism, is located in the park.

Location and Directions: From the Interstate 695 beltway, take Interstate 795 (the Northwest Expressway) west. In seven miles, take the Franklin Boulevard exit, heading east. At the second traffic light, turn left onto Reisterstown Road, also known as Route 140. Just past the shopping center, turn right at the sign into Hannah More Park. Veer right around the former academy building, and continue to the playground and ball fields.

Kinder Farm Park

Kinder Farm Park is a 288-acre sprawl of ball fields, ponds, trails, meadows, and woodland situated off Jumpers Hole Road, in Millersville. Parents with young children will likely agree that the park's gem is its playground—one of the most vast in the Baltimore area. It spreads across several levels and includes about a dozen unique play stations. Crawling tubes, climbing ropes, a large sandbox, and two tube slides built into a hillside vie for the kids' attention. I counted 10 sliding boards—none at a height that I would consider dangerous. A favorite activity of the toddlers was crawling on plastic animals, including dinosaurs, a toad, and an alligator.

Be aware that, keeping track of two children simultaneously can be a challenge since the park is so spread out, especially when it is crowded (and it often is). Restrooms and vending machines are located on the premises. Many picnic tables and grill sites are located nearby. Large pavilions are available for rental. Parents visiting the playground may want to bring along the baby jogger, as there are many walking trails in close proximity, including the paved 2.4-mile-long Perimeter Trail.

Also included in Kinder Farm Park is the Harvey Garcelon Sports Complex, which includes playing areas for baseball, softball, soccer, and basketball. Four ponds are scattered around the grounds for catch-and-release fishing, though a state fishing license is required. Paved trails for biking and unimproved trails for hiking and horseback riding are also available. Older kids will enjoy the disc golf course.

Kinder Farm Park offers a calendar full of youth-oriented programs. A representative selection includes a birdhouse-building workshop, a stargazing party, an evening bird identification walk,

▲ Tubes and slides at Kinder Farm Park

▲ The expansive playground at Kinder Farm Park

and wildlife story time. Parents who live near Kinder Farm Park may have interest in the community gardens, where each year 120 plots (each 20 feet by 30 feet) are leased to the public for personal gardens. The growing season is from mid-March through November.

Kinder Farm Park is the result of land bequeathed to Anne Arundel County in 1979 by the Kinder family, who for generations farmed the land and raised cattle there. The park is about one-third of their total holdings. The park office is a brick farmhouse built in 1926, and many of the original silos and outbuildings still stand.

Location and Directions: At 1001 Kinder Farm Park Road, in Millersville, just north of Severna Park. From Baltimore, take Interstate 97 south. In Severna Park, take Benfield Boulevard east, and continue for 2.4 miles. Turn left onto Jumpers Hole Road and continue for 1.2 miles. Turn left onto Kinder Farm Park Road, and continue to the parking areas.

Hours and Admission: Park hours are Wednesdays through Mondays from 7 a.m. to dusk. Park office hours are Mondays, Wednesdays, Thursdays, and Fridays from 9 a.m. to 4 p.m., and Saturdays and Sundays from 10 a.m. to 3 p.m. The park and office are closed on Tuesdays. Admission is free.

Website and Phone: www.kinderfarmpark.org; (410) 222-6115.

Lake Waterford Park

Located near larger and more popular recreational venues like Downs Park and Kinder Farm Park, Lake Waterford Park often gets lost in the mix. But this little peach of a park offers lots of opportunities for fun and games. The centerpiece is a gemlike, 12-acre pond that hosts flocks of waterfowl and schools of bass, panfish, and catfish. Trout are stocked in spring. Shoreline fishing is allowed, but boats are prohibited. Kids will enjoy the sprawling "boundless" playground where they can hone their climbing and balancing skills. The park has pavilions to rent, basketball courts, tennis courts, a football field, softball diamonds, and nice trails for hiking. Organized hikes and programs dealing with various nature-based topics are regularly offered.

Location and Directions: At 830 Pasadena Road, in Pasadena. From Baltimore, take Interstate 95 south and Route 100 east. Take the Catherine Road exit. From the ramp, turn right onto Catherine Road and continue about three-quarters of a mile to the park entrance.

Hours: Daily from 7 a.m. to sunset, with extended hours during fishing season. Park office hours are Monday through Friday from 9 a.m. to 2 p.m.

Website and Phone: web.aacpl.net/rp/parks/lwp; (410) 222-6248.

Lyn Stacie Getz Creative Playground

At 14,000 square feet, the Lyn Stacie Getz Playground is one of the largest in the area. It's located where Route 24 meets Ring Factory Road, near Bel Air. The playground is mostly constructed of wood and offers an unusual number of ramps, runways, stairs, and balancing apparatus. There is a climbing wall, a pyramid to crawl through, and a clock tower to scale. Rope walks and fun obstacles are everywhere. A couple of swing sets are available for a change of pace, and a generous sandbox comes well stocked with sand toys. Benches line the park for waiting parents, and a few picnic tables are freckled about.

The Getz playground was constructed in 2001, and serves as a model for what can be accomplished when a community comes together to benefit children. In all, 750 volunteers took part in the project. The names of the donors are splashed across a surrounding picket fence. The entire playground was built over a period of five days by local volunteers and soldiers of the U.S. Army Ordnance Center and

School. Currently portable toilets are located in the parking lot, but plans are afoot to construct a restroom building on the premises.

The playground serves as a memorial to Lyn Stacie Getz, a Bel Air native who was killed in a New York City apartment fire in 1999, and to Paula Craven and her son Jay, who died in the crash of TWA Flight 800, in 1996. Large donations to the facility were made by both sets of parents.

Location and Directions: At the intersection of Route 24 and Ring Factory Road, just east of Bel Air. From Baltimore, take Interstate 95 north. Take Exit 77B, Route 24, west toward Bel Air. Continue for about four miles. Turn left onto Ring Factory Road, and make a quick left into the parking lot of the playground.

Hours: Daily from dawn to dusk.

North Point State Park

This pretty park, located southeast of Baltimore, will appeal to those who enjoy less-developed recreational areas. The park is located on the tip of a peninsula jutting into the Chesapeake Bay, sandwiched between the Back and Patapsco Rivers. Its 1,370 acres are mostly fields, wetlands, and marsh, with trails snaking about the unusual ecosystems. Kids will enjoy seeing the abundant birds flitting about the marsh reeds. Much of the land is designated as wilderness in co-operation with the Nature Conservancy. There are lots of interpretive signs schooling visitors in wetland ecology and animals that live here. A one-third-mile-long trail leads to an observation deck. Watch for the iridescent bluebirds along the park's entrance road.

Most visitors will eventually end up at the waterfront area, which offers panoramic views of the Chesapeake Bay, including two lighthouses within eyeshot. A small and so-so swimming and wading area gets crowded in summer. Fishing is available from a wooden pier near the park office. A fun thing to do is to walk out onto the concrete recreation pier.

The area around the waterfront comes with an intriguing past. It used to be the site of the Bay Shore Amusement Park, Baltimore's favorite waterfront escape from 1906 to 1947. A trolley from downtown Baltimore brought excursionists here on an 18-mile rail line. In its heyday, it deposited over 1,000 visitors at the park each hour. Historical photographs show elbow-to-elbow revelers. The amusement park had many rides, but the favorite was the "Sea Swing," which was erected in the water. It rotated riders wildly in a circle, throwing them into the chop. It was closed because of liability concerns (even then!). The resort included a dance hall and 500-seat restaurant. A diving board at the end of the still-standing pier sent swimmers into the deep waters. Two remnants of the amusement park remain: the beautiful Edwardian trolley shed, which is now used for group events, and a fountain recently restored to its original state. Both are worth a visit, as is the visitors' center behind the fountain, which has some historical photographs of the amusement park. The park was also the site of a skirmish during the War of 1812.

Location and Directions: North Point State Park is located on Route 20, just south of Edgemere, in southeastern Baltimore County. To get there, take Exit 42 (Edgemere/Fort Howard) from the Interstate 695 beltway and follow Route 20 (North Point Road) south. If you are traveling north on the beltway, take Exit 43 and follow signs for Route 20 south. The entrance to the park is well marked.

Website and Phone: www.dnr.state.md.us/publiclands/central/northpoint.html; (410) 329-0757.

Oregon Ridge Park

Oregon Ridge Park is the largest tract of public land administered by Baltimore County, spanning over 1,000 acres of wooded hillsides. It has a nature center and swimming lake discussed elsewhere in this book. A walk through the park is presented in the Hikes chapter. But Oregon Ridge Park is so rich in activities, it warrants further discussion.

What parents of toddlers favor most about Oregon Ridge Park is its playground—the "Purple Playground" as my daughter calls it. It's quite large and pretty to look at, with the slides and other apparatus being purple, teal, and blue. The playground equipment is exceptionally safe. Runway areas are well lined with safety bars, and the sliding boards have high edges. The unit in general seems to contain children much better than most—a boon for this parent of a risk-taking 3-year-old son. Plenty of picnic tables are scattered about the playground, and a large pavilion nearby is available for rent. The only pitfall: no restrooms.

Situated next to the playground is the Oregon Ridge Dinner Theater, which is now a public hall for community events such as children's shows, dog shows, and meetings. Beside the dinner theater is a former ski lodge (notice the now-defunct ski slopes and lift remnants on the nearby hillside) now used as a conference and meeting center. Next to the lodge is an outdoor concert hall where the Baltimore Symphony Orchestra performs in summer. Each summer the BSO hosts some concerts for children. Spread a blanket, bring a picnic, and enjoy great music.

The park also offers a tiny par-three golf course, horseshoe pits, and softball and other sports fields. There is more open space than could ever be used, and the trail system is among the area's best. A spectacular and resplendent hot-air balloon launch happens here each year during Preakness week. The Oregon Grille restaurant is located near the park entrance, but may be more upscale than most parents care for.

Location and Directions: At 13401 Beaver Dam Road, in Cockeysville. From Baltimore, take Interstate 83 north. Take Exit 20-B, Shawan Road, heading west. At the first light, turn left onto Beaver Dam Road, and follow signs to the various facilities.

Hours and Admission: Hours vary according to season. Entrance is free, though some activities require a fee.

Website and Phone: www.co.ba.md.us/agencies/recreation/oregonridgelodge; (410) 887-1818.

Patapsco Valley State Park—McKeldin Area

Some parks are laden with playgrounds and ballfields, and are clearly intended for hard-core recreational use. Others are kept relatively unfettered by athletic facilities and development, and are set aside for outdoor enthusiasts seeking a more spiritual experience. Planners of the McKeldin Area of Patapsco Valley State Park have skillfully managed to dovetail these two notions with aplomb. This park of stunning beauty is loaded with hiking trails, secluded picnic areas, and quiet spots, yet interspersed throughout are more traditional recreational facilities such as basketball courts and playgrounds. It's all woven together tightly enough to appeal to everyone.

The park sprawls across 1,000 acres in southeastern Carroll County, just off Marriotsville Road. The park facilities are situated in the crotch of the Patapsco River, where the north and south branches flow into the main stem, carving deep ravines in the hillsides. The park is primarily used by hikers, mountain bikers, birders, and folks using the picnic pavilions. There is also a large group camp here that attracts scout troops. Two playgrounds are simple and unobtrusive. The park offers many fine picnic pavilions, with smaller ones renting for as little as $10. A nice disc golf course rambles throughout sparse woodland and meadows. The park has an unusual number of comfort stations, a boon for parents concerned with potty-training.

McKeldin is a great place to bring the kids to spot wildlife. The woods are rife with deer that enter the grassy meadows for feeding at dusk and dawn. Rabbits, groundhogs, and other small critters can readily be observed. I've seen the occasional beaver submarining through the waters along the north branch of the river. McKeldin is also a favorite birding location for local clubs. Coming here makes for the perfect excuse to dust off those old nature guidebooks and trick the kids into thinking that you know ecology.

All visitors should venture to McKeldin Falls. Though not a waterfall per se, it's a nice tumbling section of the Patapsco River that can be accessed either by hiking trails or by taking the access road through the park to its farthest reach. The pool below the falls looks inviting, but no swimming is allowed. Keep an eye peeled for herons in the water and kingfishers clinging to overhanging tree branches. The park is rich in hiking trails, which include gentle ones running along the river and more ornery ones through the hills. The four-mile Switchback Trail traces a nice circuit, and is detailed in the Hikes chapter. Getting a detailed trail map from the park office is highly recommended if you plan to do any substantial hoofing.

Location and Directions: Off Marriotsville Road in southeastern Carroll County. From Baltimore, take Interstate 70 west. Just past Ellicott City, take the Marriotsville Road exit and head north. Entrance to the park is about four miles up Marriotsville Road on the right, just past the Patapsco River crossing.

Hours and Admission: Daily from 9 a.m. to sunset. Admission is $2 per person on holidays and weekdays, with seniors 62 or over and kids in car seats free. On weekdays, admission is $2 per car, and is paid on the honor system.

Website and Phone: www.dnr.state.md.us/publiclands/central/patapscovalley.html; (410) 461-5005.

Patapsco Valley State Park—Tire Park

The area's finest tire park is located in the Hilton Area of Patapsco Valley State Park, in Catonsville. A tire park is a playground built with scrap tires. Tires are difficult to recycle or dispose of, and converting them to playground equipment is an idea that Maryland's Department of Natural Resources has been toying with for over a decade. This tire park, built in 1994, is the successful end result of their forward way of thinking. It spans two acres and utilizes over 7,000 tires. About 1,000 went into assembling playground apparatus, and the remaining 6,000 were shredded and used as cushiony ground cover. Other tire parks are located in Calvert Cliffs State Park, Gunpowder Falls State Park, and Cunningham Falls State Park.

Playing on a playground assembled from scrap tires seemed unappealing to me at first, but soon after using the facility I had a change of heart. Tires can be used to build wonderful climbing towers that wouldn't work with wood or plastic. They're fun to run across when lined up. They are soft and have an added degree of safety when compared to more conventional playground equipment. Patapsco Valley State Park wisely integrated other playground equipment into its tire park to offer a full ensemble of play opportunities. There is a large sliding board in a wooden tower, smaller slides, some balance beam apparatus, and two zip lines that draw large crowds. The tires simply fill in the framework.

Located near the tire park is a pavilion that hosts nature events, a group campground, and some hiking trails. A fun playground diversion is to hike down to the swinging bridge, a 200-foot-long suspension walkway over the Patapsco River. To get there, walk out to Hilton Avenue, turn right, and follow it about 100 yards to the entrance to the All Saints Convent. Just before the entrance gates, turn right onto the hiking trail that follows a cleared right-of-way. Follow the trail about one-quarter mile down a steep hill and cross over a railroad track (watching carefully for trains). The swinging bridge is directly ahead, with restrooms across the bridge.

Location and Directions: In the Hilton area of Patapsco Valley State Park, in Catonsville. From the Interstate 695 beltway, take Exit 13, Frederick Road, west. Continue for about one mile through Catonsville. Turn left at the light onto Rolling Road, and stay straight onto Hilton Avenue. The entrance to the tire park is located about 1.5 miles down Hilton Avenue to the right.

Phone: (410) 461-5005.

Piney Run Park

Piney Run Park is a very scenic destination spot in southern Carroll County. My first visit there was to research this book, and I kicked myself for not going sooner. Park facilities are spread across a hillside overlooking a 300-acre reservoir, built in 1974 for water resource purposes. The park is a nice place to commune with nature, and may be Carroll County's best spot to spread a blanket and share some cheese and crackers with the family.

Developments at Piney Run Park include tennis and basketball courts and two playgrounds. The primary playground consists of three sections of apparatus—one a swing set—built into large sand pits. The equipment is a bit outdated, and my children were more enamored of a huge climbing boulder nearby. A more contemporary play area is located near the boat rental center. Restroom facilities are available and pavilions can be rented.

The appeal of the park, however, seems to be its lack of development. Many visitors to the park come to fish or boat on the picturesque reservoir. Rentals of canoes, kayaks, rowboats, and paddle boats are available, and are detailed in the Boat Rental chapter. A 24-passenger pontoon boat is also available for rent, and ideal for birthday parties. The lake is stocked with trout, largemouth bass, striped bass, crappie, and the elusive and pugnacious tiger musky. Fishing is allowed from boats and along much of the shoreline, though a state fishing license is required.

For landlubbers, Piney Run Park has a nice network of hiking trails along the lake's west bank. The longest is the 3.5-mile-long Inlet Trail that leads to a long arm of the reservoir. The one-half-mile Lake Trail explores the shoreline near the boat launch. A 3.6-mile lattice of equestrian trails is located on the east shore of the lake.

One facility not to miss when visiting Piney Run Park is the nature center. It's very homespun and hands-on, and was obviously created with children in mind. Details can be found in the Nature Centers chapter.

Location and Directions: At 30 Martz Road, near Sykesville. To get there, take Interstate 70 west from Baltimore, and then Route 32 north. In Eldersburg, turn left onto Route 26 and continue for 2.1 miles. Turn left onto White Rock Road (at a park sign) and continue for 1.9 miles. Turn left onto Martz Road and continue to the park entrance.

Hours and Admission: The park has most facilities open daily from April 1 to October 31, from 6 a.m. to sunset. Admission is $4 per car for Carroll County residents and $5 per car for other visitors. Seniors 62 and older are free. Add $3 if you bring your own boat.

Phone: (410) 795-3274.

Rocks State Park

Rocks State Park is an oasis of wilderness in northern Harford County. The park is one of the more attractive in the region. It straddles Deer Creek, a pretty stretch of tumbling trout stream, and is studded with high rock crags. The park is best known for its King and Queen Seat, a 190-foot rock outcrop overlooking Deer Creek that is popular with rock climbers. It features such climbing routes as Vertical, Breakfast of Champions, Breakaway, and Superbulge. A fun thing to do is hike the short (but steep) trail from the road pull-out to the lookout and watch experienced climbers struggle up the rock face. Parents should take extra precautions here, since the terrain is rocky and dangerous, and falling deaths do occur. The lookout was once a ceremonial meeting spot for the Susquehannock Native Americans.

The other major draw of Rocks State Park is Deer Creek, which attracts waders, swimmers, and tubers. Those wanting to tube should bring their own as they are not available for rent. Some rapids on Deer Creek are categorized as Class III in high water, which means your rump will bump; portage may be the proper course of action. This flurry of water activity along Deer Creek annoys anglers, who come to test their mettle against trout, smallmouth bass, and panfish.

Rocks State Park features three picnic areas—Hills Grove, which is open year-round, and Wilson and Rock Ridge, which are open from April through October. Each picnic area features tables, grills, restrooms, and playground facilities. There is a $2 per person charge to enter a picnic area from April through October, though seniors and kids in car seats are free. Each picnic area also offers a large group pavilion for rent. The Ma and Pa Railroad, which once connected Baltimore with York, Pennsylvania, wove along Deer Creek through what is now Rocks State Park; visitors can hike along the former rail line and check out some of its remnants.

Location and Directions: In northern Harford County, about nine miles northwest of Bel Air. From Baltimore, take Interstate 95 north. Take Exit 77B, Route 24, west toward Bel Air. Continue on Route 24 through Bel Air, Rock Spring, and Forest Hill. Rocks State Park is along Route 24, about five miles past Forest Hill.

Website and Phone: www.dnr.state.md.us/publiclands/central/rocks.html; (410) 557-7994.

Susquehanna State Park

When Captain John Smith sailed up the Susquehanna River in 1608, he came across the land of what is now Susquehanna State Park and proclaimed that "heaven and earth seemed never to have agreed better to frame a place for man's commodious and delightful habitation." Little has changed in these lightly trodden hills framing the river. Susquehanna State Park remains nothing short of bucolic, and one of the few places in the Baltimore area where a slice of tranquility can always be had.

Naturalists are drawn to the park's serenity and solitude, and outdoor recreationists like the extensive network of hiking and mountain-biking trails. Getting a trail map from the park office before setting out is recommended. A favorite destination is the Susquehanna Ridge Trail, which bounces along the waterfront hills, affording fantastic views of the river. It does offer some challenging uphills. Walking a lightly traveled road that runs along the river may be a more agreeable hike for the less intrepid. The park features an exceptional campground, which is described in the Camping chapter.

Picnicking opportunities abound here, and fishing is popular along the river, especially in spring when the shad are running. Wading is not recommended in the deceivingly swift-moving river, however, since currents swirl with ferocity and the rocky bottom is slippery. A safer fishing spot for children is along Deer Creek, which traverses the northern section of the park.

▲ The Grist Mill at Susquehanna State Park

The park wears its history like a badge of honor. The water-wheeled Rock Run Grist Mill has been restored and is open for public inspection. Displays inside tell about farming and milling in the 1800s, and demonstrations are given. Just up from the mill is the white-washed Jersey Toll House, which once served a covered bridge that crossed the river at this point. On the hill overlooking the mill is Rock Run House, a stunning 1804 mansion once owned by John Carter, a partner in the mill. It is also open for tours.

Visitors to Susquehanna State Park may want to stop in the Steppingstone Museum, on Quaker Bottom Road. This museum features rural arts and crafts from the period 1880 to 1920. It provides insight into rural life a century ago, and also offers special programs and demonstrations. The museum is open on weekends between May and the first Sunday in October, from 1 p.m. to 5 p.m. Admission is $2 and children 12 and under are free.

Location and Directions: Three miles northwest of Havre de Grace, in Harford County. From Baltimore, take Interstate 95 north. Take Exit 89, Route 155, and head west. To get to the Steppingstone Museum, turn right in about one-quarter mile onto Earlton Road and left onto Quaker Bottom Road. To get to the Rock Run Grist Mill and campground, continue on Route 155, turn right onto Route 161, and go right onto Rock Run Road. Follow signs for the various attractions.

Website and Phone: www.dnr.state.md.us/publiclands/central/susquehanna.html; (410) 557-7994.

Thomas A. Dixon Aircraft Observation Area

One of the Baltimore area's teeniest parks also packs the biggest punch. The Dixon Aircraft Observation Area, located adjacent to the Baltimore-Washington International Airport, in Dorsey, comprises only a few acres and offers only a modest playground and sitting pavilion. But on nice days crowds descend here in droves. The reason is the park's location; it's situated literally yards from where jets touch down at BWI Airport. On certain days, and during certain times, the landings come one after another, and each one is a spectacle of sight and sound that holds kids at rapt attention. It is my son's favorite local park.

One hitch to this park is that aircraft are not guaranteed to be landing at this particular runway, and there is no way to be sure before your visit. Coming solely to see the planes is a crapshoot. A fun

▲ Playground meets airport at the Thomas A. Dixon Aircraft
Observation Area

alternative thing to do is use the nearby BWI Trail, an 11-mile-long paved hiking and biking trail circling the airport grounds. It's a great place to bike, walk, push a stroller, in-line skate, or ride a scooter. On nice days, an ice cream truck sets up camp in the park's parking lot, offering yummy snow balls and other treats. A fun game to play when planes are landing is to try to guess what airline will touch down next (hint: you rarely go wrong saying Southwest).

Location and Directions: On Dorsey Road (Route 176), in Dorsey. From Baltimore, take Interstate 95 south, then take Route 195 east toward BWI Airport. Just before the airport, take Route 170 south, and continue for about two miles. Turn left onto Route 176, Dorsey Road, and continue about two miles to the park, on the right.

Watkins Regional Park

Families venturing south of Baltimore should consider stopping off at Watkins Regional Park, located in Prince George's County, near Upper Marlboro. This 850-acre behemoth of a park is bursting with things kids adore. Standard park fare is well represented—playgrounds, ball fields, basketball courts, picnic pavilions, and tennis courts (including five indoor courts in a bubble). But Watkins Park offers activities that far surpass the plain-Jane recreational fare.

The Old Maryland Farm is an interpretive and educational agricultural facility open to the public. It includes agricultural exhibits, livestock viewing (including donkeys and llamas), and display gardens. Pony rides, hay rides, and farm demonstrations are

▲ Playgrounds aplenty at Watkins Regional Park

regularly provided. The farm is open on Tuesdays through Fridays from 10 a.m. to 2:30 p.m., Saturdays from 9 a.m. to 4:30 p.m., and Sundays from 11:30 a.m. to 4:30 p.m. Call for times for pony rides and hayrides.

Another favored attraction is the Chesapeake Carousel, built by master craftsman Gustav Dentzel, a German immigrant known for his elaborate wood carvings. The carousel operated at Chesapeake Beach through 1972 and was brought here in 1985. It's open

◄ The historic carousel at Watkins Regional Park

daily (except non-holiday Mondays) from 10 a.m. to 7 p.m. from Memorial Day through Labor Day, and then on weekends in September. Cost is $1 for residents of Prince George's and Montgomery Counties, and $1.25 for others.

Kids would probably agree that the park's crowning feature is the Watkins Express, a bright-red, miniature excursion railroad. The lumbering, 10-minute journey takes riders through a pretty patch of woodland. The Watkins Express has been in operation for over 30 years, and replicates the 1863 C.P. Huntington locomotive. The train operates on the same seasonal schedule as the carousel. Cost is $1 per ride for residents, and $1.25 for non-residents. Watkins Park also offers miniature golf ($2 for residents and $2.50 for non-residents), a nature center, lots of hiking trails, and a humongous playground.

Location and Directions: In Upper Marlboro, about one mile west of Six Flags Amusement Park. From Baltimore, take Interstate 97 south. Take Route 3 south through Bowie. Route 3 turns into Route 301. Continue on Route 301 to Central Avenue (Route 214). Turn right onto Central Avenue, and continue for about four miles. Turn left onto Watkins Park Drive (Route 193). The park entrance is about one mile on the right.

Website and Phone: www.pgparks.com/places/parks/watkins. html; (301) 218-6700.

D.C. Attractions

What to do in the District of Columbia with children is well covered in such guidebooks as *Frommer's Washington, D.C., with Kids* by Beth Rubin and *Washington, D.C., with Kids, 2002-2003* by Linda Perlis and Sandra Burt. As a bonus to this book, I've included five lesser-known D.C. attractions that may give you reason to brave D.C. Beltway traffic.

C&O Canal National Historical Park

Great Falls is a thunderous cascade in the Potomac River that is among our nation's most photogenic natural attractions. Located practically within earshot of the D.C. Beltway, it's where, each second, thousands of gallons of Potomac River water sluice through a narrow gorge and cascade over a 72-foot drop, the largest fall-line elevation displacement on the East Coast. The falls straddle the Maryland–Virginia border, but a nice place to view it is from the section of the C&O Canal National Historical Park near Potomac.

Great Falls is not viewable from the parking area or surrounding concessions. You will have to follow a trail and boardwalk to the Olmsted Island overlook, which offers a spectacular vantage. The footbridge to the island was destroyed by Hurricane Agnes in 1972, and rebuilt 20 years later. Don't forget the camera. You may also see rock-climbers scaling the surrounding cliffs and kayakers puttering about below the falls. Occasionally a brazen boater will actually shoot the falls. If you're looking for a more dramatic portrait of Great Falls, visit a few days after a major rainstorm, when the water level typically peaks.

Other neat things are clustered here. Stately Great Falls Tavern, a former 19th-century lock-tender's house and later an inn for city dwellers seeking country air, has been converted to an interesting museum on canal history and falls geology. Local to-do information can also be found there. Kids may want to ride in a mule-drawn canal boat and pass through an actual lock. The 60-minute ride costs $8 for adults, $6 for seniors, $5 for kids 4 - 14, and is free for those under 4. Hikers can amble a stretch of the 184.5-mile-long canal towpath that passes through here. The path is gravel, stone-flat, stroller-friendly, and a fine way to remove yourself from the crowds around the falls area. Those seeking a more arduous hike should try the four-mile-long Billy Goat Trail, which can be accessed by following the towpath downstream and looking for the blue blazes.

Visitors should heed warning signs about wading in the river, as swift currents and turbulence sweep visitors to their deaths each year. Parents should also keep a tight rein on young children and keep pets on a leash. For break time, a concession stand is available.

Location and Directions: At 11710 MacArthur Boulevard, in Potomac. From Baltimore take Interstate 95 south, and take the Interstate 495 beltway west. Just before crossing into Virginia, take the Clara Barton Parkway west. Continue for about one mile, and where it dead-ends, turn left onto MacArthur Boulevard. Continue about three miles to the park.

Hours and Admission: The Great Falls Tavern Visitor Center is open daily from 9 a.m. to 4:30 p.m., with extended hours in summer. Cost to enter the park is $5 per car.

Website and Phone: www.nps.gov/choh; (301) 767-3714.

Mason Neck Peninsula

Spotting a bald eagle is an exciting event for both children and adults. Thanks to the tenacious advocacy of conservation groups and government agencies, eagles have returned in force to the lower 48 states. The best place to spot a bald eagle in the Baltimore area is on the Mason Neck peninsula, located about 20 miles south of Washington, D.C., on the banks of the Potomac River.

The 10,000-acre peninsula consists of an assortment of public lands and a few housing developments. A recent survey revealed 109 eagles around the peninsula. In each of my dozen or so trips to Mason Neck, I've logged anywhere from a handful to 28 bald eagles.

Kids will be thrilled to see an eagle at close range. The best bet for this happening is along the trails that hem Pohick Bay. This sliver of inlet is narrow enough to draw eagles close to the observer. To access the trails, go to Pohick Bay Regional Park and park near the docks. First, make a scan for eagles from the parking lot. Eagles will most likely be seen either perched in the upper strata of waterfront trees (on both sides of the inlet) or circling overhead. Occasionally, one will stake claim to a fallen log along the shoreline. Look hard and far away, paying particular attention to black splotches in distant trees.

Follow the blue-blazed trail from the lot's far end. It winds about one-half mile to a prime viewing area. Where the trail sidles up to the waterfront, pay particular attention to the treetops canopying the water. At one point, the trail arcs away from the waterfront to accommodate a private residence. The trail ends at a headland, where viewing is ideal. Backtrack briefly and trek up a cleared pipeline right-of-way, turn right onto a trail blazed blue and orange, and then turn right onto a dirt road. This dirt road leads about one-half mile to another headland farther up Pohick Bay—a second prime viewing area. Along the dirt road, scan the waterfront treetops to your right. Finish by backtracking to the car.

Another sweet spot for eagle-viewing is Mason Neck State Park, located on Belmont Bay. This park comes with a visitors' center and viewing platforms. Belmont Bay is more expansive than Pohick Bay, allowing for longer and broader sight lines and a greater viewing canvas. Eagles, however, tend to be farther away. Birders often gather here armed with spotting scopes; ask to sneak a peek. If the tide is low, walk up the beach about one-third mile to the Kanes Creek blind, paying close attention to the trees around the creek entrance.

Prime eagle-viewing season at Mason Neck is from October through March, when the congregation is greatest. Most eagles depart with the spring thaw, though some remain year-round to nest. Eagles mate for life. Eggs are laid in April or May, and incubate for about one month. Eaglets grow quickly and attempt their first flight at about three months, though only about 60 percent survive their coming out. The bald eagle's telltale white head doesn't develop until full maturation, usually after five years. A good portion of the eagles at Mason Neck are immature, and will be solid black with some lighter mottling in the belly. A spotting scope is ideal to see an eagle, but a decent pair of binoculars should suffice.

Location and Directions: To get to Mason Neck peninsula, take I-95 south past Washington, D.C. In Lorton, Virginia, take Exit 163, Route 642. Turn left onto Route 642, and follow signs to the various parks. All attractions are off Gunston Road. Small fees may be charged.

National Postal Museum

Readers may have experienced the vast and overcrowded museums that frame Washington, D.C.,'s mall area. For a change of pace, try the lightly trodden National Postal Museum, conveniently located across 1st Street from Union Station, the popular hub many Baltimoreans pass through to get into D.C. The museum puts an interesting spin on a mundane topic, and manages to make displays enjoyable to children. The museum, administered by the Smithsonian Institution and the U.S. Postal Service, is probably not large enough to warrant a visit in itself, but can be combined with a visit to other nearby attractions, including Union Station, the Capitol, and the Capital Children's Museum (800 3rd Street, N.E.).

The National Postal Museum is part of the old City Post Office building, built in 1914, at a time when municipal buildings exuded elegance and charm. Enter the museum through the side door near the intersection of 1st Street and Massachusetts Avenue, next to the Capitol City Brewing Company. As you pass through the former waiting area of the post office, notice the ornate teller booths, brass fixtures, ornamental wood carvings, marble tables, and old mailboxes lining the walls. Once inside, follow signs for the museum, descending an escalator.

Visitors enter the museum through a main atrium with a 90-foot cathedral ceiling. On display are replicas of different ways the mail has historically been transported, ranging from a biplane to mail cars to a horse-drawn coach to a Southern Railroad transport car. Don't miss the exhibit memorializing globetrotting Owney, the stray mutt adopted by an Albany, New York, post office in 1888. Owney escorted mail bags all around the world.

Visitors follow a corridor through the remaining exhibits. Kids will enjoy walking through the evening forest, complete with piped-in spooky sounds, though the relevance to mail delivery was lost on me. The postal museum features lots of displays on mailboxes and stamps and letters and how mail is moved, but it's all very fascinating. Dozens of displays line the corridor, several of them temporary. Point out to your kids the mail sled used in frozen regions and the models of ships used to move mail overseas and across the country.

Adults will like seeing Amelia Earhart's brown leather flight suit, and the postal outfit worn by John Ratzenberger (i.e., Cliff Clavin) on the sitcom *Cheers*. And whereas the National Museum of Natural History gives you the inimitable and priceless Hope Diamond, the National Postal Museum shows you the package it was once mailed in. My favorite display is the room showing the different duck stamps that have been issued over the years. Kids will probably want to linger in the interactive area that has lots of computer games, some holograms, and neat displays on popular mail-order companies such as L.L. Bean, Burpee, and Tiffany and Co.

The National Postal Museum has two nice stores—one selling books, apparel, and trinkets, and another specializing in stamps and stamp collecting gear. Kids can pick up a special self-guiding tour brochure at the front desk. When you are finished, pop into the Capitol City Brewing Company for a sandwich and suds, or just peek in to see the extraordinary vault from the building's previous life. Another great nearby luncheon place is the food court in the basement of Union Station, situated across the street.

Location: At 2 Massachusetts Avenue, in the northwest quadrant of the city, beside Union Station. Your best bet is to take public transportation into Union Station (e.g., the MARC train or the red Metro subway line).

Hours and Admission: Daily from 10 a.m. to 5:30 p.m. Closed on Christmas.

Website and Phone: www.si.edu/postal; (202) 357-2991.

Smithsonian's National Museum of Natural History

It's no secret that the Smithsonian's National Museum of Natural History is a world-class venue that parents have to pry their kids out of. But not everyone knows that the museum recently completed a 10-year overhaul, adding new displays, removing outdated ones, opening an IMAX theater, and giving the entire joint a spit-shine. If you haven't explored the grand granite corridors lately, it may be time to return.

The most impressive change is the interactive nature of the exhibits. Lots of computers and video equipment help bring displays to life. Hundreds of stuffed specimens, outdated and mildewy (some shot and donated by Theodore Roosevelt), were removed—a symbolic reflection that the natural history museum is no longer just a repository for killed animals, but rather an interactive experience between man and nature. You'll notice wild and soothing sounds being piped in, and lots of color sprinkled about. The atmosphere went from fugue to flamenco.

▲ Inside the rotunda at the National Museum of Natural History

The biggest and most appreciated change may be construction of the IMAX theater. Short flicks on topics like dinosaurs, Africa, and Mt. Everest are shown on a 60-foot-high screen. Tickets are $7.50 for adults and $6 for kids and seniors, and advance purchase is recommended, especially during busy times.

A museum as extensive as this one (124 million specimens cataloged) demands a plan of attack. Families trying to see it all in one day may end up cranky and frustrated. Get a floor map upon entering and choose displays that interest you and your children.

Kids love dinosaurs and bones, which plays to the museum's strengths. A virtual treasure trove of fossils, bones, and skeletons is on display in various exhibits (see museum map for details). Observant return visitors may notice that Hatcher, the famous 65-million-year-old triceratops, received a costly computer-generated face lift. Visitors should also rest assured that the 13-foot-tall African bush elephant, the largest ever mounted, still stands sentinel in the entry rotunda.

Kids will gravitate to the exhibits on geology, gems, and minerals. Everything from large chunks of purple amethyst to brightly hued geodes to oddly shaped rocks with tongue-twisting names are on display. The 45.52-carat, deep-blue Hope Diamond is the crown jewel of the exhibit. It's the largest blue diamond in the world with a value exceeding $100 million. I always wondered whether the actual rock is the one on display. Also try not to miss the Discovery Room, where kids can handle lots of different rocks and fossils.

The one must-see exhibit for junior biologists is the O. Orkin Insect Zoo, where dozens of weird and funky bugs, spiders, scorpions, and centipedes are on display. A staff entomologist allows visitors to cradle a tarantula or hissing cockroach. A replica termite mound is available to crawl through, and an interactive display educates visitors on what insects inhabit the typical house (think silverfish, fleas, cockroaches, etc.) Kids thrive on the insect zoo, but it may give parents the willies.

For a lunch break, the Atrium Café is on the museum's basement floor. Service is cafeteria-style, and a meal typically runs about $8 with drink. The museum stores here are particularly good. Parents will love browsing the extensive book section or seeing vases and pieces of art from far-flung locales. If you don't see anything to buy your little cherubs, don't fret; kids have their own store across the hallway. It's jammed with toys and games that are fun and educational. Check out the "yap rock" on display near the stores; "yaps" are coins from the Pacific island of Yap that are the size of monster truck wheels.

Location: At the intersection of 10th Street and Constitution Avenue, in the northwest quadrant of Washington, D.C. The museum is located near the Smithsonian Metro stop, which is on the orange line. The closest orange line station to Baltimore is in New Carrollton.

Hours and Admission: Daily from 10 a.m. to 5:30 p.m. Closed on Christmas. Admission is free, though a ticket to the IMAX theater ranges from $6 to $7.50.

Website and Phone: www.mnh.si.edu; (202) 357-2700.

U.S. Naval Observatory

While droves of tourists descend upon downtown D.C. attractions, finding one off the beaten path is a serendipitous pleasure. One such attraction is the U.S. Naval Observatory, a scientific agency that is our country's pre-eminent authority on time-keeping and celestial observation. On certain Monday evenings, the agency offers to the public free tours of its buildings and grounds, which, weather permitting, includes a startling peek through a high-powered telescope deep into the heavens.

The observatory spreads across 72 lush and leafy acres in northwest D.C., along Massachusetts Avenue. It includes several attractive buildings and lots of observation facilities. The main office building is stately, with high windows and tall ceilings. A mansion on the grounds is home to the vice president of the United States.

Tour participants get to see lots of time-keeping devices, including the Master Clock of the United States that keeps time to a billionth of a second per day. The clocks are all very fine, but kids will get their kicks from the telescopes. With agreeable weather, visitors will view the moon and whatever planets are out and about through a hefty Alvan Clark refractor scope with 12-inch lens, which is housed in an attractive dome. The view is, as one would expect, outstanding! If the skies are clouded over, visitors will instead check out a mammoth, 30-foot-long refractor telescope with 26-inch lens that dates to 1873. Through this venerable optical device, scientists of the Naval Observatory discovered the two moons of Mars—Phobos and Deimos. The floor of the observatory that houses this telescope has the largest elevator in the city.

Public tours are offered on alternating Mondays between 8:30 p.m. and 10 p.m., and last about 90 minutes. Before the telescopes and time pieces are shown, tour participants get to see a short video summarizing the history and mission of the Naval Observatory. Parents should keep in mind that, although there is no specified age limit, tours involve traipsing around the hilly observatory grounds in the dark. Advance passes are required for tours, and can be obtained via its website or by calling (202) 762-1438. Because of the September 11, 2001, terrorist attacks, tour participants must adhere to a strict code of conduct that is delineated on the website.

Location and Directions: At Massachusetts Avenue and 34th Street. Directions and public transportation options are available on the website.

Hours and Admission: Tours are offered on alternating Mondays from 8:30 p.m. to 10 p.m. Tours are free.

Website: www.usno.navy.mil; (202) 762-1438.

Festivals

Baltimore likes to kick up its heels and have a good time. The area features plenty of festivals and fairs, many which are amenable to families. A complete listing of such events can be obtained by calling the Maryland Office of Tourism Development at (410) 767-3400. Here is a sampling of local festivals.

January

Great Scale Model Train Show
Maryland State Fairgrounds, Timonium
www.gsmts.com

Horse World Expo
Maryland State Fairgrounds, Timonium
www.horseworldexpo.com

Reverend Dr. Martin Luther King Parade
Martin Luther King Boulevard, Baltimore
www.baltimoreevents.org

White Flint's Camp and Summer Programs Expo
White Flint, Bethesda
www.shopwhiteflint.com

February

Maryland Kennel Club All-Breed Dog Show
Fifth Regiment Armory, Baltimore

World of Pets Expo
Maryland State Fairgrounds, Timonium
www.worldofpets.org

March

Bunny BonanZoo
Baltimore Zoo
www.baltimorezoo.org

Great Scale Model Train Show
Maryland State Fairgrounds, Timonium
www.gsmts.com

Greenberg's Train Shows
Maryland State Fairgrounds, Timonium
www.greenbergshows.com

Lunch with the Elephants
Lexington Market, Baltimore
www.lexingtonmarket.com

Maryland Day Celebration
Various sites in Annapolis
www.annapolis.org

April

Baltimore Waterfront Festival
Inner Harbor and surrounding neighborhoods, Baltimore
www.baltimoreevents.org

Maryland International Kite Festival
Ocean City
www.ococean.com

Spring Festival and Crafts Show
Anne Arundel County Fairgrounds, Crownsville
www.aacountyfair.com

May

Baltimore Blues Festival
Fells Point, Baltimore
www.baltimorebluesfestival.com

Baltimore Herb Festival
Leakin Park, Baltimore
www.baltimoreherbfestival.com

Children's Museum Discovery Weekend
Rose Hill Manor Park, Frederick

Civil War Living History Day
Steppingstone Museum, Havre de Grace
www.steppingstonemuseum.org

Family Discovery Day
Calvert Marine Museum, Solomons
www.calvertmarinemuseum.com

Lithuanian Festival
Catonsville Armory, Catonsville

Maryland Sheep and Wool Festival
Howard County Fairgrounds, West Friendship
www.sheepandwool.org

Preakness Crab Derby
Lexington Market, Baltimore
www.lexingtonmarket.com

Towsontown Spring Festival
Courthouse Area, Towson
www.towsontownspringfestival.org

June

Flag Day
Fort McHenry National Monument, Baltimore
www.flagday.org

Frederick Festival of the Arts
Carroll Creek Linear Park, Frederick
www.frederickarts.org

Latino Fest
Patterson Park, Baltimore
www.eblo.org

St. Nicholas Greek Folk Festival
Greektown, Baltimore

Scottish Festival
Steppingstone Museum, Havre de Grace
www.steppingstonemuseum.org

July

Artscape
Mt. Royal Avenue Corridor, Baltimore
www.artscape.org

Baltimore's Fourth of July Festival
Inner Harbor
www.baltimoreevents.org

Cecil County Fair
Fair Hill
www.cecilcountyfair.org

Family Fun Day
Mayo Beach Park, Mayo
www.web.aacpl.net/rp

Harford County Farm Fair
Harford County Equestrian Center, Bel Air
www.farmfair.org

Howard County Pow-Wow
Howard County Fairgrounds, West Friendship

Sharkfest
Calvert Marine Museum, Solomons
www.calvertmarinemuseum.com

August

Baltimore Pow Wow
Community College of Baltimore County, Catonsville Campus
www.baltimorepowwow.com

Greenberg's Train Shows
Maryland State Fairgrounds, Timonium
www.greenbergshows.com

Howard County Fair
Howard County Fairgrounds, West Friendship
www.howardcountyfair.com

Maryland Renaissance Festival
Crownsville Road, Annapolis
www.rennfest.com

Montgomery County Agricultural Fair
Montgomery Country Agricultural Center, Gaithersburg
www.mcagfair.com

September

Anne Arundel County Fair
Anne Arundel County Fairgrounds, Crownsville
www.aacountyfair.com

Apple Festival
Piney Run Park, Sykesville

Baltimore Book Festival
Mt. Vernon Place, Baltimore
www.baltimoreevents.org

Great Frederick Fair
Fairgrounds, Frederick
www.thegreatfrederickfair.com

Maryland State Fair
Maryland State Fairgrounds, Timonium
marylandstatefair.com

Mid-Atlantic Reptile Festival
Maryland State Fairgrounds, Timonium
www.reptileinfo.com

Ukrainian Festival
Patterson Park, Baltimore

Westminster Fallfest
City Park, Westminster

October

Anne Arundel Scottish Highland Games
Anne Arundel Fairgrounds, Crownsville
www.annearun.com/aasfi

Chocolate Festival
Lexington Market, Baltimore
www.lexingtonmarket.com

Fall Harvest Days
Carroll County Farm Museum, Westminster

Great Scale Model Train Show
Maryland State Fairgrounds, Timonium
www.gsmts.com

Railfest
Western Maryland Scenic Railroad, Cumberland
www.wmsr.com

Zoo BOOOO!!!
Baltimore Zoo, Baltimore
www.baltimorezoo.org

November

Baltimore's Thanksgiving Parade
Pratt Street, Baltimore
www.baltimoreevents.org

December

Annapolis First Night
Various locations in Annapolis
www.firstnightannapolis.org

Fun and Games

Museums can be fun and instructive. Nature centers are swell places to learn the basics of biology. Camping and hiking adventures take the classroom outdoors. But sometimes kids just want to kick back and have a good time without any heavy learning strings attached. Here are some ideas about where to turn.

Arundel Mills

Schlepping my kids to a shopping mall for the sole purpose of having fun was a repulsive thought prior to researching this book. But after weathering a stormy Saturday at Arundel Mills, I'm now sold on the concept. Kids love this place. Not the stores and products, but the experience. The atmosphere. The "Mills Effect," as the advertisement says.

Arundel Mills is Baltimore's version of the Mall of America. It features mostly outlet stores, and spans many, many acres in Hanover, just off Route 100. The corridors are wide-open and very conducive to running kids. They feature giant video screens playing cartoons, movies, and advertisements. Corridors are lined with exciting attractions for young kids, including one that makes you part of what appears to be a gigantic pinball machine. Another features super-sized butterflies and lady bugs. The decor is bright and cheerful.

Over 200 stores line the walkways, a few of which I would categorize as must-see. Bass Pro Shops Outdoor World has several attention-grabbing attractions. A monstrous aquarium crammed full of game fish will mesmerize kids. No tiny guppies or tetras here. We're talking 10-pound largemouth and striped bass, chain pickerel as long as my arm, and channel catfish that could munch a small dog. An exhibit near the store's mid-section reproduces a rugged mountain scene, complete with three-story waterfall and stuffed mountain lion, bighorn sheep, and pair of imposing moose. The backside of the mountain exhibit is a climbing wall, which kids 10 and older can take a crack at for $3 a climb. Climbing hours are Tuesdays through Fridays from 5 p.m. to 9 p.m., and weekends from noon to 5 p.m. Have the kids try to find Uncle Buck's red bush plane suspended from the ceiling.

The Crayola Works store, which bills itself as the Creativity Studio and Store, is worth a stop-over if you can get past the sensory overload of colors. A studio lets kids craft masterpieces using crayons, paints, and other art supplies. Skateboards, pinwheels, chairs, and toy cars are among the items that can be painted. Prices start at about $7 to take part. Organized classes are also offered, and are perfect for moms who want to shop sans kids (though a cell phone is required to drop kids here). For a real treat, let your kids scribble all over the actual car parked in the store (and remember to explain that they can't do this at home).

The Sun & Ski Sports store has another climbing wall. The Children's Place not only offers monster bargains, but has a nice play area for the kids while you shop. Jillian's is the loudest and largest arcade you'll ever set foot in. The Muvico theater touts an almost preposterous 24 screens, and there are more unusual restaurants than you can shake a kabob skewer at.

Location and Directions: At 7000 Arundel Mills Center, in Hanover. From Baltimore, take Interstate 95 south. Take Exit 43A, Route 100, east. Take Exit 10A, Route 713, south, and follow signs to mall parking.

Hours: Mondays through Saturdays from 10 a.m. to 9:30 p.m. and Sundays from 11 a.m. to 7 p.m.

Website and Phone: www.arundelmillsmall.com/index2.html; (410) 540-5100.

Baltimore Children's Theatre

Watching a play or musical can be an arduous experience for children, since many have the attention spans of tsetse flies. To the rescue comes the Baltimore Children's Theatre, a theater troupe that puts on productions specifically designed for the temperament and tolerance of children and young adults. The theater was created by Mark Andrew Beachy to inspire in children a love for acting. Kids will not only love the creative storylines, but will also be enamored of the child actors who play prominent roles in the productions. As icing on the cake, performances are sometimes preceded by games such as musical chairs, in which kids in the audience can participate.

Recent Baltimore Children's Theatre performances include *Annie, Babes in Toyland, The Wizard of Oz,* and *Charlie and the Chocolate Factory.* Tickets are $8 in advance and $10 at the door. Performances are typically held at the Baltimore Museum of Art or the Slayton House, in Wilde Lake Village Center, Columbia. The theater also offers acting classes for children of all ages, with specific classes geared towards toddlers. If your child gets bitten by the theater bug, why not audition him or her for a part in the next Baltimore Children's Theatre production. Audition details are provided at its website.

Website and Phone: www.baltimoretheatre.org; (410) 203-1757.

Baltimore Rowing Club

Few sports are as physically demanding yet aesthetically pleasing as rowing. It's called a ballet on water. Entry into this appealing sport, however, is hindered by the high cost of equipment and accessibility of water. The Baltimore Rowing Club, or BRC, has that problem solved. BRC offers a novice program for first-time rowers, 16 years or older. Four novice sessions are held each rowing season. Each session runs six weeks, and classes meet on Tuesday and Thursday evenings, and on Saturday mornings, for two hours. Besides the actual skills of rowing, participants are taught boatmanship, boathandling, and training methods. Most of the time is spent on water in eight-man shells. Many rowers will continue on into the club's intermediate programs. The cost of each session is $150.

Classes are held at the BRC's boathouse, also referred to as the Baltimore Rowing and Water Resources Center, which is an attractive red-roofed structure easily seen from the Veterans Memorial (Hanover Street) Bridge. BRC shares the facility with the city of Baltimore, which uses it for special events. The boathouse includes locker and shower facilities, and a workout room featuring weights and rowing ergometers. Rowing is done on the protected waters of the Middle Branch of the Patapsco River, just west of the Veterans Memorial Bridge. Experienced boaters venture farther out into the Patapsco River to the open water. The most seasoned oarsmen will loop around Fort McHenry and row into the Inner Harbor, making for a nice nine-mile round trip. Rowing along the dilapidated piers of blue-collar Baltimore and amidst freight ships and pleasure boats can be quite exhilarating.

The club owns a flotilla of boats, ranging from single sculls to eight-man shells. Qualified club members are allowed to use club boats. Novice rowers will learn on sweep boats, where each rower handles one oar. With experience, some will graduate to sculling, where each rower grasps two oars. Club members participate in regattas up and down the East Coast, including the Head of the Charles, the world's largest rowing regatta. The BRC also hosts a few races each year such as the Ariel Regatta and Charm City Sprints. The club shares the boathouse with several high schools and colleges.

Annual club membership is $385, which is quite reasonable considering rowers have access to boats, coaching, and workout equipment. Annual student membership is $335 ($125 for those students home for the summer and just rowing in June, July, and August). Those participating in a novice class may apply the $150 course fee to their full membership. Membership dues can be reduced by volunteering at club events.

Parents should rest assured that club leaders are sticklers for boat safety. All prospective members must pass a swimming test, and must attend regular safety clinics. Stringent safety precautionary measures are also in place for anyone going on the water.

Location and Directions: At 3301 Waterview Avenue, in South Baltimore. From downtown Baltimore, take Light Street south. In the Federal Hill neighborhood, turn right on any cross street, and continue for two blocks to Hanover Street. Turn left onto Hanover Street, and follow it across the Veterans Memorial (Hanover Street) Bridge. Just after the bridge, turn right onto Waterview Avenue. The boathouse is on the right.

Website and Phone: www.baltimorerowing.org; (410) 355-5649.

Bengies Drive-in Theatre

Drive-in theaters have gone the way of the milkman and rotary phone, but Baltimore is fortunate to have one of the few remaining ones. Bengies is located on Eastern Boulevard, in Middle River. It has been restored to look as it did in the 1950s. For five decades, Bengies has been providing fun family entertainment, and it remains one the area's top Friday night draws. Bring some lawn chairs, grab a pizza from the snack bar, and make a night of it.

Movies at Bengies are a treat to watch. Its 52-foot-high and 120-foot-wide screen is the largest on the East Coast. There's always a double feature playing, and usually a triple feature on Friday and Saturday nights. The first and often second films are typically child-friendly. Bengies has in the past shown Disney films, lots of animated features, and light teen comedies. Funny trailers and vintage cartoons entertain waiting customers between flicks. To my delight, the projectionist seems to have a preference for the Three Stooges. Make sure your car has a radio if you'd like to hear the movie.

Admission to Bengies varies depending on what is being shown and when. Admission usually runs between $5 and $7 per person. Children under 11 and in a car are free. Admission is reduced to $3 for late shows. Tuesdays (and Sundays in fall) are Pack-a-Car Bargain Nights, where up to five patrons in one car get in for the price of two.

Fifteen Fun Free Activities

1. Watching the Lighted Boat Parade from the Inner Harbor.
2. Picnicking and watching boats at Fort McHenry National Monument.
3. Checking out the Miracle on 34th Street.
4. Visiting one of the various train gardens.
5. Taking in the tulips at Sherwood Gardens in spring.
6. Playing atop Federal Hill Park.
7. Sliding and swinging at the Oregon Ridge Park playground.
8. Watching planes land at the Thomas A. Dixon Aircraft Observation Area.
9. Hiking Catoctin Mountain Park.
10. Touring Conowingo Dam.
11. Visiting frogs and snakes at the Oregon Ridge Nature Center.
12. Strolling the trails at Cylburn Arboretum.
13. Wandering around Susquehanna State Park.
14. Touring the National Wildlife Visitor Center.
15. Riding the steam trains at Leakin Park.

Bengies has a delightfully retro snack bar, but it goes well beyond typical theater fare. Subs, shrimp rolls, vegetable rolls, burgers, and chicken can be had at reasonable prices. A large cheese pizza runs $9.95. There's also lots of candy, ice cream, and fresh baked cookies. Outside food is not allowed in the theater area without a $5 permit, which must be obtained upon entry. (The sale of food is what allows Bengies to escape the bulldozers.) Bengies memorabilia can be purchased at the food stand. The theater also has a playground for the kiddies, but it closes when the movies roll.

Patrons of Bengies must adhere to a host of house rules that are strictly enforced. Most deal with safety issues (turn car engines off while viewing, no bare feet) and courtesy issues (no honking horns or running around during movies). The rules are delineated on its website. Those living north of the city should check out the Bel Air Drive-In Theatre, in Churchville.

Location and Directions: At 3417 Eastern Boulevard, in Middle River. From Baltimore, take Eastern Avenue heading east, and follow through Essex. Bengies is located just past the Glenn L. Martin State Airport on the right.

Website and Phone: www.giantoutdoorscreen.com; (410) 687-5627 for shows, and (410) 686-4698 for other information.

Earth Treks Climbing Center

Want to do something completely different with your children? How about rock climbing—indoors! Earth Treks Climbing Center, in the Columbia Gateway industrial park, offers a child-friendly environment for learning to clamber up faux cliffs. The climbing center is among the biggest and busiest on the East Coast. Don't be intimidated by the experts bounding off the 44-foot walls or hanging from the ceilings; there is a separate and more humble set-up for the young, where the wall is shorter and the surroundings more private. Parents should rest assured that safety is the first and foremost priority of the staff, as evidenced by the strict rules and safety signs posted about.

Earth Treks offers several programs geared toward children and teens. The Kids Klimb program introduces 6- to 12-year-olds to the sport. It's held on Sunday mornings throughout the year from 9 a.m. to 11 a.m., and on Saturday evenings from November through April from 6 p.m. to 8 p.m. Young ones are shown very basic climbs up easy walls led by highly experienced instructors and belayers (those

◄ No fear of heights at Earth Treks Climbing Center

controlling the support ropes). No experience is necessary, though children under the age of 10 must have a parent or guardian present. Parents will probably have more fun watching than the children will climbing. The cost for a Kids Klimb is $20 per session, and pre-registration is required. At Earth Treks, there is no gender bias: In the Kids Klimb session that I watched, girls outnumbered the boys.

A Youth Rox Climbing Series is available for ages 10 through 14. This series is more serious about teaching kids proper climbing procedures. Putting on a harness, tying into a climbing rope, belay tactics, and simple climbing skills are taught by qualified instructors. Each series involves three sessions, each one running two and a half hours on consecutive Fridays, from 6:30 p.m. to 9 p.m. The cost per series is $85.

Kids looking for more serious and regular climbing may join the competitive junior climbing team or the recreational junior climbing team. The competitive teams meet on Tuesdays from 4 p.m. to 6 p.m., and each three-month session costs $225 ($125 for members of the climbing gym). Members of this team take part in various regional competitions. Climbers must qualify for this team. The recreational team—those just climbing for fun without the climbing competitions—meets Sundays from 3 p.m. to 5 p.m., and each three-month session costs $225 ($125 for members). There are also summer programs, climbing camps, and outdoor expeditions.

◄ At Earth Treks, climbing is not just for adults

Earth Treks provides a unique location to host a kid's birthday party. Parties are held in a private area unencumbered by other gym users, and include equipment and qualified instructors. Your kids will be a hit with their friends, who get to climb the kiddie walls at will. The cost of a birthday party at Earth Treks runs from $100 for a two-hour session to $625, depending on the number of kids present and whether the party is on a weekday or weekend.

Parents can rest assured that climbers at Earth Treks are in good hands. It's owned and operated by Chris Warner, who, in 2001, became the only Maryland resident to summit Mount Everest. Staff instructors average 13 years of climbing experience and 9 years of teaching experience each. Just dropping in to watch expert climbers scaling the big walls would be a real treat for kids and adults alike.

Location and Directions: At 7125-C Columbia Gateway Drive. From Baltimore, take Interstate 95 south to Columbia. Take Exit 41, Route 175, west toward Columbia. From Route 175, take the Columbia Gateway Drive exit into the industrial park. At the third light, turn right, which will keep you on Columbia Gateway Drive. Take the fifth right into "Renaissance at Gateway," and follow signs for Earth Treks Climbing Center. Parking is available in front of the center.

Hours and Admission: Mondays through Wednesdays from 3 p.m. to 10 p.m., Thursdays and Fridays from 12 noon to 10 p.m., Saturdays from November through April from 9 a.m. to 8 p.m.,

Saturdays from May through October from 9 a.m. to 6 p.m., and Sundays from 9 a.m. to 6 p.m. A day pass costs $16, except for Fridays, when the cost is $12. Five-visit passes are available for $70, and a 30-day unlimited pass costs $70. A 90-day unlimited pass costs $185. Belayers may be rented for $20 per hour. Equipment is also available for rent, including harness ($3 per session) and shoes ($5 per session). Monthly individual membership is available for $55, and monthly family membership costs $90 (both require a one-time, $35 initiation fee).

Website and Phone: www.earthtreksclimbing.com; (410) 872-0060.

ExploraWorld

ExploraWorld is an ideal afternoon destination when foul weather restricts outdoor play. ExploraWorld is hard to categorize. It lies somewhere between children's museum, playground, and really cool schoolroom. Imagine visiting the house of very wealthy friends who lavish on their children the most up-to-date, amusing, and outlandish toys and games. Their playroom would be similar to ExploraWorld. In my daughter's lexicon, it's "totally awesome."

One exhibit allows kids to dress up in firemen's outfits and crawl all over a life-size fire truck. A sports arena, popular with the fathers, offers up foosball, air hockey, and an area to shoot baskets. Another exhibit allows kids to dress up in glamorous and showy outfits, choose a song from a list of popular selections, and dance like a fool while being filmed and shown live on a large television screen. The Chesapeake Bay exhibit lets children dig through a large sand box to uncover surprise toys. My daughter dwelled at length in the pretend hospital that allows kids safe access to medical equipment, including a real ambulance.

There's a pretend post office, puppet theater, computer lab, bubble lab, play house, and medieval castle. Parents of infants and young toddlers will not be disappointed in the soft-block area, nursery rhyme room, or special infant area. An educational undertone runs through all exhibits.

ExploraWorld is a fantastic spot for birthday parties, and offers special packages and individual rooms for the occasion. A café is also available for snacking. Though the large play area (purportedly the largest activity area in Maryland) is compartmentalized into many units, the separating walls are low-slung, allowing parents to better track their kids.

ExploraWorld is geared toward children 1 to 10 years old. Note that for safety purposes the children-to-adult ratio cannot exceed 6:1, so don't try to bring the whole neighborhood by yourself.

Location and Directions: At 6570 Dobbin Road, in Columbia. From Baltimore, take Interstate 95 south. Take Exit 41, Route 175, west toward Columbia. In about two miles, turn left onto Dobbin Road. Continue on Dobbin Road for 0.7 of a mile. ExploraWorld is on the right.

Hours and Admission: Mondays through Thursdays from 9:30 a.m. to 6 p.m., Fridays and Saturdays from 9:30 a.m. to 8 p.m., and Sundays from 11:30 a.m. to 6 p.m. Admission is $7.95 for children 2 and up; $3.95 for 1-year-olds; and free for children under 12 months. Adult admission is $2. The admission fee is reduced by $2 during the last two hours of a business day.

Website and Phone: www.exploraworld.com; (410) 772-1540.

Ken Zo's Yogi Magic Mart

Comb the aisles of Wal-Mart and turn the toy section of Target upside down. What you can buy at Ken Zo's you won't find at any of these cookie-cutter department stores. Ken Zo's has the area's largest selection of magic and illusion paraphernalia. It services everyone from tenderfoot illusionists to sleight-of-hand experts. Much of the fare is conventional, such as juggling clubs, clown apparel, novelty make-up, basic parlor tricks, and rubber snakes and rats. An entire wall is covered end-to-end with how-to and other magic-related books. Posters of esteemed illusionists cover the other walls along with autographed pictures of famous magicians and entertainers. Seasoned veterans will want to venture behind the glass case, where the more advanced and pricey tricks await purchase. The seller's philosophy: The secret is told when the magic is sold.

The store also peddles the bizarre and intriguing. It's a virtual one-stop shop for fart machines, and you surely won't want to leave without purchasing a joke replica of a severed leg. Ken Zo's is a unique place to go for kids' party gear. Inflated balloons go for $1.25 each, and there's also a wide selection of offbeat party favors and Mardi Gras beads.

Ken Zo's is owned by Ken and Bernadette Horsman, former clowns with Ringling Brothers. Their son, Spencer, is a ventriloquist prodigy who has appeared on *The Late Show with David Letterman* and *The Jerry Springer Show*, and has performed with David Copperfield. The store is a popular meeting spot for local magic clubs and often has guest speakers.

Location and Directions: At 1025 South Charles Street. From downtown, take Light Street south into Federal Hill. Just before Cross Street Market, turn right onto Cross Street and continue for one block. Turn right onto Charles Street. Ken Zo's is two blocks ahead on the right.

Hours: Mondays through Saturdays from 10 a.m. to 7 p.m.

Phone: (410) 727-5811.

Northwest Ice Rink

Of the handful of public-use ice rinks scattered about the Baltimore area, this facility, centrally located in the attractive Mt. Washington neighborhood, may be the best-known and most popular. It serves everyone from those lacing skates for the first time to Olympic-caliber athletes (J.P. Shilling, a figure skater in the 2002 winter games in Salt Lake City, trained here). It's noteworthy enough to play host to Olympic medal winners Michelle Kwan and Tara Lipinski.

Though it's a national-class figure-skating venue, plenty of time is set aside for public skating. Sessions happen daily from 11 a.m. to 1 p.m., and in the evening on certain weekdays and weekends, though hours vary. Cost is $6 per session for children and adults, and $4 for seniors 55 or over. Skate rental is available for $2 per session, though a skating store is available to purchase equipment. Group lessons are available for various types of skating and ice hockey, with special sessions for home-schooled children and adults accompanying children, where the adults skate for free. Private lessons are also offered.

Northwest Ice Rink also offers special programs for ice hockey and speed skating, and summer camp programs for freestyle skating, figure skating, and synchronized skating. Prices range from $50 to $150 per week. The rink facility includes a nice locker area and resting nook with snack bar and vending machines.

Several other public ice rinks in the Baltimore area have services similar to those offered by Northwest Ice Rink. They include the Columbia Ice Rink, Ice World in Abingdon, the Mount Pleasant Ice Arena in the city's northwest region, Patterson Park Ice Rink in East Baltimore, and the particularly impressive Gardens Ice House in Laurel.

Location and Directions: At 5600 Cottonworth Avenue, in Mt. Washington. From downtown, take Interstate 83 north. Take the Northern Parkway exit, heading east, and continue for about one-half mile. Turn left onto Falls Road and continue for just over one-half mile. Turn left onto Smith Avenue and make a quick left onto Cottonworth Avenue. The ice rink is immediately to the left.

Phone: (410) 433-4970.

Senator Theatre

There's no better place to view a movie in Baltimore than at the Senator Theatre. Located in Belvedere Square in North Baltimore, this colorful Art Deco movie house harks back to a poignant cinematic era when Gene Kelly was singing in the rain and Dorothy was befriending forest creatures. The palatial arena seats about 900 in front of a 40-foot-high screen. The projection and sound system are considered among the finest available. *USA Today* called the Senator one of the four best movie theaters in the United States. Indeed, it is one of the few vintage Art Deco movie houses in the country that has not closed down or been carved into multiple mini-theaters.

The Senator shows top-quality first-run movies that appeal to a wide audience. Showings have included *Shrek, Chicken Run, Rugrats in Paris, Lord of the Rings: The Fellowship of the Rings, E.T.,* and *Star Wars: The Phantom Menace.* Classic movies are also shown on occasion. The Senator hosts a number of special events, which have been attended by such celebrities as Muhammad Ali, Bruce Willis, Johnny Depp, Ned Beatty, Shirley MacLaine, Danny DeVito, and Kevin Bacon. Also, Baltimore-area directors—Barry Levinson and John Waters among them—often premier their movies at the Senator. Check out the "Walk of Fame" in front of the theater.

Patrons of the Senator should take heart that they are supporting a national treasure. In 2001 the National Trust for Historic Preservation named grand movie houses among the 11 Most Endangered Historic Places, and cited the Senator as an example. The Senator was subsequently featured on *The History Channel* and *CBS News Sunday Morning.*

The Senator offers a fun social opportunity for groups. From 15 to 40 people may rent one of two private viewing boxes on the mezzanine level. Groups may supply their own food and drink, though popcorn is provided. The downside is that the boxes must be leased in advance, usually before the movie selection is known. A fun tie-in would be to have a post-movie dinner at Café Zen, a funky but sumptuous Asian eatery located just around the corner. At the time of this writing, the area around the Senator Theatre was being considered for a large-scale urban revitalization project.

Location and Directions: At 5904 York Road, in North Baltimore. From Interstate 83, take Northern Parkway east. Continue on Northern Parkway for about two miles, and turn right onto York Road. The Senator is two blocks down York Road on the right. The Senator shares a parking lot with Staples, which is located across York Road and one block south of the theater.

Website and Phone: www.senator.com; (410) 435-8338.

Shadowland Laser Adventure Center

Laser tag is not an activity typically associated with wholesome family fun, but after a visit to Shadowland Laser Adventure Center, you may think differently. Shadowland provides a high-spirited and bedazzling interactive game where parents can tumble around the floor with their kids, and kids will have a sensory-driven blast. Located in Columbia, Shadowland is one of the better-organized laser tag arenas in the area. Parents squeamish about their kids using guns should note that Shadowland seems particularly sensitive to that sentiment as well.

The game is played between two or more teams, though individual performance counts as well. Participants don an impressively high-tech, Jetson-like outfit that is radio-linked to central command, and equipped with a handset that emits an infrared laser beam. On the handset is a monitor that keeps score in real time. Each participant takes on an alias, for instance Terminator or Poison Ivy, and is sent into the 6,000-square-foot, two-level playing area set up in the most Gothic of fashions. The playing area is laden with lights and sounds and an abundance of obstacles. Very simply, hit your opponents with laser beams and avoid getting hit yourself. The game involves lots of ducking, darting, and diving behind obstacles, and is physically demanding and sweat-inducing.

Shadowland has private rooms available for birthday parties that start at about $9.95 per person. They include sodas, a gift, and one or more adventures.

Location and Directions: At 9179 Red Branch Road, in Columbia. From Baltimore, take Interstate 70 west, and in Ellicott City take

Route 29 south. Take Exit 21A, Route 108, heading east. At the second traffic light, turn left onto Red Branch Road. Park next to Top Flight Gymnastics and walk to the front of the building, which is the adventure center.

Hours and Admission: Mondays from 11 a.m. to 6 p.m., Tuesdays through Thursdays from 11 a.m. to 10 p.m., Fridays from 11 a.m. to midnight, Saturdays from 10 a.m. to midnight, and Sundays from 10 a.m. to 10 p.m. Cost is $7.25 for one adventure, $14 for two, and $19.50 for three. Special discounted packages are set up for groups.

Website and Phone: www.shadowlandadventures.com; (410) 740-9100.

Spicy Skatepark

Spicy Skatepark attracts the largest congregation of skateboarders, inline skaters, and BMX bikers in the area. The skatepark is located next to the Freestate Indoor Sports Arena, off Route 40, in Whitemarsh. Spread across 12,000 square feet of macadam are a launch box, Bauer boxes, a pyramid, four starter ledges, street ramps of all sizes, and two grinding bars. And if you know what any of that means, please educate me. It can get crowded, but facilities are spread out enough to give everyone an opportunity.

▲ Busting moves at Spicy Skatepark

The park is predominantly used by skateboarders, and all skill levels are accommodated. There are modest ramps for the newbies, and a spacious and imposing half-pipe for the well-seasoned skater. Spectators may witness some impressively footloose skating, including high leaps and aerial tricks. Even if you can't tell a front-end grind from a casperflip or a backside grab, it's still fun to watch. Just be prepared to see bodies tumbling and loose skateboards scudding through the air. Parents can rest assured, however, that management requires all users to don helmets and knee pads. To get to the skatepark, you must walk through the indoor arena used for roller hockey and indoor soccer and out the back door. Knock on the plywood hut for help. At the time of publication, Spicy Skatepark had been sold and was being renovated.

Skaters to the south of the city may want to try the Sawmill Skateboard Park, located at 301 Dorsey Road, in Glen Burnie. The park is open daily from 11 a.m. to 8 p.m. The ramps and boxes, however, are metal, so you'll hear lots of clankity clankity clanking.

Location and Directions: At 5811 Allender Road, in Whitemarsh. From Baltimore, take Interstate 95 north. In Whitemarsh, take Exit 67, Route 43, east. Continue for about one-half mile and take Route 40 east. Continue for about two miles on Route 40, and turn left onto Allender Road. The Freestate Indoor Sports Arena is immediately to the left.

Hours and Admission: Summer hours are Mondays through Fridays from 1 p.m. to 8:30 p.m., Saturdays from 11 a.m. to 8:30 p.m., and Sundays from 11 a.m. to 9 p.m. Winter hours vary depending on weather. The skatepark is reserved for bikes on Wednesdays and Sundays after 4 p.m. Admission is $6 during the week and $8 on weekends. A $10 membership fee is also required for first-time users. There are weekly and monthly discounts.

Sports

Sports is a former soccer arena in Cockeysville that has been crammed full of indoor sporting activities and a generous spread of video games and carnival-type attractions. It's tantamount to nirvana for younger kids, but can be equally entertaining for fun-loving parents. Go there on a rainy day under the guise of doing something special for the kids and have a blast yourself.

The centerpiece of Sports is the 18-hole miniature golf course, which weaves around a Cinderella-type castle perched atop a low rise. Fountains spritz water and a millwheel turns ceaselessly. Miniature golf costs $5 for adults, $4.50 for kids, and $4.25 for seniors over 65. Batting cages offer machines chucking both hardballs and softballs at various speeds; $2 will get you 20 pitches, and $5 will get you 60. Baseball enthusiasts will also want to try Speedpitch, where users pitch a ball into a canvas net and a radar device estimates the pitch speed. Speedpitch costs $1 for a minute of action.

Young children will likely head to the Adventure Zone, an impressive climbing structure made up of stacks upon stacks of tubes and slides. Kids between the ages of 3 and 10 may enter if they are four feet tall or less. The Adventure Zone costs $4 per child. Parents waiting for kids in the Adventure Zone can test their mettle at Skeeball, hidden behind the playground entrance.

Older and more agile children may want a shot at the Devil's Tower, a 25-foot-high climbing wall that looms over the entire Sports complex. The wall, named after an unusual rock formation in Wyoming, seemed well-supervised and popular; $5 will get you two scrambles to the top.

Sports is also peppered with video games and other interactive attractions. A snack bar sells drinks and lunch-type food like pizza and nachos ($1.50 each). A separate room is used for birthday parties.

Location and Directions: At 10 Halesworth Road, in Cockeysville. From Baltimore, follow Interstate 83 north and take Exit 17, Padonia Road. Continue east on Padonia Road for less than one mile until it dead-ends at York Road. Turn left onto York Road and continue for about one mile. At the Shell station, turn right onto Halesworth Road. Sports is the large white-roofed building on the left.

Phone: (410) 666-2227.

Tom Mitchell's Golf Gridiron

This is Baltimore's largest and most popular family golfing center. While mom or dad play on the Executive Course, the kids can hone their putting game at one of three miniature courses, or practice working a fairway at the driving range. If golf isn't their forte, there are always the batting cages for both hardball and softball hitting practice.

The three miniature courses accommodate different skill levels. The Regular Course is well-suited for the novice, offering short and mildly challenging holes. The Championship Course is laced with more difficult obstacles, including a water trap and some interesting twists and turns. The supreme challenge lies in the Monster in the Pines Course, which has the longest lanes of any putt-putt course I've seen. The course winds along a hillside beneath a stand of shady pines.

The Executive Course at Tom Mitchell's is a fine place for beginning golfers to get their feet wet in the real deal. The course has nine holes that are very forgiving, with wide fairways and only a modest number of sand and water traps. Those wanting to play 18 holes can double-up, since each hole has two different tee areas, thus creating a back nine. Men's par for the full 18 holes is 61, while ladies' par is 62. Clubs ($10), pull carts ($3), and electric carts ($5 to $20) are available for rent. The clubhouse has some vending machines and there are two outdoor picnic areas.

Location and Directions: At 301 Mitchell Drive, in Reisterstown. From Baltimore, take Interstate 795 west for nine miles until it ends. Continue on Route 140 west and take a quick left onto Mitchell Drive. The golf center is located at the end of the drive.

Admission: Miniature golf is $3 for the Regular Course, and $5 for the other two. Balls for the driving range cost $4 for a small bucket, $6 for a large, and $11 for a jumbo. Those using the batting cages get five balls for a quarter. The Executive Course costs $11 for nine holes, and $16 for 18 holes. Seniors and children 17 and under pay $7 and $11, respectively. Lessons are offered for $40.

Phone: (410) 833-7721.

Yoga Center of Columbia

Recent studies have shown that children partaking in a regular yoga program show a reduction in disruptive behavior, an improvement in physical conditioning, and an increase in emotional well-being. Yoga has also been known to control symptoms associated with attention deficit disorder. It should come as no surprise that more parents are enrolling their children in yoga classes, and more yoga centers are catering to the youthful crowd.

The Yoga Center of Columbia, one of the area's premier facilities, offers a Yoga for Kids program. One class is for children aged 4 to 8, and teaches basic yoga through fun activities and age-appropriate postures. Relaxation and body posture are stressed. Each class lasts 45 minutes and is held once a week. Each session is seven weeks, with an eighth week used to make up missed classes, and costs $56.

▲ The Pigeon Pose at the Yoga Center of Columbia
Courtesy of Mark Rothstein, copyright 2000

Another class is geared toward children aged 9 through 12, and lays a more solid foundation for body awareness and well-being. Posture, breath, and relaxation are emphasized. Each class lasts one hour and is held once a week. Each session is seven weeks, with an eighth week for making up missed classes, and costs $63.

The Yoga for Teenagers class caters to those 13 to 18 years of age. Participants still concentrate on posture, breath, and relaxation, but classes get more involved in technique, strength, and flexibility. Each class lasts 90 minutes and is held once a week. Each session is eleven weeks and costs $128.70. Sessions run year-round, and parents have been known to accompany their children. The yoga center offers occasional free introductory sessions, and drop-in fees are $16 per class.

Other yoga centers exist in the Baltimore area. Those living north of the city should check out the Greater Baltimore Yoga Center in Timonium (410-560-2980), which also offers classes for kids.

Location and Directions: At 8950 Route 108, Suite 109, in the Parkridge Plaza Building, in Columbia. From Baltimore, take Interstate 70 west, and in Ellicott City, take Route 29 south. Continue for about four miles, and take Route 108 east. The yoga center is 1.3 miles on Route 108 to the left. Parking is available behind the building.

Website and Phone: www.columbiayoga.com; (410) 720-4340.

Hikes

The Baltimore area is rife with hiking trails, ranging from easy walking paths in city parks to rugged climbs through the Catoctin Mountains. There's something for hikers of all abilities and interests. Young kids and novice hikers can get their legs trained on the paved and graveled trails presented in the Bicycling chapter. These trails also provide ideal stroller-pushing opportunities for parents seeking a workout. Those wanting to just dabble with single-track dirt trails can venture out to one of the parks discussed in the County Parks chapter.

The hikes presented here are geared toward hikers who have a decent level of stamina and who want to be challenged by rocks, roots, and in some cases, steep climbs. These are my local favorites. They range in distance from 2.5 to 4.5 miles, and typically pass through pretty wilderness and by interesting landscape features. For a more complete and informative guide to hiking trails in the Baltimore area, I recommend *50 Hikes in Maryland* by Leonard M. Adkins. I also suggest getting a trail map before embarking on any of these hikes, to make sense of the various trail systems.

Catoctin Mountain Park (3.0 miles)

If Maryland has an epic hike, it would be somewhere along the rough-and-tumble wilderness of Catoctin Mountain Park. Maryland here is at its grandest. The trails are steep and rocky, and the lookouts and scenery spectacular. Two popular hiking destinations in the park are Chimney Rock, a panoramic lookout, and Wolf Rock, an arresting boulder formation. This three-mile loop hike ties to-

▲ Panoramic mountain view from Chimney Rock at Catoctin Mountain Park

gether both features and includes a romp through some of the state's finest woodland. This hike is difficult, however, and should only be attempted by experienced hikers seeking an added challenge.

Begin the hike at the park's administrative offices, along Route 77, located about one mile downhill from the visitors center. Before hiking, scan the nearby pool of Hunting Creek for trout; they often feed in the tail of the pool or lay low in the deep section. Enter the woods near the entrance to the parking lot, at the hike mileage sign. Start the strenuous 1.1-mile uphill climb to Chimney Rock, following signs to that feature. The trail is not blazed, but is well trodden and accurately marked with signs. Be mindful of switchbacks, slick rocks, and ankle-grabbing roots. Expect your lungs and quads to be strained.

Atop the mountain, the trail flattens out before making the final ascent to Chimney Rock, at mile 1.1. The lookout offers nice views of adjacent mountains and the rolling farmland of Frederick County. Watch for dangerous crevices and drops at the lookout.

From Chimney Rock, continue northward along the ridge to Wolf Rock, at mile 1.5. This stretch of trail is generally pretty and easy going, save for some short, steep pitches. It wanders through a nice stretch of mountain laurel. A sign will announce the appearance of Wolf Rock to the right. Wolf Rock is not a lookout, but rather an intriguing formation of quartzite boulders that are fun to clamber over. That type of rock is virtually erosion-proof, which explains its lofty presence. Don't miss reading the interpretive sign about the formation, and be mindful of the steep drop-off to the left.

From Wolf Rock, continue on a meandering stretch of wide and pretty trail to an intersection at mile 1.8. Turn left, following signs for Park Central Road (or if you want to up your mileage, continue 0.7 of a mile to Thurmont Vista, a nice lookout of that town, and backtrack to this point). After turning left at the intersection, descend 0.2 of a mile to another intersection. Here, turn left, following signs to the park headquarters (not to be confused with the visitors' center). Continue downhill toward the park headquarters. At mile 2.9, turn right onto the spur leading to the parking lot, and continue 0.1 of a mile to your car. The visitors' center, about one mile uphill on Route 77, makes for a worthy post-hike rest stop.

Directions to Trailhead: From Baltimore, take Interstate 70 west. In Frederick, take Route 15 north. In Thurmont, take Route 77 west and continue for about two miles to the roadside parking lot on the right, by the park administrative offices.

Gunpowder Falls State Park— Falls Road (3.5 miles)

This stretch of the Gunpowder South Trail traces the scenic upper reaches of Gunpowder Falls as it passes through rocky bluffs and majestic hemlock stands. It is, in my opinion, the prettiest stretch of hiking trail near Baltimore. That said, this trail may be too difficult for some kids. It requires scrambling over large boulders and fallen logs, and there are some steep climbs. Do not try this if you are an inexperienced hiker. Those braving the obstacles, however, will be privy to an breathtaking slice of western Maryland in the eastern part of the state.

Begin the hike at the Falls Road parking lot. Follow the white-blazed spur trail 0.2 of a mile, over a short rise and down a steep hill, to the Gunpowder South Trail. Turn left onto the white-blazed Gunpowder South Trail, heading upstream, and continue 1.2 miles to the Prettyboy Dam. This stretch of Gunpowder Falls is the most productive trout stream in the state. Upwards of 4,000 trout per mile—mostly brown trout—have been surveyed here. Catch-and-release fishing is allowed, and you will likely encounter serious fly fishermen, so show decorum (i.e., no chucking rocks in the drink). This stretch also offers unparalleled beauty, with water sluicing between huge boulders and tumbling into deep, icy pools. Since the water originates deep in Prettyboy Reservoir, its temperature remains around 50 degrees year-round (hence all the trout).

The first quarter-mile of the Gunpowder South Trail requires lots of scrambling over rocks and roots. There are great "Pocahontas rocks," as my daughter calls them (rocks that jut over the river or trail), along this stretch. The trail soon switches to hard-packed dirt. It is very narrow and passes through a gauntlet of lovely mountain laurel, rhododendrons, berries, and the occasional lily. Diligently keep your eye on the white blazes, since small spurs turn off to the river. At about mile 0.75, the trail climbs an embankment to bypass a steep canyon area. At the hilltop, continue right on the white trail. The blue-blazed Highland Trail veers to the left, leading to another parking area.

Descend the hill and follow the river another half mile, until you encounter a huge bulwark of concrete that is Prettyboy Dam. The dam was built in 1932 and quells the river, creating a 1,500-acre reservoir. If the dam is releasing water, the lion's roar can be heard well before the dam comes into sight, and an extra dash of cool air can be felt. Rock-skipping is a mandatory activity in the pool below the dam if no fishermen are present.

Backtrack south on the Gunpowder South Trail along the river. The first large bend from the dam has a stretch of slack water. Notice the beaver dam causing this pool. Backtrack the entire 1.2 miles from the dam to the spur trail leading to the car. The fork of this spur is located just after the quarter-mile stretch of boulders. Here you can either turn right onto the spur, which leads up a hill to the parking lot (making for a hike totaling about three miles), or continue south on the Gunpowder South Trail along the river, adding another half-mile to the hike.

If you decide to lengthen the hike, continue along the river for another couple of hundred yards. Near a fantastic grove of hemlocks along the river bank, the Gunpowder South Trail turns right, away from the river, over a hill. You may follow this for about 0.2 of a mile, turning right at the T-intersection, where it leads to the iron bridge where Gunpowder Falls crosses Falls Road. For a more scenic and challenging stretch, bushwhack the boulders just past the hemlock stand (staying high and away from the river), which may require hoisting small kids over some rocks. Then descend back to the river, and follow the fishermen's trail about a quarter-mile to the iron bridge. At this point, follow Falls Road uphill, about 0.2 of a mile, back to the Falls Road parking lot.

Directions to Trailhead: From Baltimore, take Interstate 83 north. Take Exit 27, Mt. Carmel Road, west and continue for just over one mile. Turn right onto Evna Road, and continue for about two miles, until it dead-ends. Turn right onto Falls Road, and continue for just under two miles to the Falls Road parking lot. This is the second pull-off area along Falls Road and the one just before the river crossing. A white-blazed trailhead post is there.

Gunpowder Falls State Park— Hereford Area (4.0 miles)

Another agreeable and unusually picturesque hike in Gunpowder Falls State Park is in the Hereford Area, just off York Road. This hike traces a four-mile loop along the Panther Branch and Gunpowder South Trails. From the parking area, descend to the river on the white-blazed Gunpowder South Trail, heading downstream. In about 100 feet, turn right onto the blue-blazed Panther Branch Trail, which you will remain on for about 2.5 miles. The trail initially ascends a fern-laden hill and dips into a nice gully or two. The trail jukes and jives over the mountainside, making lots of turns. Follow the blue blazes carefully and you should be fine. (Remember that a double-blaze signifies a turn.) The one poorly marked turn is at mile 0.5, where you should turn right.

Continue on the Panther Branch Trail across the ridge top, passing an intersection with the pink-blazed Sandy Lane Trail. At mile 0.7 the trail juts left onto what appears to be a lightly used pathway. At mile 0.9 it passes through an orderly stand of tall pine trees. At mile 1.1 the trail crosses a sunny meadow and hooks up with Panther Branch, which begins as a trickle but picks up steam as it nears its mouth. The stream was supposedly named for a wild cat that once haunted a nearby cave. The Panther Branch Trail runs beside the stream over its entire course. The trail passes many rock remnants, which are what's left of former mills, some of them gunpowder mills. A gunpowder mill is thought to have exploded here in the 19th century.

Near the mouth of Gunpowder Falls, at mile 2.2, the trail bounces over a small rise and terminates at the white-blazed Gunpowder South Trail. Turn left onto the Gunpowder South Trail and continue about 1.8 miles to the car. The Gunpowder South Trail passes through the lush riparian area of a calm stretch of Gunpowder Falls, offering nice views of the river. Obvious through this stretch of river is the abundance of beaver inhabiting the area. Notice the many downed and partially gnawed trees and the numerous mud chutes where beaver get in and out of the water. If hiking at dawn or dusk, you may see one lying low in the river. Listen for the loud Kerplunck! as it submerges. This section of trail is relatively flat and easygoing, with some minor meanderings over hills. A few nice rock outcrops line this stretch.

As you near the end of the loop, cars on Interstate 83 can be heard. It may seem like you're home free, but be warned that one substantial climb separates you from your vehicle. To add miles to this hike, continue out and back on the white-blazed Gunpowder South Trail across York Road.

Directions to Trailhead: From Baltimore, take Interstate 83 north. Take Exit 27, Mt. Carmel Road, and head east for about one-half mile. Turn left onto York Road and continue for about 1.7 miles to the trailhead. Parking is available along York Road just before crossing Gunpowder Falls.

Oregon Ridge Park (4.3 miles)

Oregon Ridge is a well-used county park offering a vast array of recreational opportunities, most of which are clustered around Beaver Dam and Shawan Roads. Oregon Ridge Park also includes some scenic and relatively untrammeled backcountry areas where shoe leather is your ticket to entry. This hike circles the outer boundary of the park, and offers decent footing but a few nasty climbs.

Begin the hike at the parking lot of the Oregon Ridge Nature Center. Cross the bridge located just left of the nature center's entrance. The bridge crosses a ravine which is actually a pit where geothite (a black ore used to make pig iron) was mined over 150 years ago. The nature center was built atop the spoils pile. Immediately after the bridge, turn right onto the red-blazed Loggers Trail, and follow it through the thick deciduous forest. Do not veer onto the tan-blazed Ridge Trail or the Disabled Trail. After about mile 0.5, the Loggers Trail begins a substantial climb. Do not take any of the spur trails shooting off to the right. Atop the hill is a T-intersection at a pipeline right-of-way. Turn right and make a quick left back into the woodland, staying on the red-blazed trail the entire time. Don't forget your wildflower and bird guidebooks, as this pipeline clearing presents ideal viewing of both.

At about mile 1.0, the Loggers Trail intersects a white-blazed Short Cut Trail which leads off to the right. Stay on the red-blazed Loggers Trail, and continue for another one-quarter mile until an intersection with other trails. At about mile 1.25, bear right onto the yellow-blazed Ivy Hill Trail, heading downhill. The yellow-blazed trail continues its descent, crosses another pipeline right-of-way, and sidles up to a tiny brook called Baisman Run. At about mile 2.0, the trail happens upon Ivy Hill Pond, a perfect place for a halfway rest break. The pretty scene's only blemish are the ailing hemlock trees circling the pocket of water. They are victims of woolly adelgid, a small but lethal insect that sucks sap from the hemlocks, causing premature defoliation.

From the pond, continue on the yellow-blazed trail, following Baisman Run downstream. The trail along this stretch, though still yellow-blazed, is called the S. James Campbell Trail, honoring the man who preserved and donated this tract. Over the next half-mile, the trail bounces back and forth over the creek, requiring skipping across rocks. At about mile 2.6, the trail begins a lung-taxing climb, which ends at about mile 3.0. Continue across the high ridge (the one motorists see from Interstate 83) for another half-mile. Cross another pipeline right-of-way, and in a few hundred feet, the yellow trail will intersect with the red-blazed Loggers' Trail. Turn right onto the Loggers' Trail, which almost immediately veers left to the clearing atop the former ski slope. After taking in the breathtaking views of Hunt Valley, notice the remnants of the former ski-lift facility.

From the ski slope, descend on the Loggers' Trail. At about mile 4.0, the trail encounters a T-intersection, with a picnic grove to the right. Turn left, remaining on the red-blazed trail uphill. In about 100 feet, the red-blazed trail turns right. Do not follow this trail. Instead, continue another 100 feet, and turn right onto the Lake Trail, which is blazed orange. This trail continues for about one-quarter mile around the quarry-cum-swim hole, and can be a bit rough in places. Children may need a hand from parents, and there are some vulnerable places where the ground slopes into the lake. If safety is a concern, backtrack to the previously mentioned picnic grove and hike around the front of the lake, following the road back to the parking lot.

For those continuing on the Lake Trail, caution is needed. The trail, however, offers nice vantages of the swimming area. At one point, crossing a log bridge is required. The trail emerges from the woodland on the west end of the lake. The nature center's parking lot is a few hundred feet to the left. A stop at the well-maintained nature center is the ideal way to wrap up such a nice hike.

Directions to Trailhead: From Baltimore, take Interstate 83 north. Take Exit 20-B, Shawan Road, heading west. At the first light, turn left onto Beaver Dam Road, and make a quick right, following signs to the nature center. Park in the nature center parking lot.

Patapsco Valley State Park—
McKeldin Area (4.5 miles)

Naturalists will want to hike the Switchback Trail at the McKeldin Area of Patapsco Valley State Park. The trail circumnavigates this scenic park, allowing access to some far-reaching woodland and nice streamside riparian habitat. It's a prime nearby spot to view wildlife and learn native flora.

Begin the hike in the parking lot nearest the park entrance. Walk the road back toward the park entrance. Just past the entrance station, enter the woods on the white-blazed Switchback Trail, which is clearly marked with a sign. Follow the trail as it slices through pretty woodland and then descends a sharp hill, making a U-turn. An alcove to the left, just past this turn, is the remnant of a former flagstone quarry that operated here.

You are on the floodplain for the South Branch Patapsco River. This area provides excellent bird habitat, and is an ideal place to make additions to your life list, especially during the spring warbler migration. Don't forget your bird guidebook and binoculars. At the U-turn is a grove of towering sycamore trees, identifiable by what appears to be peeling bark. In spring, the northern parula, an uncommon, diminutive blue and yellow bird, can be found twitter-

▲ Child-friendly hiking at the McKeldin Area of Patapsco Valley State Park

ing in the highest canopy. Watch for bluebirds and indigo buntings in some of the clearings through this stretch.

Follow the Switchback Trail as it meets and parallels the river. A purple-blazed trail departs from the Switchback Trail at about mile 0.6 and rejoins the trail at mile 0.9. Stay on the white-blazed trail unless you're looking for a good hill workout. The trail passes over a sharp rise and crosses a road at about mile 1.0. Just past the road is the Switchback Trail's confluence with the orange-blazed McKeldin Rapids Trail. Follow the McKeldin Rapids Trail to the right for about one-quarter mile to one of the area's prettiest cascades. Below the falls is a large pool ideal for fishing and rock-skipping, though swimming is off-limits. This area is unusually rocky, which makes for fun play, but is also loaded with water snakes. Herons and kingfishers (short, stocky, blue and white water birds often seen perched on tree limbs overhanging water) are numerous through this stretch.

Backtrack on the McKeldin Rapids Trail to the white-blazed Switchback Trail. Turn right and continue on the Switchback Trail. The trail bounces up and down a hillside, passes through a disc golf course, and comes to rest at the spot where the South Branch Patapsco River meets the north branch. Continue on the Switchback Trail as it follows the north branch upstream. The Switchback Trail runs along the river for the next 1.5 miles, providing easy and scenic hiking with good footing. The North Branch Patapsco River comes from Liberty Reservoir, and usually flows at a low rate of speed. This stretch of the river is ruled by beaver. Look for gnawed and fallen trees. Keep an eye out for a beaver drifting on the river like a floating log, or submarining underwater (especially at dusk or dawn).

Avoid taking the red-blazed Plantation Trail that enters from the left. Keep following the white blazes along the north branch. At about mile 3.5, it passes over loose rocks and boulders that require extra attention. Just past this stretch, the Switchback Trail makes a sharp left, leaves the riverside, and climbs a very steep incline. The top of the hill affords nice views of the river valley. Avoid taking the red-blazed trail once again, and continue following the white blazes as the Switchback Trail rollercoasts through a beautiful patch of woodland.

At mile 4.0, near the top of a final climb, the trail meets up with a paved road at a restroom. Next to the comfort station, look far past Pavilion 550 for a fine view of Liberty Reservoir and the dam face. Continue on the paved road for the final one-half mile, following it to the paved parking area where the hike originated. Watch the fields as you pass, and if it is dawn or dusk, count the number of deer you see through this stretch.

Directions to Trailhead: From Baltimore, take Interstate 70 west. Just past Ellicott City, take the Marriotsville Road exit and head north. The park entrance is about four miles up Marriotsville Road on the right, just past the crossing of the Patapsco River.

Patuxent Wildlife Research Center (2.5 miles)

At 12,800 acres, the Patuxent Wildlife Research Center comprises what is reportedly the largest undeveloped tract of land on the East Coast between Boston and the Carolinas. It's the nation's premier spot for biological and ecological research, employing hundreds of scientists from around the world. While the vast majority of the land is off-limits to the public, the few open areas present great hiking opportunities. This hike is relatively short and on well-groomed trails, making it ideal for families introducing children to the activity.

Begin the hike at the National Wildlife Visitor Center, a world-class facility worth a look-see. Follow the paved Loop Trail past the parking lot for about 0.1 of a mile, noting the nice views of Lake Redington and Cash Lake. Pick up the well-marked Goose Pond Trail, and continue another 0.2 of a mile to the pond. This

◄ Letting loose along the trails of the Patuxent Wildlife Research Center

▲ Full-grown northern cricket frog, a common sight at the Patuxent Wildlife Research Center

puddle of an impoundment is employed for waterfowl management practices (note the wooden duck houses). Walk the border of the pond to see lots of green and leopard frogs leaping into the drink. A close look will reveal squadrons of thumbnail-sized northern cricket frogs bouncing around your feet, which are fun to catch (though doing so requires quick hands).

From Goose Pond, pick up the Laurel Trail and continue for 0.4 of a mile. This trail bisects a mature deciduous forest and was named for the mountain laurel that lines its path. Keep an eye peeled for deer and songbirds through this stretch. At marker 18, note the grid marker used for biological studies here. Where the Laurel Trail terminates, turn right onto the Valley Trail and continue 0.6 of a mile to Cash Lake. The Valley Trail bounces through a wooded area thick with oak and beechwood trees. At marker 13, note the tree that was struck by lightning and probably has bats living beneath the loose bark. The Valley Trail terminates on the Cash Lake Trail, around the waterfront. Turn left and continue about 0.2 of a mile, crossing two footbridges, to the barrier-free fishing pier and restrooms. The pier makes a good rest/lunch spot. Depending on the season, waterfowl may be prolific here. Look for geese, grebes, mergansers, swans, and lots of different ducks (don't forget your bird book).

When finished resting, backtrack on the Cash Lake Trail around the north face of the lake. The trail runs for about 0.7 of a mile, hugging the waterfront the entire length except for the last 100 yards. Notice the signs of beaver activity, including the log beaver home. Cash Lake Trail will deposit you at Goose Pond. From there, turn left, following the Goose Pond Trail back to the paved Long Trail, and return to the visitor center.

Directions to Trailhead: From Baltimore, take the Baltimore-Washington Parkway south. Past Laurel, take the Powder Mill Road exit and turn left onto Powder Mill Road, heading east. Continue for about two miles on Powder Mill Road and turn right onto Scarlet Tanager Loop. Continue 1.4 miles to the visitors' center and parking area.

Soldiers Delight Natural Environment Area

Soldiers Delight may be the area's best kept natural secret. Since it lacks any big-ticket draw—no waterfalls, no rivers, no lakes—most recreationists stay clear. But its pure beauty and unique terrain endear it to the true naturalist. Soldiers Delight is a serpentine barren, a rock type that inhibits typical vegetative growth; the result is terrain that resembles a high-elevation Montana prairie rather than a deciduous Piedmont woodland. This unique geologic formation is responsible for 39 species of rare, threatened, or endangered plants growing here, in addition to rare insects, rocks, and minerals.

Serpentine is an unusual green metamorphic rock that is found throughout the park. In Harford County, it's quarried under the name Maryland green marble, and adorns the inside lobby of the Empire State Building. The Gothic-looking Mt. Vernon Methodist Church, in downtown Baltimore, was built of serpentine. The presence of serpentine in the Soldiers Delight area, however, had more far-reaching repercussions. The valuable mineral chromite was discovered intermingled with the serpentine, and in the nineteenth century, almost all the chromite in the world was mined here. Chromite was used to make chromium products, dyes, and paint pigments.

Soldiers Delight supposedly got its name from soldiers who were stationed here and loved the wide-open terrain. The park hosts seven miles of trails, all accessible from the overlook parking area. Trails are decently marked, though an attentive eye is required to stay on track. Instead of leading you on one particular hike, I will describe the options and let you choose. A trail map, available at the Visitors Center, is recommended.

West of the overlook parking area is a three-mile, white-blazed loop trail that is a bit more rugged than other hikes here, but very attractive. It's the best trail to take to see the unusual terrain. The one blemish on this hike is a power line that bisects the park, though the clearings created by the lines offer great opportunities

◀ Exploring biodiversity at Soldiers Delight Natural Environment Area

for viewing wildlife, particularly birds. Also scan the far clearings for feeding deer. The white trail leads past the abandoned Red Dog Lodge, built in 1912 of native stone, and a visitors' center that is well worth a stopover.

Those seeking a more kindly hike should stick to the trails east of Deer Park Road. From the parking area, cross the road, staying right, and follow the trail emblazoned with red, orange, and yellow blazes. Follow the yellow blazes for a three-mile loop trek that leads to the far reaches of the park. You can shorten the hike to two miles by following the orange blazes, or take a leisurely one-mile stroll by tracking the red blazes. The trails are single-track dirt and offer agreeable footing. Skipping across tiny brooks may be necessary.

All three trails to the east of the parking area pass the entrances to the former Choate mines, where most of the world's chromite was mined from 1839 through 1886, and again during World War I. The shaft plunges 200 feet, sloping to the southeast, before opening up into the main mining area where 3,000 tons of chromite was removed. Hikers can explore the entrance to the shaft. Also, what appear to be construction projects along the trail are really efforts to stave off encroachment of Virginia pines into this fragile ecosystem.

Directions to Trailhead: From the Baltimore Beltway, take Route 26, Liberty Road, west. In Wards Chapel, just before crossing Liberty Reservoir, turn right onto Wards Chapel Road. Continue two miles on Wards Chapel Road to its dead end. Turn right onto Deer Park Road and continue one-quarter mile to the overlook parking lot.

Susquehanna State Park (3.2 miles)

Susquehanna State Park is a quiet and lightly trodden expanse of forest and meadow in Harford County, within an hour's drive of downtown Baltimore. The park is tied together by a generous web of single-track hiking trails leading to neat pockets of wilderness and nice lookouts of the Susquehanna River. This 3.2-mile route will provide hikers with a nice taste of what the park has to offer. Note that this hike requires several stream crossings, which may result in wet shoes (though rock-hopping across may be a possibility in low water). Also note that this trail passes through a hunting area, so take precautions when hiking in fall and early winter.

Park by the grist mill in the Rock Run Historic Area. Follow Rock Run Road uphill for about 100 yards. Turn right and enter the woods on the Susquehanna Ridge Trail, which is blazed red and blue. Follow this trail for about one mile as it undulates on a ridge along the Susquehanna River, offering sweet views to your right. Taking this trail requires an immediate but fun crossing of Rock Run. Notice some historic artifacts along this stretch of trail, including stone fences that once delineated property boundaries.

At about mile 1.0, turn left onto a well-used, but unnamed, spur trail blazed with the number 4 (do not follow the red-blazed trail that continues off to the right). Shortly after turning left, you will pass through a dilapidated and abandoned farm. To the right is a creepy red barn, and to the left a derelict silo and remnants of a stone building. Refrain from poking around the tumbling structures (in a show of respect to spiders, snakes, and falling debris).

Just beyond the farm structures, at about mile 1.25, the trail blazed with a 4 terminates at a field. Turn left onto the blue-blazed Farm Road Trail and follow it uphill as it traces the treeline. This was the access road to the former farm. Watch for deer, songbirds, and butterflies as you follow the treeline, and don't forget a post-hike tick check. Eagles, hawks, and turkey vultures can often be seen soaring above. You may have to strain to see the blue blazes on the trees. At the end of the field, a footpath veers to the right. Do not take this path. Instead, continue on the blue-blazed trail that enters the woodland to the left. It descends gradually to Wilkinson Road.

At about mile 2.0, the Farm Road Trail crosses the road, bounces over a small ridge, and meets Rock Run Road. Cross over Rock Run Road at mile 2.5, and cross the Rock Run stream. How it got its name should be obvious. This is a great spot to pull up a slab and rest, look for salamanders under rocks, or throw stones in the water. Just past the Rock Run crossing, the blue-blazed trail terminates at the yellow-blazed Rock Run Y Trail. Turn left onto the yellow-blazed trail and continue for about one-half mile back to the Rock Run Historic Area and your car. The yellow-blazed trail sneaks behind the Rock Run House, a stunning 1804 mansion once owned by John Carter, a partner in the nearby grist mill operation. When finished hiking, be sure to check out the wildlife observation platform along the river, and take a peek in the grist mill if possible. The Rock Run House is sometimes open for tours.

Directions to Trailhead: From Baltimore, take Interstate 95 north. In Havre de Grace, take Exit 89, Route 155, and head west. In about two miles, turn right onto Route 161, and go right again onto Rock Run Road. Continue on Rock Run Road to its terminus at the grist mill, along the river.

Wincopin and Quarry Trails (2.5 miles)

A century ago, the hills around the town of Savage were heavily quarried. When the rock operations closed down, a diamond was left behind—a lush sliver of land wedged between the Little Patux-

◀ Searching for slimy critters along the Wincopin Trail

ent and Middle Patuxent Rivers. This pinch of property has become part of Savage Park, and offers one of the area's richest diversities of flora and fauna. Hiking the sparsely used Wincopin and Quarry trails is a great way to explore Savage Park. Note, however, that this 2.5-mile hike requires a relatively steep ascent and descent, and a few short stretches of challenging footing.

From the parking lot, follow the red-blazed Wincopin Trail, which quickly turns from pavement to dirt. At about mile 0.25, turn left onto the green-blazed Quarry Trail. Cross over a high, wooded plateau, and descend a steep hill to the Little Patuxent River. Turn right at the bottom, following the green blazes. This section of the trail was laid over a former railroad bed. The derelict stone structure visible along this segment is what remains of the place where railroad cars were once loaded with quarried rock.

Where the two river branches meet, the Quarry Trail cuts sharply right and follows the Middle Patuxent River. Before making the turn, wander out onto the stone remains of a former railroad bridge for a nice vantage of the confluence. Just downstream of this point is Savage Mill, a former textile mill that once produced such things as sails, tents, and backdrops for Hollywood silent movies. It's now a trendy antiques and shopping outlet. Just past the confluence, look right for a puddle-pond filled with green and pickle frogs. About one-half mile past the pond, follow the Quarry Trail up a steep hill, where it reconnects with the red-blazed Wincopin Trail. Turn right onto the Wincopin Trail, and hike about one-half mile back to the parking area.

Directions to Trailhead: From Baltimore, take Interstate 95 south. Take Route 32 east and Route 1 south. Take the first right onto Howard Street into Savage. Continue for about one mile and turn right onto Savage Guilford Road. Continue for another mile and turn left onto Vollmerhausen Road. Then proceed for about one-half mile to the parking lot on the left.

Historical Walks

The Baltimore area comes with a rich past. These four walks will lead readers through culturally rich and historically significant neighborhoods that have grasped their roots firmly, and have survived modernization with their historical character intact. Each walk is between one and two miles long. For more developed walking tours of the Baltimore area, see *Urban Hikes in and around Baltimore*, by this author.

Annapolis

This quaint, but chic, Chesapeake Bay town is most known for nautical themes: the U.S. Naval Academy, sailboats, Chino-wearing boat owners, and yacht clubs. But Annapolis also offers the nation's finest collection of colonial architecture, preserved in pitch-perfect fashion. This walk will reveal what an eastern seaboard maritime town may have been like centuries ago.

Begin at the **Market House**, an open-air market situated on Randall Street, near the city dock. A market has stood on this site since the early 1700s, and the present building was erected in 1858. The Market House provides the ideal spot to purchase pre- or post-walk drinks and snacks.

Continue north on Randall Street for two blocks. Located just past the Market House is **Middleton Tavern**, a venerable eating establishment that was built around 1750 as an inn and watering hole for the seafaring. George Washington, Thomas Jefferson, and Benjamin Franklin all bent elbows here. Just past Middleton Tavern, Randall Street crosses Prince George Street. On the far right side of the intersection is a white, wood-frame house. Next door, at 130 Prince George Street, is a cream-colored clapboard house with

119

green shutters. This is the **Sands House**, built in the late 1600s, and believed to be the oldest structure in Annapolis.

Where Randall Street meets King George Street, cut back diagonally onto East Street. The attractive **Waterwitch Fire Station** is one block to the left. It's thought to be the only fire station in the country designed in the Tuscan style. Farther up and to the right is the **Brice House**, a grand example of five-part colonial Georgian architecture for which Annapolis is famous. Five-part design features a central housing unit flanked by two wing units, each connected to the central unit by a segment called a hyphen. Construction of the house began in 1767 for James Brice, who later became mayor of Annapolis and acting governor of Maryland.

Cross Prince George Street and look right. The noble brick dwelling five houses up is the **William Paca House**, another five-part mansion, this one once belonging to a signatory to the Declaration of Independence. The house and gardens are among the finest in Annapolis, and are open for tours. Annapolis was once called the "Athens of America," thanks to estates like this. A 200-unit hotel was built over the gardens in the early 1900s, but was razed in 1965 and the garden returned to its original state. Continue on East Street toward the State House. Look left down **Fleet Street**. Many of these tiny rowhouses lodged soldiers during the Revolutionary War.

East Street dead-ends at State Circle, home to the **State House**, the center of Maryland's state government. The State House was built in 1771 and remains the oldest active state house in the nation. It was here that George Washington tendered his resignation as commander-in-chief of the Continental Army, and where the Treaty of Paris was signed, signifying the end of the Revolutionary War. The diminutive brick **Old Treasury Building** hunches to the east of the state house. Dating to 1735, it's the oldest public structure still standing in Annapolis.

Turn right onto State Circle, and make another right onto Maryland Avenue. This was historically the city's most fashionable street, and today is chock-a-block with specialty shops, galleries, boutiques, and coffee shops. The immaculate **Hammond-Harwood House** is one block down to the right. It's generally considered the finest example of colonial Georgian architecture in the country, and one of the finest medium-sized houses in the world. It's the seminal work of Annapolis architect William Buckland, and is open for inspection. It remains surprisingly intact from its original 1774 appearance, with the only modifications being a new roof, some window work, and a few coats of paint. Henry Ford tried to purchase this house and move it to his Michigan estate, but Annapolis said no-can-do. Across the street is the **Chase-Lloyd House**, another Buckland gem open for tours.

Turn left onto King George Street, continue for one block, and make another left onto College Avenue. To the right is the campus of **St. John's College**, the third oldest institution of higher education in the country behind Harvard University and the College of William and Mary. Its distinctive liberal curriculum centers around the "Great Books" series, considered to be the classic works of western civilization. The campus was home to the **Liberty Tree**, a tulip poplar that stood for 400 years and served as a primary meeting place for patriots planning the American Revolution; the tree succumbed to high winds in 1999.

Continue on College Avenue, past the **Governor's Mansion**, to Church Circle, home of historic **St. Anne's Episcopal Church**. A church has stood on this site since the city's creation. Also on the circle is **Reynold's Tavern**, a busy meeting place in colonial Annapolis that was built in 1737 for hatmaker William Reynold. The tavern provides a nice example of a masonry peculiarity known as all-header bond: each brick is laid with the short end facing outward. Immediately past the tavern, look down Franklin Street. **The Banneker-Douglass Museum**, situated in a former church built by freed slaves, is located a half-block down. The museum commemorates African-American history in Annapolis.

From Church Circle, turn right onto Duke of Gloucester Street and continue for five blocks. The wedge-shaped **Maryland Inn** still offers a snug bed and meal as it did in 1784. It was the first structure in Annapolis built as a hotel, and was erected on land used by the town drummer, a person who conveyed information to the townsfolk via a series of complex drum beats. Where Duke of Gloucester Street crosses Conduit Street is the **Rainbow Row**, a series of brightly hued rowhouses that once served as an annex to the **Mann's Hotel**, located at the end of the chain. George Washington lodged here in 1783.

The **Maynard-Burgess House**, which recently underwent an intensive archeological investigation by the Historic Annapolis Foundation to trace its past, is situated just past Conduit Street. Results of the study are on display in the structure. Across from the house is the **Annapolis City Hall**, which was first used as a social hall where George Washington attended galas. The building was gutted by a blaze in the Civil War but its original structure remains. The **Ridout House**, at 120 Duke of Gloucester Street, is another fine, five-part Georgian dwelling. It's still privately owned by the Ridout family. George and Martha Washington were personal friends of the Ridouts and frequently stayed here. Supposedly, the family is in possession of a nightcap worn by Martha.

Farther along Duke of Gloucester Street is **St. Mary's Church**, the primary place of worship for colonial Catholics (practicing Catholicism in public was officially forbidden in colonial times). Behind the church is the stately **Carroll House**, which stands sentinel over Spa Creek. It was home to Charles Carroll, the wealthiest colonist and only Catholic signer of the Declaration of Independence. Climb onto the Spa Creek drawbridge and look back for a nice view of the house and grounds.

Just before the Spa Creek, turn left onto Compromise Street and continue two blocks to the Market House. **The Museum Store**, run by the Historic Annapolis Foundation, stands at 77 Main Street and is worth a visit. It's in the former **Victualling Warehouse**, where supplies awaiting transport to troops were stored during the Revolutionary War. The hike ends on the City Dock at the end of Ego Alley, a thin strand of water where tight-fitting yachts like to strut their stuff to passers-by. Check out the **Kunta Kinte Memorial** in front of the Market House. Kunta Kinte was the slave immortalized by Alex Haley in *Roots*. In researching his book, Haley learned that Kinte, an ancestor of his, was brought to Annapolis and sold into slavery at this particular spot. The walk ends inside the Market House, where a cool drink and refreshing snack can be had.

Directions: From Baltimore, take Interstate 97 south. Near Annapolis, take Route 50 East. Take Exit 24, Rowe Boulevard, south. Continue toward downtown Annapolis. After crossing College Creek, veer right just before the Louis L. Goldstein Treasury Building, and then turn left onto Northwest Street. Go around Church Circle, and turn right onto Duke of Gloucester Street. Find on-street parking or a parking garage in this general vicinity, and proceed a few blocks downhill toward the Market House.

Ellicott City

When the Ellicott brothers set out in 1771 to establish a vibrant flour mill community, they found the ideal location among the verdant hills of what is now Baltimore and Howard Counties. The town was built on rocky and craggy hillsides interwoven with lots of creeks and resembled a European village. Milling has waned, but today Ellicott City has been transformed into a charming hamlet of coffee shops, antique stores, and boutiques.

Begin the walk at the Oella Avenue parking lot, located about 100 yards west of Frederick Road. From the parking lot, turn left onto Oella Avenue, and right onto Frederick Road toward downtown Ellicott City. The large stone abutments near the parking lot were used to carry tracks for the **#9 trolley line** over the Patapsco River. The former trolley line linked Ellicott City with Catonsville, and is now a rails-to-trails walking and biking path. For an interesting diversion, walk up a flight of stairs from the parking lot and north on the trolley trail about 200 yards to see the "**deep cut**," where rail engineers blasted through a bulwark of rock, creating 60-foot-high walls. Teetering above the deep cut is **Alhambra**, the mansion once belonging to John Ellicott, a member of the town's founding family.

Look southward on Frederick Road. You can't miss the tall silos and eight-story industrial edifice coughing flour out its windows. This is the former Wilkins-Rogers plant, which produced Washington-brand baked products. It's also the site of the town's first flour mill, built by the Ellicott brothers. Continue on Frederick Road into Ellicott City. Just before crossing the Patapsco River, look on the far hill for the unusual white structure. **Castle Anglo** is a Gothic Revival residence built in 1831 by a French artist to replicate, on a smaller scale, an actual castle from his homeland. It's now a private residence.

After the river, cross beneath the **Oliver Viaduct** into downtown Ellicott City. This viaduct carries the still-active **B&O Railroad** over Frederick Road. This was the western terminus of our nation's first rail line, a 12-mile stretch built to connect the flour mills of Ellicott City with the port of Baltimore. Just past the viaduct to the left is the **B&O Railroad Station Museum**. The station, which was built in 1831 and thought to be the first commercial rail station in the country, is now a modest museum deserving of a stopover. This rail station served as the finish line for the legendary Tom Thumb race, which pitted a steam engine against a horse-drawn carriage. The carriage won, thanks to mechanical malfunctions with the steam engine, but the race ushered in the era of mechanized travel. The woodshed-like structure attached to the west face of the rail station is said to have been the first "indoor" outhouse in America. The stone and brick plaza in front of the station was the site of regular slave auctions.

Ellicott City's main business district begins just past the rail station. Antique shops, restaurants, coffee houses, book shops, and curio shops line the street, attracting browsers. The town's charm is attributable to the historical infrastructure that remains. The stone building across from the rail station is the former **Patapsco Hotel**, which later served as an ice storage facility. It collapsed in 1926 when the owner removed vital steel structural beams to create more storage space. It was rebuilt stone by stone. The tall building next door is the former **Opera House**, where John Wilkes Booth, the assassin of Abraham Lincoln, began his short-lived theatrical career.

Continue uphill on Frederick Road and turn right onto Church Lane. The triangular structure at this intersection is the former **firehouse**, built in 1889 and nicely restored as a museum. It replaced the bucket brigades, in which citizens lined up and passed buckets of water from the river to the fire location. The firehouse was purposely built on a downhill slope so that horses could get a running start to the blaze.

Continue on Church Street up a steep hill. Look left down Emory Street. The stone building with green cupola is the **former county prison building** used from 1878 until the modern facility was built in Jessup a century later. Just beyond Emory Street, look right toward the far hillside across town. The spire of **St. Paul's Roman Catholic Church** can be seen. This is where, in 1914, Babe Ruth married a 17-year-old waitress named Helen Woodford. Ruth was from Baltimore and was playing for a Baltimore minor league team at the time. Farther along Church Street and to the right is a brown guardrail. In fall and winter this vantage point offers postcard-perfect views of **Oella**, a former mill town fringing the Patapsco River. The former mill building and a string of millhouses can be seen.

Straight ahead, near Sarah's Lane, are the ominous ruins of what was once the finest female educational institution in the country. In its day, the **Patapsco Female Institute** was as highly regarded as Harvard and Yale. Many prominent Americans, including Robert E. Lee, enrolled their daughters there. It operated as a school from 1837 through 1890, and later as a hospital, hotel, nursing home, and theater.

Turn left onto Sarah's Lane. To the left is **Mount Ida**, a mansion once belonging to William Ellicott, one of the town's founding fathers. Continue another block and turn left onto Court Place, which runs alongside **Howard County's courthouse**. Where Court Place dead-ends, turn right onto Court Avenue. This stretch of wood-frame buildings is **Lawyer's Row**, legal offices dating to the late 19th century.

Wind along Court Avenue for one block until it dead-ends on Frederick Road. Turn right onto Frederick Road and continue for one block to the **Thomas Issac log cabin**. Dating to 1780, this is the oldest intact structure in town. The small, gable-roofed building behind the cabin served as Ellicott City's courthouse from 1840 to 1843. Notice how it sits on a lower level than the present Frederick

Road, reflecting the route's original elevation. Just across Ellicott Mills Road, look for the **gray millstone** lodged upright. It was taken from one of the original mills. The simple white building behind the stone is a former mill. The planking where the mill wheel was attached is clearly visible.

Backtrack down Frederick Road through town. **Tersiguel's** is an upscale French restaurant situated at the corner of Frederick Road and Forrest Street. It was once home to Dr. Mordecai Gist Sykes, who was the town's dentist for decades and the mayor from 1889 to 1897. Every two weeks, he would ride his high-wheeled bicycle to his office in Sykesville, located about 20 miles to the northwest.

Tiber Alley meets Frederick Road near the hill's bottom. The stream flowing beneath the buildings to the right is called **Tiber Branch**, named after the Tiber River that cuts through Rome. Ellicott City, like Rome, is built on seven hills, so the stream was named accordingly. Look up high while returning beneath the Oliver Viaduct. On a piece of vertical planking are tick marks showing high-water levels from various floods. Crane your neck to see the 21.5-foot high-water mark from the flood of 1868, which took 36 lives and swept away or damaged every building in its path.

Continue along Frederick Road over the Patapsco River, turn left onto Oella Avenue, and make a quick right into the parking lot. This marks the end of the walk.

Directions: From the Interstate 695 beltway, take Exit 13, Frederick Road, west. Continue for five miles into Ellicott City. Take a right onto Oella Avenue just before crossing the Patapsco River. Continue on Oella Avenue for about 100 yards, and make a right into the parking lot.

Frederick

Frederick may be an hour's drive from downtown Baltimore, but it's well worth the trek if you want to see a charming and well-preserved town that has deftly maintained its historical leanings. Begin the walk at the intersection of Market Street (the town's primary north–south corridor) and **Clarke Place**. Proceed east on Clarke Place for two blocks. The street is lined with stately, century-old Victorian mansions evoking the town's glorious past; 104 Clarke Street is the oldest house on the block. Across the street is the **Maryland School for the Deaf**, the state's premier institution for the hearing-impaired. Helen Keller lectured here in 1931. The stone building situated behind the fountain is the **Hessian Barracks**, where troops were housed during the Revolutionary War. The Hessian Barracks also served as a military prison, a hospital, a silkworm cocoonery, and as the staging grounds for the Lewis and Clark expedition.

Turn left onto Carroll Street and proceed for five blocks. This street was once lined with numerous mills. Some remain, and have been converted to antique shops. The tiny yellow building along the rail tracks is a former freight terminal, built on the site of the nation's first freight terminal. At Carroll Creek, take the stairs down to creek level to view the town's most unusual attraction. The **Community Bridge** is a mosaic of illusions painted in the *trompe l'oeil* style, which translates to "that which deceives the eye." What appears to be an aged stone bridge with climbing ivy and fountains is really a concrete bridge painted to look that way. The illusion is quite startling; I've seen sparrows try to land on the painted fountain.

Continue on Carroll Street past Patrick Street. Patrick Street, to the left, is the town's main artery for antiques, and is a worthy diversion for antique hounds. The **Frederick News-Post** building at this intersection was erected in 1910 as the central depot for the city's trolley system. The trolleys entered and left the building through its main bay entrance along Patrick Street.

Continue straight on Carroll Street. Turn left onto Church Street and continue for two blocks. A shiny gold church steeple bearing a cross is visible from this intersection. It belongs to **St. John the Evangelist Catholic Church**, which was built in 1833 by Irish immigrants. Four years later it became the first Catholic Church consecrated in the United States. One hundred years to the day the church was consecrated, lightning struck its steeple. The tower burned, but the remaining structure escaped unscathed.

The **Visitation Academy** stands behind a high wall at the intersection of Carroll and Church Streets. This private school was started in 1824 by five sisters from nearby Emmitsburg and is still in use today. Before becoming a school, the site served as a training grounds for militia under the instruction of Robert E. Lee's father. Note the lovely mansions along Church Street. The **Frederick County Historical Society** occupies 24 East Church Street, a former residence and orphanage. Stop in for interesting information on the town. Across the street is the **Evangelical Lutheran Church**, whose twin steeples are the centerpiece of what is known as Frederick's "clustered spires." This church served as a makeshift hospital during the Battle of Antietam, when many of the 23,000 casualties were brought here.

Winchester Hall stands at 12 East Church Street. This attractive Greek Revival building once housed the Frederick Female Seminary, which later became the Woman's College of Frederick. The institution subsequently moved to the northwest side of town and became Hood College. **Kemp Hall** is the three-story building facing Market Street, but whose side runs along Church Street. This is where the state legislature met in 1861 to decide whether Maryland should remain loyal to, or secede from, the Union. Some historians suggest that Abraham Lincoln wanted the legislature to meet here instead of Annapolis because delegates of the southern Maryland districts—typically Confederate sympathizers—would not be able to make the lengthy journey to vote. If this was his strategy, it proved successful: Maryland voted to remain in the Union.

Turn right onto Market Street and continue for three blocks. This stretch of Market Street is lined with nice shops and eateries. The building now occupied by the **Brewer's Alley** brew pub was built in 1873 to be both Frederick's City Hall and its opera house. Theodore Roosevelt once addressed an audience here, as did William Howard Taft. From the front steps, abolitionist Frederick Douglass delivered his landmark speech, "Self-Made Man."

Turn left onto 4th Street, and make another left onto Court Street. Just past 2nd Street, Court Street comes upon **Court Square**, home to the current **City Hall**, which was built in 1862. This square is where repudiation of the British Stamp Act played out, resulting in the execution of three Tories convicted of treason. The fine dwellings surrounding the square are now mostly businesses or law offices. The house at **108 West Church Street** once belonged to Dr. John Tyler, who performed the first cataract operation in America. He opened his practice in 1786. The cast-iron dog on the front stoop was stolen by Confederate soldiers during the Civil War, with the intention of melting the iron into bullets. It was later found on the Antietam battlefield intact, and returned to its rightful owner.

Continue on Court Street past Court Square. The former **Francis Scott Key Hotel** stands on the northeast corner of Court and Patrick Streets. Presidential candidate John F. Kennedy ate here while campaigning in 1960, as did Eleanor Roosevelt in 1933. Across the street is the Weinberg Center for the Arts, a former movie house identified by its Art Deco marquee. This elegant cinema once featured crystal chandeliers, velvet rocking chairs, mosaic tiles, and marble columns. It was the first in Frederick to be air conditioned. The theater succumbed to a ravaging "100-year" flood in 1976, when its famous Wurlitzer organ was found floating in the orchestra pit. It's now a community arts center.

Turn right onto Patrick Street. The **Frederick County Courthouse** stands to the left. A plaque identifies the original location of the **John Hanson House**. Hanson was actually elected the first president in the United States in 1781, and served a one-year term. But Hanson served under the Articles of Confederation, and not the

Constitution, which wasn't ratified until 1788. History remembers George Washington as our first president because he was elected pursuant to the Constitution.

The **Barbara Fritchie House** is located at 154 West Patrick Street. Fritchie gained folk-hero status when, at the age of 95 and while ill, she was said to have defiantly waved her Union flag in front of Confederate troops marching by her house. Her popularity increased when John Greenleaf Whittier immortalized her in a popular poem bearing her name. Winston Churchill and Franklin Delano Roosevelt visited the house in 1943 while en route to nearby Camp Shangri-La (now Camp David).

Immediately past the Barbara Fritchie House, turn left onto a walking path that runs along Carroll Creek. A tavern once stood on this spot, where George Washington, Benjamin Franklin, and General Edward Braddock met in 1755 to discuss the attack on Fort Duquesne, near Pittsburgh. Braddock met his demise during that battle, whereas Washington distinguished himself enough to set his future course.

Turn right onto Court Street, walk one block, and turn left onto All Saints Street. Proceed one more block and turn right onto Market Street. Continue for two blocks until the intersection with Clarke Place, where the hike ends.

Directions: From Baltimore, take Interstate 70 west. In Frederick, take Exit 54, Market Street. After the exit ramp, turn left onto Market Street, also called Route 355, toward downtown Frederick. Proceed for about one-half mile and park near the intersection of Market Street and Clarke Place.

Mt. Vernon

Few visitors to Baltimore wander beyond the glitz and festivity of the Inner Harbor. Much of the city's beauty and history, however, lie north of Lombard Street. This walk will reveal to readers the treat that is Mt. Vernon Square, once the wealthiest and most luxurious neighborhood in the city.

Begin the walk in Mt. Vernon Square, at the **Washington Monument**. The 178-foot-tall monument, completed in 1829, was the first in the country commemorating our premier president. Robert Mills designed the column of the monument, which is made of Cockeysville marble. He later designed the more famous Washington Monument in Washington, D.C. The original intent was to place this monument in the downtown area, along the waterfront, but many townspeople feared what would happen if it tumbled over. It was instead placed on a barren hillside overlooking town. The city's upper crust, however, began building luxurious homes around the monument, effectively creating Mt. Vernon.

Walk west on the south side of Mt. Vernon Place (to the right as you face downtown) for one block to **1 West Mt. Vernon Place,** which hosted many luminaries, including Warren Harding, Mrs. Herbert Hoover, and King Edward VII of England. It now holds the Walters Art Museum's Asian arts collection. Notice the nice wood-carved doors on **3 and 5 West Mt. Vernon Place**.

The breathtaking **Garrett-Jacobs House** stands at 7-11 West Mt. Vernon Place. Once owned by the Garrett family of B&O Railroad fame, it was the largest and most costly residential dwelling in the city. It included over 40 rooms, including a theater. The crown jewel of the house is a brilliant Tiffany stained-glass sun window above a wood-carved staircase, which remains today. The building now belongs to the Engineering Society of Baltimore. Such movies as *Her Alibi, Diner, Twelve Monkeys,* and *The Accidental Tourist* have had scenes filmed here.

Turn right onto Cathedral Street and continue a short distance to the other end of the square. Both 702 and 704 Cathedral Street have historical significance. At **702 Cathedral Street** Abraham Lincoln spent one evening in 1864 when he was in town to deliver a speech at the Maryland Institute; and **704 Cathedral Street** was where iconoclastic writer H.L. Mencken and his wife, Sarah, lived for five years following their marriage and until her death from tuberculosis.

Turn right down the north side of West Mt. Vernon Place. This block features another stretch of fantastic rowhouses. The wide white dwelling at **8 West Mt. Vernon Place** is the oldest building on the square, and once played host to the Duke and Duchess of Windsor. It's now the Mt. Vernon Club, a private organization for women.

At the Washington Monument, turn left onto the west side of Washington Place (Charles Street), and continue for one block. The lovely 1906 **Beaux Arts apartment building**, to the immediate left, brings a European flair to the square. It had a decades-long waiting list in its heyday. Beyond it stands the **Stafford Hotel**, once home to the elite, including F. Scott Fitzgerald. It's now subsidized housing, but is being considered for renewal. The ostentatious French chateau next door is the **Graham-Hughes House**, still a private residence.

At the end of the square, circle the **statue of John Eager Howard**, and return to the Washington Monument along the east side of Washington Place. Mt. Vernon was built on the former estate of Howard, which offered sweeping views of the harbor. Four blocks north on Charles Street is a beautiful and tall red-brick building with a mansard roof. This is the **Belvedere Hotel**, which was built on the site of Howard's former Georgian mansion. It was named Belvedere, meaning "beautiful view."

The home of one of Baltimore's oddest museums is at 717 Washington Place. The **Museum of Incandescent Lighting** was the obsessive byproduct of dentist Dr. Hugh Francis Hicks, whose main source of pride was his collection of 60,000 light bulbs. Included is the bulb that lit the table where the Japanese signed the surrender ending World War II, and a floodlight used on the set of an Elvis movie. Hicks passed away in 2002. The display, to date housed in the basement of his dentistry practice, is temporarily closed as it awaits a move to one or more other local museums. The green-tinted **Mt. Vernon Methodist Church**, built in 1873, gives off eerie Gothic vibes, but is worth a peek if the front doors are open.

Continue past the Washington Monument and head south on Washington Place, which becomes Charles Street. Just past the monument, to the left, lining East Mt. Vernon Place, is the **Peabody Institute**, the first institution in the nation dedicated to training professional musicians. The list of musicians who have studied or performed here reads like a "Who's Who" in American musical history. Notice the cast-iron grillwork embellishing the white-washed **Shapiro House** at 609 Washington Place. Many houses in this neighborhood had such adornments, but most were stripped off and donated to scrap metal drives during various wars.

Across Washington Place is the **Walters Art Museum**, well worth a stop over. It grew from the personal collection of William Walters, who made his fortune in liquor and railroads. Walters collected local art, but fled to Europe during the Civil War, where he cultivated a broader range of tastes and greatly expanded his holdings of art. Upon his return, he opened his house so that the public could view his collection (and donated the entry fees to charity). Upon his death, he willed the collection to his son, who later bequeathed it to the city.

Continue south on Charles Street through a fantastic stretch of eateries, businesses, and historical buildings. Turn and backtrack to Mt. Vernon Square at your pleasing. The **First Unitarian Church** stands at the northwest corner of Charles and Franklin Streets. Built in 1818, it is the country's oldest Unitarian church still in use. Just beyond it is the **Archbishop House**, where Cardinal Gibbons lived for 50 years.

Behind the Archbishop House (and well worth a one-block walk down Mulberry Street) is the **Basilica of the Assumption of the**

Blessed Virgin Mary, or the Baltimore Cathedral. Architectural historian Nikolaus Pevsner called it "North America's most beautiful building." It was designed by Benjamin Latrobe, who also designed the United States Capitol Building, but this cathedral is generally considered his masterpiece. If possible, peek in the front door for a look-see. Across Cathedral Street from the Basilica is the main headquarters of the **Enoch Pratt Free Library**, which opened in 1882 as one of the country's first public libraries. The present building was erected in 1933. Most big-city public libraries built at that time featured grand entrances with statues, columns, and dramatic stairways. Designers of this library chose instead to keep the facade simple and at street level so that the passing public could look in the display windows.

Return to Charles Street and continue downtown. This stretch was once lined primarily with residential houses, but when a horrible fire annihilated most of downtown Baltimore in 1904 (destroying 1,500 buildings and causing $3 billion in damage, as calculated in today's dollars), many businesses were forced to relocate here. In 1915, the Charles Street Association, Baltimore's first neighborhood organization, was formed to resist this transformation. At 333 North Charles Street is the **Woman's Industrial Exchange**, the oldest remaining one in the country. Here soldiers' wives once sold crafts and baked goods to earn extra money. Meg Ryan and Rosie O'Donnell dined here in a scene from *Sleepless in Seattle*. **Downs Stationery**, at 317 North Charles Street, is the only pre-World War II business remaining along this stretch of Charles Street. It was once the social center of the Mt. Vernon elite and is where the all-important debutante list and social calendar were kept.

The attractive triangular building at the corner of Charles and Saratoga Streets is the former **YMCA building**, erected in 1873. Across Saratoga Street is the **Old St. Paul's Episcopal Church**, the only property in Baltimore city that has remained under original ownership since the initial survey was completed in 1730. The former **Masonic Temple** stands at 223-227 Charles Street, and is now used by the Tremont Hotel for conferences. This area represents the northernmost boundary of the 1904 fire. Most buildings south of here were destroyed and rebuilt, which explains the more recent styles of architecture. Notable exceptions are the **Fidelity Building** at the northwest corner of Lexington and Charles Streets and the **Central Savings Bank,** located catercorner, both of which survived the conflagration. From this point, backtrack to Mt. Vernon Square, where the hike ends.

Directions: From downtown Baltimore, take Charles Street north. Mt. Vernon Square is about one mile north of the Inner Harbor.

Holiday Activities

An entire book could be dedicated to holiday activities in the Baltimore area. For a comprehensive list, check the December issue of *Baltimore's Child* magazine. Here are a few family-friendly holiday doings with a wide appeal that may be a step above the rest.

Baltimore on Ice Skating Rink

A delightful holiday activity is to go skating at the Rash Field ice rink, with the lovely downtown Baltimore urbanscape as your backdrop. Rash Field separates Federal Hill Park from the harbor waters, and was once home of the Southern High School football team (the scoreboard still stands). In warm-weather months it plays host to public fairs, running races, and an annual beach volleyball competition, but in winter it is taken over by the skaters.

Skating rates are reasonable, given the locale. Two-hour sessions for adults are $5 during peak hours, and $4 during non-peak hours. Skate rental is only $2 per pair. Skaters must sign up for specific sessions. A food concession is available to the skaters, offering pizza slices, drinks, and pretzels for $2 each. A restroom is available (OK, it's just a port-a-john).

Private parties may rent the rink during certain off-hour times for special occasions. I visited while a teenager was celebrating her birthday with about 50 friends. Rink rental costs $175 per hour, and you may bring your own food. There is a sitting area for relaxation.

When you have finished skating, walk to the east end of Rash Field, where a well-manicured garden is punctuated by a tall, wooden sailing-mast statue. This is a memorial dedicated to the captain and three crew members who perished in the capsizing of the *Pride of Baltimore*. This was Baltimore's goodwill ship, a clipper schooner that logged over 150,000 miles circling the globe, promoting Baltimore to over 125 cities. In 1986, while traveling about 250 miles north of Puerto Rico, it was struck by a violent squall that capsized it and claimed the four lives. Eight others were rescued by a passing Norwegian tanker.

Location: Rash Field, on the south bank of the Inner Harbor.

Hours and Admission: Hours vary in accordance with weather and ice conditions. Admission for each two-hour session is $5 per adult on Friday evenings, Saturdays, Sundays, and holidays; and $4 per adult on weekdays. Children 4 and under are $2 at all times. Skate rentals are an additional $2.

Christmas Tree Farms

Don't just pick a wilted Christmas tree off the corner lot that is already dropping needles. High-tail it to the nearest tree farm and chop down your own perfect specimen. Your kids will deem you a holiday hero and you may even save a buck or two. Don't forget to pack a thermos of hot chocolate and some holiday treats for when the deed is done.

Here's a list of Christmas tree farms in the Baltimore area. Complete information on each can be found at the Maryland Christmas Tree Association's website at www.marylandchristmas trees.org. Be sure to call first to determine whether the farm has the particular tree you prefer, whether they take credit cards, allow pets, or offer refreshments.

Baltimore County
All Timber Hill Farm, Parkton, (410) 343-1940
Elliott's Ventura Farm, Butler, (410) 771-4510
Freezer's Farm, Marriottsville, (410) 461-5654
Frostee Tree Farm, Perry Hall, (410) 687-3344
Green Hill Farm, Baldwin, (410) 592-7813
Martin's Tree Farm, Hampstead, (410) 374-8114
Mt. Carmel Tree Farm, Parkton, (410) 329-8032
Ruhl's Tree Farm, Phoenix, (410) 666-2924
Stansbury Christmas Tree Farm, Jacksonville, (410) 666-2531

Carroll County
Davidson Christmas Tree Farm, Upperco, (410) 239-6556
Feldhof Farm, Westminster, (410) 876-7680
Fra-mar Tree Farm, Hampstead, (410) 374-2868
Hirt Tree Farm, Westminster, (410) 876-8839
JCK Christmas Tree Farm, Taneytown, (410) 876-TREE
Judy's Nursery, Westminster, (410) 876-7647
Otterdale View Christmas Tree Farm, Union Bridge, (410) 775-0176
Pine Valley Farms, Sykesville, (410) 795-8314
Quality Evergreens, Manchester, (410) 374-1499
Sewell's Farm, Taneytown, (410) 756-4397
Silver Meadow Farm, Woodbine, (301) 829-9198
Thomas Tree Farm, Manchester, (410) 374-9538

Harford County
Applewood Farm, Whiteford, (410) 836-1140
Deer Creek Valley Tree Farm, Street, (410) 692-9793
Environmental Evergreens Tree Farm, Darlington, (410) 457-4842
Evergreen Farm, Havre de Grace, (410) 939-0659
Jarrettsville Nurseries, Jarrettsville, (410) 557-9677
Maranatha Tree Farm, White Hall, (410) 692-2517

Howard County
Greenway Farms, Woodbine, (410) 442-2388
Larriland Farm, Woodbine, (410) 442-2605
TLV Farm, Glenelg, (410) 489-4460

Lighted Boat Parade

Kids love boats and parents love free events. That makes the lighted boat parade a can't-miss activity. Held on the first Saturday of December, boats bedecked in cheery lights and holiday garb file at a barge's pace from Fells Point, through the Inner Harbor, and back again. Agreeable weather attracts upwards of 50 vessels, ranging from sea kayaks to tall ships. Often included in the festoon are extravagant private yachts, U.S. Coast Guard vessels, lots of dress-up Santas, an Elvis impersonator crooning "Blue Christmas," and a naval vessel electronically purveying the score of the afternoon's Army–Navy football game (but, interestingly, only if Navy wins). Kids will love watching the colorful boats appear from the distant darkness. If the weather is clement, the carousel beside the Maryland Science Center will be operating.

Be warned, the parade typically begins with the firing of a cannon from the lead vessel. On one occasion, cannons were fired throughout the evening. Each cannon blast reverberates around the harbor in startling fashion. Parents with children who spook easily should beware.

Location: The parade is best viewed from the Inner Harbor colonnade. Thinning crowds near the Maryland Science Center make it an ideal viewing area. Federal Hill Park, situated to the south of the harbor, provides an unusual bird's-eye vantage of the event.

Hours and Admission: Usually held the first Saturday in December, at 6 p.m. Admission is free.

Miracle on 34th Street

If Baltimore is the capital of kitsch, then 34th Street in December is the epicenter. Residents of the 700 block cloak their homes in an over-the-top display of luminescence and decoration that is not to be missed. Tens of thousands of lights are strung up, several canopied over the road. Life-size snowmen and Santas perch on the rooftops, and nativities adorn the tiny front lawns. Automated Santas belt out Christmas carols and illuminated Grinches hang from

▲ Miracle on 34th Street, a Baltimore tradition of kitsch for kids

house facades. This is the street is where Baltimore focuses the lion's share of its Christmas energy.

Visitors to 34th Street should not miss house numbers 722 through 726, which shine the brightest. Kids gravitate to 724, which has a large, scale-model train looping around the front porch and occasionally disappearing through the front wall into the living room. At 726 there are more singing Santas than one would think lawful. Look for Santa's workshop on the roof of the audio-visual building next door.

Another house not to be missed is 708, which is home to a pair of artists who dabble in the avant-garde. Over the holiday season, they convert their living room into a show gallery for their funky wares, and invite visitors in for a view (and perhaps a purchase). Look for the snowmen crafted from bicycle wheels and the Maryland blue crabs molded from cast-off wrenches. The house is easily identifiable by the hub-cap Christmas tree in the front yard.

What makes a visit to 34th Street so special is the homespun friendliness of the residents: they love to chat and share Christmas merriment. Some advice to prospective visitors: tens of thousands of people converge on 34th Street during the month of December. Some come by tour bus, others by limo, and others on foot. It gets crowded. Simply driving down the street will not expose visitors to the total experience. I suggest finding on-street parking nearby and

▲ A city horse, known in Baltimore as an Arabber, taking in the lights at the Miracle on 34th Street

hoofing the street. Since weekend evenings can be elbow-to-elbow, try visiting on weekday evenings.

Location and Directions: In Hampden, on the 700 block of 34th Street, between Keswick Road and Chestnut Street. From downtown, take Interstate 83 north. Take the Falls Road exit and continue to Hampden. Turn right onto 36th Street. In four blocks, turn right onto Keswick Road and continue two blocks to 34th Street.

Hours and Admission: Lights are flicked on the first Saturday after Thanksgiving, and stay up through the new year. Viewing hours are 6 p.m. through 10 p.m. nightly, sometimes longer during Christmas week. Admission is free.

Symphony of Lights

Drive-through holiday light displays are becoming increasingly popular around Baltimore, and are always a hit with young kids. One of the finest is Symphony Lights, in Columbia's Merriweather Post Pavilion's Symphony Woods. Guests are greeted by over 70 humongous lighted displays, up to three stories high. There is a teddy bear carnival, polar bears and penguins, a steamboat atop a blue sea, an enormous rocking horse, elves making toys, and, my personal favorite, reindeer leaping through the air.

The drive is about 1.5 miles, and takes about 20 to 30 minutes. The display attracts more than 100,000 visitors over a holiday season. Drivers can tune their car radio to a particular FM station to hear holiday music during their visit. The impressive display takes six weeks to install, with 18 people working full-time. Nine miles of electric cable and over one-quarter million light bulbs are involved. Similar holiday light shows can be seen at Sandy Point State Park, in Annapolis; Watkins Regional Park, in Upper Marlboro; and Seneca Creek State Park, in Gaithersburg.

Location and Directions: In Merriweather Post Pavilion's Symphony Woods, in Columbia. From Baltimore, take Interstate 70 west. In Ellicott City, take Route 29 south. Continue on Route 29 for about five miles, and take the Broken Land Parkway exit heading west. Follow to Symphony Woods.

Hours and Admission: Hours are 6 p.m. to 10 p.m. on Sundays through Thursdays, and 6 p.m. to 11 p.m. on Fridays and Saturdays through mid-December. From mid-December through early January, hours are daily from 6 p.m. though 11 p.m. Admission is $12 per car.

Train Gardens

Some items are quintessentially Baltimore: formstone rowhouses, marble stoops, duckpin bowling, and painted window screens. Add to this list of icons the Christmas train garden.

Baltimore's Christmas train gardens are extravagant scale-model train layouts deployed during the holiday season. They usually take on a winter theme. Larger train gardens cover hundreds of square feet and incorporate over a dozen model trains of varying scales, chugging in sync around Christmas trees and through tunneled mountains. They include model villages and lots of tiny figurines. Lights of every hue flicker, and the sound of locomotives fills the air. Train gardens are exciting for adults and mesmerizing for children. Visiting a train garden has been a Baltimore holiday tradition for decades.

Lovers of train gardens have the Germans to thank. Immigrants from that country brought to the new world the habit of assembling beneath their holiday tree a nativity scene. Over time, these small, decorative displays expanded to include toy trains and scale villages. Like a holiday waistline, they grew and grew. Firehouses latched onto this unique Christmas tradition, and by the 1950s, almost every station in Baltimore claimed ownership of their

◀ I beg your pardon, you *can* promise them a train garden

own train garden, some very impressive. They were a source of community pride. Neighbors contributed volunteer labor. Visitors elbowed to get a look, and tour buses laden with gawkers visited from out of state. Fast-forward five decades, and just a handful of Christmas train gardens remain. The few that do, however, are spectacular and worth a visit.

Train gardens once had a decisive religious flair, but recent versions are more secular in nature. Some incorporate attention-grabbing contemporary cartoon characters to appeal to the young. Others impress with unusual details. For instance, Arbutus Volunteer Fire Company's train garden includes a miniature drive-in theater showing an actual movie (during my visit, it was Chevy Chase's *Christmas Vacation*). Several train gardens feature buttons children can push to operate certain exhibits.

Some Christmas train gardens offer children more than model trains. Kids visiting the train garden at Ellicott City Fire Department No. 2 often leave with a candy cane and plastic fireman's hat. Children there may also wander into the garage to view the real fire trucks and emergency vehicles, including an immaculately restored vintage model. The train garden at the B&O Railroad Museum sprawls across its entire roundhouse and is surrounded by dozens of real-size locomotives, boxcars, and passenger cars.

Most train gardens are free of charge, though donations are commonly solicited to defray costs. Some firehouses allow visitors to bring an unwrapped toy for donation to a charitable organization.

Here is a list of Christmas train gardens in the Baltimore area:

1. Arbutus Volunteer Fire Company, 5200 Southwestern Boulevard, Arbutus.
2. B&O Railroad Museum, 901 West Pratt Street, Baltimore.
3. Ellicott City Fire Department No. 2, 4150 Montgomery Road, Ellicott City.
4. Engine House No. 45, Baltimore City Fire Department, Cross Country Boulevard and 2700 Glen Avenue, Baltimore.
5. Long Green Volunteer Fire Department, Long Green and Manor Roads, off Dulaney Valley Road, Baltimore County.
6. Pleasant Valley Volunteer Fire Department, 2030 Pleasant Valley Road, Carroll County.
7. Riviera Beach Volunteer Fire Company, 8506 Fort Smallwood Road, Riviera Beach.
8. The Shops at Kenilworth, Kenilworth Drive, Towson.
9. Wise Avenue Volunteer Fire Company, 214 Wise Avenue, Dundalk.

Washington Monument Lighting

The holiday season in Baltimore officially commences with the lighting of the Washington Monument. Strands of lights strung from this towering obelisk illuminate the surrounding urbanscape in dramatic polychromatic fashion. The evening features choirs, plenty of food vendors, and strolling musicians. A nightcap of fireworks adds more color and festivity to the occasion. This event is a good place to spy Baltimore celebrities. Mt. Vernon Square, one of Baltimore's prettiest locations, features some of the city's finest architecture and lots of statues and fountains.

Location and Directions: At Mt. Vernon Square. From downtown, take Charles Street north to the Washington Monument.

Hours and Admission: The event is usually held on a weekday evening during the first week in December. Events usually begin around 5:30 p.m. Admission is free.

Inner Harbor Attractions

The Inner Harbor is Baltimore's happy face. It's where the city shines brightest and where a laugh and good time can always be had. Families visiting Baltimore should make the Inner Harbor their first (but surely not last) stop, for it bristles with kid-friendly opportunities. Here are the best of the best.

American Visionary Art Museum

Let's face it: not all kids can appreciate traditional art museums (nor adults, for that matter). They may come across as too quiet, static, and . . . well . . . boring. For a delightful change, try the American Visionary Art Museum on for size. Located at the base of Federal Hill Park, this unique institution promotes the intuitive works of self-taught artists, often featuring pieces that deviate from what some may consider mainstream art. To put it bluntly: the stuff is funky! The works tend to be colorful, oddball, fun, loud, and eye-catching. Imagine popsicle-stick houses and robots and sand sculptures and whirlygigs. What makes this museum so ideal for young children is that it could possibly inspire creativity and imagination in them in a way Monet and Manet never could.

Kids will immediately be drawn to the 40-foot-tall, kaleidoscopic, wind-powered contraption called "Wind Sculpture," which stands near the museum's entrance. It was developed by a 76-year-old mechanic and farmer named Vollis Simpson. His purpose in contriving this spectacle was to salute Federal Hill, and the concepts of life, liberty, and the pursuit of happiness. If you're lucky, the splashy mosaic car will be parked outside. The museum has an equally funky gift shop that is the home to Joy America Café, an upscale eatery where the well-presented dishes are akin to works of art.

Location: At 800 Key Highway, near the northeast corner of the base of Federal Hill Park.

Hours and Admission: Hours are Tuesdays through Sundays from 10 a.m. to 6 p.m. Closed on Thanksgiving and Christmas. Admission is $8 for adults, $6 for students and seniors, and free for children under 4.

Website and Phone: www.avam.org; (410) 244-1900.

Baltimore Maritime Museum

Children fancying anything nautical should not miss the Baltimore Maritime Museum. The museum features two ships, a submarine, and a lighthouse, each open for exploration. The most interesting sight is probably the U.S.S. *Torsk*, which is one of two remaining tench-class fleet submarines in the nation (the other is docked in Pittsburgh). The *Torsk* is moored next to the aquarium, where it bares its painted teeth to passing tourists. Touring a submarine is a sobering—and for some, claustrophobic—experience. The lack of amenities, personal space, and headroom is startling. Kids will eat up the complexity of the engine rooms and all the pipes and electrical systems running throughout the sub.

The *Torsk* was built in Portsmouth, New Hampshire, and launched in September 1944. It patrolled the Pacific Ocean during World War II, and is most noted for firing the last torpedo, and sinking the last Japanese vessel, of the war. The *Torsk* has made almost 12,000 dives, more than any other U.S. submarine.

Claustrophobes should pass on the *Torsk* and head right to the lightship *Chesapeake*, which is docked next door. Lightships are floating lighthouses, anchored where placing a stationary lighthouse is not feasible. The 133-foot-long lightship Chesapeake was built in Charleston, South Carolina, in 1930. It originally sat off Fenwick Island in Delaware for a few years, before being moved to the mouth of the Chesapeake Bay. There it served admirably until 1965, when it was replaced by a platform light. Its beacon shone for five more years at the mouth of the Delaware Bay, before being relegated to full-time duty as a tourist attraction. The lightship has also been used for marine research.

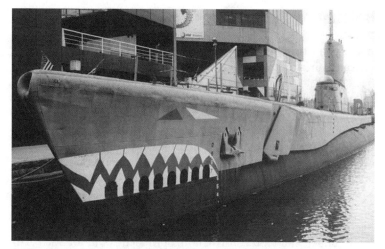

▲ The U.S.S. *Torsk*—part of the Baltimore Maritime Museum

Just behind the Marine Mammal Pavilion of the aquarium is the 327-foot-long U.S. Coast Guard Cutter *Taney*, a World War II battleship. Commissioned in 1936, the *Taney* served mostly in the Pacific theater. It was docked in Pearl Harbor during the December 1941 attack, and survived unscathed. It is the only Pearl Harbor ship still afloat. Besides serving military duty, the *Taney* also put in time as a weather ship, a military training vessel, and as a member of the ship posse that searched for Emilia Earhart. It was also used to track down boats involved in drug trading.

The final member of the Baltimore Maritime Museum is the Seven Foot Knoll Lighthouse, located on the waterfront behind the Pier 5 Hotel. Built in 1855, it's Maryland's oldest lighthouse. For 135 years, its welcoming beacon greeted ships entering Baltimore's harbor. It was moved to its present lair in the early 1990s and made into a tourist attraction. Inside the lighthouse are exhibits on the Chesapeake Bay and lighthouse lore.

Location: At various locations throughout the Inner Harbor.

Hours and Admission: Winter hours are Fridays through Sundays from 10:30 am to 5 p.m. Spring, summer, and fall hours are Sundays through Thursdays from 10 a.m. to 5:30 p.m., and Fridays and Saturdays from 10 a.m. to 6:30 p.m. Admission is $5 for adults, $4 for seniors, $2.50 for kids 6-14, and free for kids 5 and under.

Website and Phone: www.baltimoremaritimemuseum.org; (410) 396-3453.

Baltimore Public Works Museum

If you want to show your budding civil engineer what's happening beneath our city streets, you have two options. You can dig up your front yard (not recommended!) or go to the Baltimore Public Works Museum. This attraction is off the Inner Harbor's beaten path, near Little Italy, but is well worth a brief diversion for the science-minded. The museum is housed in what has to be the most architecturally beautiful sewage pumping station in the country (it still operates as one). The edifice is of Edwardian design with a hodgepodge of other architectural styles interwoven, including Victorian elements.

A quadrant of the pumping station houses the museum. The displays are simple but interesting. There's an engaging spread of historical photographs dealing with public works projects such as road, tunnel, and dam construction. Sprinkled about are such artifacts as gas meters, a gas streetlight, surveyors' instruments, decades-old architectural sketch books, and lots of construction tools. One passageway is configured to feel like a rail tunnel. A computer laboratory offers visitors the chance to solve urban design challenges.

The finest display is a presentation on how water from such outlying reservoirs as Prettyboy and Loch Raven gets purified and transported to city houses. A tiny theater shows a 12-minute film on the history of public works. A store sells books and fun toys. I found the staff to be energetic and helpful. While in the museum, take time to gaze upward at the impressive, solid-steel crossbeams and Victorian windows.

▲ Baltimore Public Works Museum

Young children will be more drawn to the outside Streetscape exhibit, where they can clamber on steps, ramps, and pipes. This display is a real-scale re-creation of what's going on beneath a typical city street, in this case the nearby intersection of President and Pratt Streets.

Location: 751 Eastern Avenue, beside the Pier Six Concert Pavilion.

Hours and Admission: Winter hours are from October 1 to May 31, Wednesdays through Sundays from 10 a.m. to 4 p.m. Summer hours are from June 1 to September 30, Tuesdays through Fridays from 10 a.m. to 4 p.m., and Saturdays and Sundays from 10 a.m. to 6 p.m. Admission is $2.50 for adults, $1.50 for children 6-17, and $2 for seniors. Children 5 and under are free.

Phone: (410) 396-5565.

Barnes & Noble

After experiencing Baltimore's Inner Harbor, you may want to read more about its history. Head to Barnes & Noble Booksellers, located in the Power Plant building, which is easily identifiable by its four prominent smokestacks. This former electric generating plant once powered the network of trolley cars that roamed Baltimore city. Barnes & Noble offers the usual mountain of books, but has an unusually wide selection of regional titles, including many on the harbor. The walls of the store are slung with historical photographs of Baltimore, and patrons can walk through the restored, copper-painted furnaces. Of special interest to children is a humongous 3,000-gallon aquarium, located at the top of the escalator, which includes angelfish, discus, and unusually large tetras. The tank replicates an Amazon rainforest habitat, and is the result of an arrangement between the bookstore and the National Aquarium in Baltimore.

Location: At 601 East Pratt Street, in the Power Plant building, between the ESPN Zone and the Hard Rock Café.

Hours: Daily from 9 a.m. to 11 p.m.

Website and Phone: www.barnes&noble.com; (410) 385-1709.

Carousel

Inner Harbor's carousel is tucked in a nook behind the Maryland Science Center, and often goes unnoticed by tourists. Families with young children, however, will want to seek it out, because it's a favorite of kids. The carousel was built in 1906 by the Herschell-Stillman Company in upstate New York, and was restored to working condition and brought to Baltimore in 1979. It's painted each year by students of Hammond High School. Most carousels feature horses to ride, but this one offers a veritable menagerie. Kids will love deciding whether to hop on a pig, dog, or rooster. The carousel operates when weather permits, and snacks are available for waiting parents. This carousel has a twin in Ocean City.

Ed Kane's Water Taxis

Cruise ships like the *Bay Lady* and *Lady Baltimore*, along with a pair of lofty sailing vessels, offer waterborne tours of the Inner Harbor. They are fun and offer a unique "from-the-water" perspective of Baltimore, but they often come at a steep cost. Here's an insider's tip: As an alternative, buy the $5 all-day pass ($3 for children) to Ed Kane's Water Taxis, and tour the harbor to your heart's content for the price of a ham sandwich.

Water taxis are the ubiquitous, slow-moving harbor boats ferrying tourists here and there. Ed Kane has been operating the taxis for over 20 years. His armada includes over a dozen boats of varying design and capacity. Larger ones can convey up to 84 passengers. Riders may not be offered piped-in music or refreshments like the more expensive cruises, but the water taxis are a gem for the budget-minded tourist.

A water taxi ride that strays from the innermost harbor will reveal Baltimore's industrial underbelly that most harbor tourists are not privy to. Riders will see the Domino Sugar plant, where Caribbean container ships may be seen dispensing raw sugar for processing. Next door is the former Proctor & Gamble plant, now a high-tech business park. Riders will see moth-balled ships, rotting piers, and other sights of great intrigue to children. The most far-flung destination served by water taxi is Fort McHenry, which is well worth a visit, being one of Baltimore's prettiest and most historic parks.

Boats are only operated when weather permits. Children 10 and under must be accompanied by an adult. Purchase of a ticket is good for any Ed Kane taxi on any route on a particular day. Seaport Taxis is another company that operates water taxis around the Inner Harbor; their rates, routes, and schedules are similar to Ed Kane's Water Taxis.

Locations: Ed Kane's Water Taxis currently serve 15 landing sites. They include: the National Aquarium in Baltimore, the U.S.S. *Constellation*, the Maryland Science Center, the American Visionary Arts Museum, Little Italy, Harborview Marina, Tidewater Marina (with connecting service to Fort McHenry), Fells Point, Boston Street in West Canton, Harris Creek at the Anchorage Marina, and Canton Waterfront Park.

Hours and Admission: Hours vary with day and season. Check website for specifics. Admission is $5 for adults and $3 for children 10 and under.

Website and Phone: www.thewatertaxi.com; (410) 563-3901 or (800) 658-8947.

Federal Hill Park

(For a description, see the City Parks chapter.)

HiFlyer

Inner Harbor visitors may scratch their heads at seeing a small dirigible hovering low over the city, tethered by a steel cable. What they are looking at is the HiFlyer, a new and unique attraction associated with Port Discovery. The HiFlyer is a spherical, helium-filled balloon with enclosed gondola. It hoists 25 to 30 people at a time to about 450 feet above the city streets, letting them breathe in the city views for about 15 minutes before descending. An elevated HiFlyer balloon is the highest observation point in Baltimore. Riders will see Baltimore's patchwork neighborhoods from a sea gull's vantage.

The HiFlyer is illuminated from the inside at night, giving it the appearance of a Chinese lantern. It looks attractive decoupaged against the city backdrop. Nighttime is a nice time to ride, as patrons are offered breathtaking and sweeping views of the city lights. The HiFlyer was developed by world-famous English balloonist Per Lindstrand. Other HiFlyer attractions are located in England, Sweden, Spain, Portugal, the Canary Islands, China, Japan, and Zimbabwe. At the time of this writing, consideration was being given to moving the HiFlyer closer to the waterfront.

Location: Next to Port Discovery, which is at 35 Market Place, just north of the waterfront.

Hours and Admission: Summer hours are Sundays through Wednesdays from 10 a.m. to 10 p.m., and Thursdays through Saturdays from 10 a.m. to midnight. Hours from Labor Day to October 31 are Sundays through Wednesdays from noon to 8 p.m., and Thursdays through Saturdays from noon to midnight. Hours from November 1 to December 31 are Fridays and Saturdays from noon to 8 p.m., and Sundays from noon to 5 p.m. Daytime admission is $12 for adults, and $8.50 for children 3-12. Evening admission (after 8 p.m.) is $15 for everyone.

Website and Phone: www.portdiscovery.com/generalinfo/balloon. html; (410) 949-2359.

Light Street Pavilion

Come lunch time, visitors to the Inner Harbor typically make a bee-line for the Light Street Pavilion. Situated near the northwest corner of the harbor, the pavilion features several sit-down restaurants and a nice food court. Phillips Seafood, Baltimore's benchmark seafood eatery, will likely have a lengthy wait, but those hankering for decent seafood will probably not leave disappointed. Lunches range from $5.99 to $13.99. J. Paul's serves saloon-type dishes. Paolo's is more upscale Italian. An eatery popular with children is Johnny Rocket's, a replica 1950s sandwich and milk-shake diner. Most families, however, end up at the food court, where inexpensive but tasty fare can be had. Think pizza and Chinese take-out and burgers and such. Lee's Ice Cream, on the lower level, is a decent dessert destination.

The Light Street Pavilion houses many shops and kiosks that children will find enjoyable. One not to miss is the Discovery Channel Store, which is a veritable science museum. It's worth a gander even if you aren't planning on buying. The Baltimore Zoo has a fun store in the pavilion, and the young athletes will enjoy seeing authentic Orioles and Ravens gear at Stadium Sports. The numerous kiosks hawking various wares come and go with abandon, but there are always a few that interest kids. It will behoove out-of-town visitors to stop at the Celebrate Maryland store, purchase a container of Old Bay seasoning, and use it on your next batch of french fries or mashed potatoes. You will remember how wonderful Baltimore is long after leaving town. Also, wander through the Pratt Street Pavilion located next door.

Location: At the southeast intersection of Light and Pratt Streets.

Hours: Light Street Pavilion hours vary with season and day. A schedule can be found on its website.

Website and Phone: www.harborplace.com; (410) 332-4191.

Maryland Science Center

Run, don't walk, to the Maryland Science Center. The facility opened its doors in 1976 as the premier attraction in the refurbished Inner Harbor, and remains a top-flight facility that has proven appeal for kids and adults alike. It was developed to inspire in children and adults an interest in the sciences, math, and technology, and does so through interactive and instructional exhibits that are just plain fun. The center is where engineers, physicists, astronomers, paleontologists, and yes, even rocket scientists, take root. The science center continually updates its exhibits to keep them fresh and topical.

Scattered about the three levels of the science center are many permanent and temporary displays. At the time of this writing, a popular exhibit was Dino Digs, where children become paleontologists and uncover fossils in a "dig pit." Actual dinosaur fossils and footprints are scattered about, revealing lessons on the animals' pasts. The cast footprint of the sauropod looked large enough to bathe my son in. The Science Arcade is another favorite exhibit. Playful lessons on such topics as light, sound, mechanics, and magnetism are taught

▲ Kids become prey at the Maryland Science Center

through toys and hands-on contraptions. Kids can generate their own water vortex, and the Bernoulli blower not only keeps a beach ball suspended in midair, but makes a terrific hair blower.

The Chesapeake Bay exhibit schools visitors on the natural resources found in and around that estuary, stressing conservation. The Outer Space Place exhibit is home to the Hubble Space Telescope National Visitor Center, and plumbs the mysteries of space while keeping visitors abreast of what's happening with the famous orbiting telescope. The exhibit is frequently updated with images transmitted back to earth. Asteroids in the Atrium is another galactic-related exhibit. The center also features a demonstration area where children are enlightened, through live presentations, in the areas of sound, chemistry, electricity, and other realms of science. Older kids may want to try out the simulator machine, which offers a choice of four virtual reality rides for $4 each.

The Kids Room is a recently renovated romping area where kids can burn off pent-up energy. Its most recent incarnation includes, among other fun things, an earthquake LEGO table, a waterbed for infants, a dress-up area, and a kelp forest to crawl through. The room is geared for kids up to 8 years old.

Integral with the Maryland Science Center is an IMAX theater and planetarium, both included in the full admission price. The IMAX theater has a screen five stories high and is surrounded by 38 speakers. Movies shown range from educational films about various animals or geographic locations to Disney productions to a Rolling Stones concert. Many films are short and appropriate for smaller children who are not ready to weather a two-hour movie. Children tend to be held captive by the screen and sound.

In the Davis Planetarium, 8,500 stars and hundreds of other images are projected onto the 50-foot dome ceiling. Several different performances are held. One show geared toward young children involves singing and make-believe characters. A more advanced show delves into the identification of constellations and planets. Another explores the potential of life on other planets. Regardless of what is being shown, young children will be dazzled by the lights, and older children will find themselves contemplating the vastness of space.

Location: At 601 Light Street, in the southwest corner of Inner Harbor.

Hours and Admission: Hours are Mondays through Fridays from 10 a.m. to 5 p.m.; Saturdays from 10 a.m. to 6 p.m.; and Sundays from noon to 5 p.m. The center offers extended hours on certain evenings for IMAX or planetarium events. Full admission is $15.50

for adults, $10 for children 3-12, and $14.50 for seniors 60 and over. This admission includes all exhibits, an IMAX movie, and the planetarium. Admission to just the exhibits and planetarium is $12 for adults, $8 for children 3-12, and $11 for seniors 60 and over. Admission to one IMAX show is $7.50 per person ($9 after 6 p.m.). Children under 3 are free.

Website and Phone: www.mdsci.org; (410) 685-5225.

National Aquarium in Baltimore

The National Aquarium in Baltimore is one of the harbor's more pricey attractions, but worth every penny. This world-class facility provides visitors with a glimpse of what lurks in our oceans, lakes, and rivers. It opened in 1981 as the world's largest aquarium, and in 1990 added the Marine Mammal Pavilion. Another expansion is being considered. No less than 10,000 organisms call the aquarium home.

Aquarium visitors follow a pathway that leads past all displays (and helps corral the children). First up is the Wings in the Water exhibit, which features an entrancing array of stingrays and small sharks gliding hypnotically around a 265,000-gallon pool. The second level includes a series of live micro-ecosystems found in and around Baltimore, including a pond crammed full of bullfrogs and turtles, and a coastal surf area inhabited by unusual needlefish and spadefish. Level three is a kid's favorite, featuring, among other things, an electric eel, giant Pacific octopus, and venomous but colorful clownfish.

Level four includes a simulated Amazon River ecosystem. Look for dwarf caimans, giant river turtles, and schools of shimmering tropical fish. Missing the imposing giant anaconda would be difficult. Level four houses the ever-popular diving puffins. Level five is a stunning replication of a rainforest. Visitors pass beneath a leafy canopy and are serenaded by tropical birds and monkeys. Appreciate, but be mindful of, the piranhas in the water and poison dart frogs on the trees. The path then leads visitors to a room surrounded by a 225,000-gallon tank loaded with various species of sharks circling interminably. Feel what it's like to be stalked by a Great White.

The aquarium includes a "touch pool," where children can handle sea creatures such as whelks, starfish, and horseshoe crabs. There is always a compelling special exhibit to take in; recent ones involved jellyfish and seahorses. The Marine Mammal Pavilion is joined to the main aquarium by an over-water walkway. It offers

Parking at the Inner Harbor

Parking around the Inner Harbor does not have to be an intimidating or pricey affair. Early arrivers will likely find meter parking along Key Highway. Meters are 15 minutes for each quarter, and have a four-hour time limit. A bank of about 150 metered sites just east of the harbor along Light Street have similar rates. Additional meter parking is available on Covington Street, between Federal Hill Park and the American Visionary Art Museum. Meters near the top of the street are 75 minutes for a quarter and have a 10-hour time limit. This is a bargain by harbor standards.

Several parking lots are also available. First try the new five-story President Street Garage at the intersection of President and Pratt Streets. Prices are $5 for the first hour, $7 for two hours, and $12 daily maximum. There is an $8 flat rate if you arrive after 2 p.m. Across Pratt Street from this garage is a small lot. Fees range from $6 to $8 for all day. If you park at one of these two spots, take time to visit the Star-Spangled Banner Flag House, which is next door. This is where Mary Young Pickersgill threaded the Old Glory that flew over Fort McHenry during the 1814 bombardment. It was the one that inspired Francis Scott Key to pen the lyrics for "The Star Spangled Banner."

A closer parking lot is along Pratt Street, just east of the ESPN Zone. There is a Columbus Center sign there. Rates are $4 for the first hour, $8 for two hours, and $12 daily maximum. Other parking garages near the Inner Harbor are available in downtown Baltimore and near the Rusty Scupper. If you're looking to relieve some thickness from your wallet, there is a convenient lot at the corner of Conway and Light Streets that will set you back $20.

Free parking is always available on the streets of the Federal Hill neighborhood, located just south of the harbor. Parking restrictions here are complicated, however, and the fines are steep. Allowable parking depends on time of day, day of week, and whether an event is happening at either stadium. Deciphering the restriction signs is a formidable task.

▲ A signature attraction, the National Aquarium in Baltimore

regular dolphin shows that are always a hit with kids. Outside the aquarium building is a seal tank free to the general public. It's worth a stopover, even if visiting the aquarium is not in your plans.

Feeding the creatures is a popular event for visitors, but times and locations vary. Check at the front desk for details.

The National Aquarium in Baltimore absorbs tourists like a sponge does water. Weekends, particularly fair-weather ones, are typically mobbed. Best weekend viewing is when it first opens. Don't think that weekdays will find the aquarium less crowded, because students on field trips proliferate then. During the week, it's best to visit after 3 p.m.—when school lets out. On nice days, the aquarium often sells out by midday. Also, parents with young kids should note that strollers are not allowed in the aquarium, as they tend to clog up the escalators. They may be checked at the door, however, where a backpack will be offered as an alternative. Plan for at least two hours inside, but crowds can push that time upward.

Location: Along Pier 3, at 501 East Pratt Street.

Hours and Admission: Hours for July and August are from 9 a.m. to 8 p.m. daily. Hours for March, April, May, June, September, and October are from 9 a.m. to 5 p.m. daily, except for Fridays when it remains open until 8 p.m. Hours for November through February are from 10 a.m. to 5 p.m. daily, except for Fridays, when it remains open until 8 p.m. Admission is $17.50 for adults, $9.50 for children 3-11, and $14.50 for seniors 60 or older. Children under 3 are free.

Website and Phone: www.aqua.org; (410) 576-3800.

Paddle Boats

A century ago, the piers along Pratt Street were lined with fancy passenger steamships and majestic wooden cargo ships laden with Baltimore harbor seafood and Eastern Shore vegetables bound for ports around the world. Today, the piers are the domain of paddle boats and electric boats available for rent. Though these craft are more modest in stature than their predecessors, renting one provides a unique and fun perspective on the Inner Harbor.

The paddle boat concession is located just west of the World Trade Center. Rental prices for 30 minutes are $7 per boat for one person, $8 for two people, $9 for three people, and $10 for four people. Be forewarned that parties of three or four may end up chugging around the harbor in a boat resembling a big green dragon with a red mane.

The Trident Electric Boat concession is located just east of the World Trade Center. Rental prices for 30 minutes are $12 for two people and $18 for three. Take note that electric boats are not as fast as they sound; I've passed them in a paddle boat.

Port Discovery

Port Discovery bills itself not as a kid's museum, but rather as a kid-powered museum. Describing this interactive panacea of fun and games as hands-on may be an understatement. Port Discovery is considered among the world's finest such facilities. *The Observer,* a London-based newspaper, ranked it among the top 12 children's museums in the world, sharing billing with museums in such cities as Tokyo, London, Amsterdam, and Paris. *Child* magazine ranked it the fourth best in the nation. Part of its allure and success may have to do with the good folks of Disney, who had a hand in its design.

The attractions at Port Discovery are numerous and ever-changing. The MPT Studioworks exhibit puts kids behind the scenes of a television studio. Sensation Station offers children various sensory experiences, and is designed for the under-6 crowd. In Adventure Expeditions, visitors travel back in time to find a lost pharaoh's tomb on the banks of the Nile River. Kids play detective and try to solve a mystery in Miss Perception's Mystery House. Kidsworks is a three-story obstacle course built into an urban tree house. Other exhibits include an art studio and a special interactive branch of Baltimore's Enoch Pratt Free Library.

Of special note is Port Discovery's Kid-Powered Toy Store, which offers a wide array of books, crafts, clothing, and creative games. It was voted Baltimore's Best Kids' Toy Store by *Baltimore* magazine. Admission to the museum is not required to shop at the store. Port Discovery is generally geared toward children between 6 and 12 years of age. At the time of this writing, consideration was being given to moving Port Discovery to a location closer to the waterfront.

Location: At 35 Market Place, between Lombard and Baltimore Streets, just north of the waterfront.

Hours and Admission: From Memorial Day to June 30, hours are daily from 10 a.m. to 5 p.m. From July 1 to Labor Day, hours are daily from 10 a.m. to 6 p.m. (except Fridays, when it stays open until 8 p.m.). From Labor Day to Memorial Day, hours are Tuesdays through Saturdays from 10 a.m. to 5 p.m., Sundays from noon to 5 p.m., and closed Mondays (except school holidays). Admission is $11 for adults, $8.50 for children 3-12, $10 for seniors, and free for children under 3.

Website and Phone: www.portdiscovery.com; (410) 727-8120.

Top of the World Observation Level and Museum

The I.M. Pei-designed World Trade Center stands on the north fringe of the Inner Harbor. At 28 stories, it's the tallest pentagonal building in the world. (The largest by area is the Pentagon, in northern Virginia.) On the 27th floor of the World Trade Center is the Top of the World Observation Level and Museum. Visitors here are treated to jaw-dropping views of the Inner Harbor, Baltimore city, and in some directions, adjoining counties. From this vantage, paddle boats in the harbor look like water beetles and Federal Hill appears as a speed bump. Look for the Francis Scott Key Bridge to the east and the stadiums of the Baltimore Orioles and Baltimore Ravens to the south. To the west, try to find the 288-foot-high Bromo Seltzer Tower, once headquarters for the Emerson Drug Company, producer of the blue-bottled antacid. The tower replicates the Palazzo Vecchio, in Florence, Italy. Interpretive signs on the observation deck provide insight into the history of the port of Baltimore and the city in general, including its economic renaissance.

I.M. Pei designed the World Trade Center so that two of the exterior walls meet at a vertical line along the waterfront. When viewed from across the harbor, it supposedly resembles the bow of a ship. The Maryland Port Administration has its main offices in the World Trade Center, as do other firms dealing in commerce and finance.

Location: 401 East Pratt Street, on the north bank of Inner Harbor.

Hours and Admission: Hours from September through May are Wednesdays through Sundays from 10 a.m. to 6 p.m. Hours from June through August are daily from 10 a.m. to 9 p.m. Admission is $4 for adults, $3 for seniors, and $2 for children 3-16. Kids 2 and under are free.

Phone: (410) 837-8439.

U.S.S. *Constellation*

Climb aboard the 186-foot U.S.S. *Constellation* for a hands-on view of the country's only surviving Civil War–era naval vessel, and the last all-sail ship built by the U.S. Navy. The naval sloop-of-war, built in 1854, is the centerpiece vessel of the Inner Harbor. Visitors are allowed to explore the various decks of the ship, including the gun deck lined with cannons. Don't miss crawling down to lower decks. The *Constellation* offers special tours. Children 10 and up may partake of the Powder Monkey Tour, which shows what life was like for the teenage boys, called powder monkeys, who served on ships such as this. The "Ship as a Machine Tour" provides hands-on insight into how large sailing vessels are propelled and controlled. The staff also provides programs for classes and youth groups. A museum dedicated to the *Constellation* is located beside the ship.

The Constellation was a military star in her day, fighting valiantly in the Mediterranean Sea and later in the shipping lanes off Cuba during the Civil War. Her civilian accomplishments are equally heralded. She once captured three slave-carrying ships en route to the United States, helping to unshackle over 1,000 Africans. Later, she delivered famine relief to Ireland, and served as a training vessel for the U.S. Navy.

The Constellation recently returned to her Inner Harbor berth following a 31-month, $7.5 million restoration. Overseen by the Constellation Foundation, it was the largest non-naval wooden-ship restoration project ever carried out in the United States. To preserve the hull, rotting boards were replaced by a laminated shell. And to achieve 19th-century authenticity, one of the gun decks was removed and the stern was reconfigured.

Location: Along Pier 1, at 301 East Pratt Street, which is near the northwest corner of the Inner Harbor.

Hours and Admission: Hours for May 1 to October 14 are from 10 a.m. to 6 p.m. daily. Hours for October 15 to April 30 are from 10 a.m. to 4 p.m. daily. Extended hours may occur during June, July, and August. Closed on Thanksgiving, Christmas, and New Year's Day. Admission is $6.50 for adults, $3.50 for children 6-14, $5 for seniors 60 and over, and free for children 5 and under. Tickets are discounted on certain Friday evenings.

Website and Phone: www.constellation.org; (410) 539-1797.

Vaccaro's

It's been a long day at the harbor and the kids have worn you out. You're irritable and that heel blister is rubbing. Time for some personal pampering. For a special treat, head to Little Italy, just one block east of the Inner Harbor, and seek out Vaccaro's. This quaint Venetian pastry shop is considered Baltimore's finest dessert stop. The tiramisu, cannolis, and eclairs are otherworldly. If you hear pleasurable groans from across the dining room, someone likely just tried the peanutto fudge gelato. Even cappuccino tastes a bit yummier when sipped at Vaccaro's. The treats may be calorie-laden, but remember all the walking you just did. The establishment is very family-friendly and the prices are surprisingly reasonable.

Location: At 222 Albemarle Street.

Hours: Daily from 7:30 a.m.

Phone: (410) 685-4905.

Libraries

Libraries are underutilized institutions. Although patrons do borrow books, they don't take nearly enough advantage of programs offered to the public, which are varied and fun. A sampling of programs offered by my local branch library includes toddler story time, puppets for infants, infant massage, a gardening question-and-answer session, how to adopt a greyhound (dog, not bus), seasonal decorations, meet the Ravens mascot, musical presentations, and one for the parents: wine tasting! Quite a mish-mash of fun. Here's a list of city and county public libraries in the Baltimore area, and the website link to their program schedules. Each library's website also provides information on its branch locations.

Anne Arundel County Public Library
web.aacpl.lib.md.us

Baltimore County Public Library
www.bcplonline.org

Carroll County Public Library
library.carr.org

Cecil County Public Library
www.ebranch.cecil.lib.md.us

Enoch Pratt Free Library
www.pratt.lib.md.us

Frederick County Public Libraries
www.fcpl.org

Harford County Public Library
www.harf.lib.md.us

Howard County Library
www.howa.lib.md.us

Museums

What to do on rainy days often presents a parenting quandary. Containing children within the bounds of four walls is never an enviable task. Parents should rest assured that the Baltimore area offers plenty of museums that should capture a child's attention in weather both fair and foul. Here are the best of the best.

American Visionary Art Museum

(For a description, see Inner Harbor Attractions chapter.)

Babe Ruth Birthplace and Museum

Kids infatuated with sports memorabilia will relish a trip to the Babe Ruth Birthplace and Museum. Nowhere else in the Baltimore area will they find more bats and balls, more mitts and uniforms, more ticket stubs and game programs, and more historical photographs under one roof. The museum occupies four rowhouses on Emory Street in the quaint Ridgely's Delight neighborhood. The house at 216 Emory Street is where the Babe drew his first breath. That house is the country's only athlete's birthplace that is designated as a national historic landmark.

As expected, many of the museum displays are dedicated to the Sultan of Swat—both the ballplayer and the folk hero. There's his 1930 road uniform, plenty of photographs and news clippings, video presentations, and a re-creation of the bedroom in which he was born. Also on display is the ball from the fabled incident when Babe delivered on his promise to hit a home run for a boy dying of bone marrow inflammation; Babe's exploit supposedly resulted in a full recovery. The museum emphasizes Ruth's early Baltimore years, including his tenure at St. Mary's Industrial School for delinquents and his short stint with a local minor league club.

Nostalgic, sports-minded parents will be happy to know that the Babe Ruth Birthplace and Museum is not limited to Babe ephemera. The Baltimore Orioles and the erstwhile Baltimore Colts enjoy equal representation. An entire room is dedicated to Cal Ripken's remarkable effort—playing in 2,632 consecutive games—and includes the "2131" banner unfurled at Camden Yards to commemorate his record-breaking spectacle. A diorama pays tribute to Memorial Stadium, and another to players who have smacked 500 or more career home runs. Look for the Orioles' 1983 world championship trophy, Jim Palmer's Cy Young and Gold Glove awards, and Eddie Murray's 500th home-run ball.

Die-hard Colts fans will love seeing Bert Jones's jersey, Johnny Unitas's shoulder pads, Weeb Eubank's fedora, and various game balls and warm-up jackets. The crowning artifact is the Vince Lombardi trophy the Colts earned for its 16-13 victory over the Dallas Cowboys in Super Bowl III. The Babe Ruth Birthplace and Museum was voted "Best Kids' Birthday Party Place" by *Baltimore* magazine. Being near Oriole Park at Camden Yards, the museum makes for an ideal pre-game side trip. At the time of publication, plans were afoot to relocate this museum to the warehouse at Oriole Park at Camden Yards.

Location and Directions: At 216 Emory Street, about two blocks west of Oriole Park at Camden Yards. From Interstate 95, take Interstate 395 and follow signs for Martin Luther King Boulevard. Turn right onto Pratt Street and continue for two blocks to Emory Street on the right.

Hours and Admission: Summer hours are daily from 10 a.m. to 5 p.m. (7 p.m. during home Orioles games). Winter hours are daily from 10 a.m. to 4 p.m. Closed on New Year's Day, Thanksgiving, and Christmas. Admission is $6 for adults, $4 for senior citizens, and $3 for children 5-16.

Website and Phone: www.baberuthmuseum.com; (410) 727-1539.

Baltimore Maritime Museum

(For a description, see Inner Harbor Attractions chapter.)

Baltimore Museum of Art

Energetic children and fragile works of art do not always make for a snug fit. The Baltimore Museum of Art (BMA), however, has gone to great lengths to overcome this hurdle, and offers a world-class art venue that is family-friendly in many ways. The imposing Classical Revival museum includes the Sadie Adler May Education Center, which, through hands-on workshops and special events, educates children in the visual arts. The museum also occasionally provides young children with dress-up costumes that coordinate with certain scheduled exhibits. For instance, during a showing of the dancing statuettes of Edgar Degas, children were able to dress up as ballerinas and dance around in a special room.

The museum also offers permanent collections that appeal to youth. An exhibit just inside the main entrance features artifacts from Oceania, Africa, and Native America. It includes unusual wood-carved masks, dolls, headdresses, ornaments, drums, jewelry, and unusual pottery. School groups tend to congregate here.

Children usually dally in the Cheyney Miniature Room, which features finely crafted scale models of period American and English rooms. Examples include a New England dining room (1800–1815); a southern plantation living room (1780–1810); an English manor (1600–1620); a Shaker community house (1820–1860); and, everybody's favorite, a New England sea captain's study (1820–1850), complete with spotting scope, maps, and teeny ships-in-bottles.

The loveliest BMA interior space is around the atrium, where wide, marble floors circle a glass-walled courtyard. Walls here are set with breathtaking mosaics dating to the 6th century. The mosaics were excavated from the town of Antioch, situated near the Turkey-Syria border. Wrought-iron benches here make for an ideal quiet spot. Rodin's statue of *The Thinker* contemplates nearby. The atrium area is where my daughter learned to walk.

Children will also gravitate to the Ryda and Robert H. Levi Sculpture Garden and the Alan and Janet Wurtzburger Sculpture Garden. They combine for about three acres of groomed gardens freckled with contemporary statues, providing a choice place for kids to burn off pent-up museum energy. Note that child-carrying backpacks are not allowed in the museum, though strollers are acceptable. A trip to the BMA can be enjoyably coupled with a stroll through the campus of Johns Hopkins University, which adjoins the museum grounds.

Location and Directions: At 10 Art Museum Drive, along the south face of the Johns Hopkins University campus. From downtown, take Howard Street north. Just past 29th Street, turn right onto Art Museum Drive.

Hours and Admission: Wednesdays through Fridays from 11 a.m. to 5 p.m., and Saturdays and Sundays from 11 a.m. to 6 p.m. On the first Thursday of each month, the museum stays open to 8 p.m.

Closed on Mondays, Tuesdays, New Year's Day, July 4th, Thanksgiving, and Christmas. Admission is $7 for adults (19-64), $5 for seniors (65 and over), $5 for college students with identification, and free to anyone 18 years of age or under. Admission is free for everyone on the first Thursday of each month.

Website and Phone: www.artbma.org; (410) 396-7100.

Baltimore Museum of Industry

Making industrial history interesting to children is a tall order, but the Baltimore Museum of Industry succeeds with aplomb. The hands-on and role-playing nature of the museum proclaims "children welcome!"

The museum demystifies where certain products come from through an array of captivating displays. Young children visiting the museum may wander into the Kid's Cannery and unwittingly be put to work. The exhibit teaches them what blue-collar life was like for Baltimore immigrants in 1883, especially those who had jobs in the waterfront canneries. Children are assigned to a work station and given a tag with the name of an actual Baltimore resident from that era. Some kids shuck clay oysters from real oyster shells. Others

◀ Funky statues and exhibits can be found at the Baltimore Museum of Industry

◀ Working in an oyster cannery at the Baltimore Museum of Industry

label the tin cans. Still others stuff the clay oysters into cans as they zip by on a conveyer. Participants work 15-minute shifts, and can switch duties. At the end of the stint, each is given a "wage" and shown what that amount of money would have bought.

In the Children's Motor Works exhibit, participants construct a model of a 1914 truck using an assembly-line operation. The actual prototype truck is part of the museum's collection.

The Baltimore Printing Company, a replica of an 1888 print shop, is another popular attraction. Using authentic machinery, children can "ink the chase" and roll finished printed papers off the presses. The print shop contains the Mergenthaler Linotype, the world's first typesetting machine, which was invented in Baltimore. The Garment Industry Workshop provides insight into the industry that at one time employed a quarter of all Baltimoreans. The museum includes stunning and authentic re-creations of a century-old pharmacy, bank, and corner grocery—when craftsmanship was more valued. A colorful Art Deco theater shows a 15-minute film on the Industrial Revolution in Baltimore

One room features lots of vintage commercial vehicles, a World War II bomber hanging from the ceiling, and fascinating wall displays touting Baltimore's "firsts" (e.g., first umbrella company in the country, first gaslight, first disposable bottle cap, first railroad.

Hidden in the northeast corner of the room is a play area for children offering blocks and other toys. Peer out the glass wall for sweeping harbor views of Fells Point and downtown Baltimore. Docked just outside the museum is the SS *Baltimore*, which was built in 1906 and is thought to be the oldest remaining steam tugboat on the East Coast. In nice weather, colorful sailboats from the nearby Downtown Sailing Center ply these waters.

The Baltimore Museum of Industry occupies the 1865 Platt Oyster Cannery building, the only surviving cannery structure along Baltimore's waterfront. It was named "Best Hands-On Museum" by *Baltimore* magazine, and received the Dibner Award for Excellence given by the International Society for the History of Technology. The museum is accessible by water taxi from the Inner Harbor or Fells Point.

Location and Directions: At 1415 Key Highway. From Interstate 95, take the Key Highway exit and follow signs to get onto the highway. Continue on Key Highway for about one-half mile to the museum on the right.

Hours and Admission: Mondays through Saturdays from 10 a.m. to 5 p.m., and Sundays from noon to 5 p.m. Closed on Thanksgiving, Christmas Eve, and Christmas. Admission is $7 for adults; $5 for students and seniors; and $23 maximum for the entire family.

Website and Phone: www.thebmi.org; (410) 727-4808.

Baltimore Public Works Museum

(For a description, see chapter on Inner Harbor Attractions.)

Benjamin Banneker
Historical Park and Museum

Benjamin Banneker is one of history's greatest scientific practitioners, and aptly named the First Black Man of Science. He was born in 1731, the son of a former slave, and grandson of an indentured servant, and lived most of his life in a one-room cabin on the grounds of what is now the historical park. The Banneker family was able to obtain this 120-acre plot of land by growing tobacco. On this homestead, Benjamin Banneker taught himself complex scientific principles. Among his accomplishments: he built the first clock in the United States, carving the pieces of wood (the clock kept accurate time for 50 years); mastered astronomy to the point of being able to predict eclipses and other celestial activity; played a key role in the survey of Washington, D.C.; and published an annual almanac that garnered international recognition.

The museum and historical park opened in 1998 as a memorial to Banneker. The exhibit hall is spacious and attractive, with stained-glass windows and an open-beam ceiling. One exhibit showcases some of Banneker's personal effects that were excavated from the homestead, including a glass lens and instruments. Other displays feature astronomy and interesting rocks and minerals. Emblazoned onto the floor of the museum is an historical map of Washington, D.C., with tiny scale-model monuments that kids can try to place correctly. A modest gift shop sells shirts, hats, books, cards, and other gifts.

Banneker's historical park also moonlights as a nature center. Stuffed and mounted animals are on display, and programs dealing with environmental and natural history topics are offered. The grounds of the historical park are well worth a visit. Lots of picnic tables are spread about, and bluebird houses are strategically placed along the grass boundary. Mild-mannered trails weave through deciduous woodland leading to good birding habitat. The trail network interconnects with the paved number 9 Trolley Trail that leads to Ellicott City's historic district (follow it downhill). Banneker is buried at an unknown location on his homestead grounds.

Location and Directions: At 300 Oella Avenue, in Ellicott City. From Baltimore, take the Interstate 695 beltway west of the city. Take Exit 13, Frederick Road, west. Follow Frederick Road for about three miles, passing through Catonsville, and turn right onto Oella Avenue. The historical park is located about one-half mile up Oella Avenue on the left.

Hours and Admission: Tuesdays through Saturdays from 10 a.m. to 4 p.m. There is no admission fee, though a donation of $3 for adults and $2 for children is recommended.

Website and Phone: www.thefriendsofbanneker.org; (410) 887-1081.

B&O Railroad Museum

Nowhere in the country is there a better marriage between museum and train-obsessed child. The reality of walking around, and climb-

▲ Inside the roundhouse at the B&O Railroad Museum

ing through, dozens of locomotives, boxcars, passenger cars, and cabooses will make any child quiver with delight. The facility is considered the preeminent rail museum in the country, and occupies
the Mount Clare Station, a lovely brick building complex dating to
1829. The former station served the country's first public railroad—a 13-mile line that terminated in Ellicott Mills (now Ellicott
City). It's also where America's first steam locomotive, the Tom
Thumb, was built. If that weren't enough, Mount Clare Station was
the receiving terminal of the country's first telegraph message, sent
in 1844 by Samuel Morse.

The museum has three primary exhibits. Lined up in formation on the outside grounds are long, colorful, historic trains. You'll
see the American Freedom Train, several long-distance passenger
trains, electrical locomotives, a pitch-perfect restoration of a string
of B&O Pullman cars, and a workhouse short-line train. In the rear
shop yard are more iron horses, including the world's most powerful steam engine, and a disfigured, torpedo-shaped car used to
move molten iron, which, as one employee declared, "has a bad case
of the uglies."

The primary train-viewing area is inside the roundhouse,
which is the largest circular industrial building in the world. (In actuality, it is a circle approximated by 22 sides.) With inlaid wood floors
and high, sun-grabbing windows, it's also one of the most beautiful
buildings. About two dozen actual and replica engines, cabooses, box
cars, and passenger cars line the walls of the roundhouse. Children

may climb aboard some. Of special note are the Tom Thumb reproductions: the "William Mason," a spit-shined brass and steel engine that ushered in the age of rail aesthetics; and the "Shay," a cog steam engine, which is the original "Little Engine That Could," used to haul coal through mountainous West Virginia terrain. A few model trains are available in this area for children to operate.

Perhaps the museum's most mesmerizing exhibit is the HO-gauge train set-up spread out across the second floor of the annex. It's one of the largest and most captivating train layouts in the country, featuring a model town, mountainous terrain, and replica rail yard. Keen observers will notice that a portion of the display shows a historical depiction of the actual B&O rail line that runs beside the Potomac River in western Maryland. Bleacher seats allow for relaxed viewing.

Actual train rides are periodically offered at the museum. The annual holiday Santa train is particularly popular, but 32,000 youthful enthusiasts showed up at a recent Thomas the Tank Engine showing. Check the museum's website for upcoming events. A gift shop serves up, among other things, lots and lots of Thomas the Tank Engine paraphernalia.

Location and Directions: At 901 West Pratt Street, within walking distance of the Inner Harbor attractions. From Interstate 95, take Interstate 395 and follow signs for Martin Luther King Boulevard. Turn left onto Lombard Street and continue for a few blocks. Turn left onto Poppleton Street and continue one block, across Pratt Street, into the museum's parking lot.

Hours and Admission: Daily from 10 a.m. to 5 p.m. Closed on New Year's Day, Easter, Thanksgiving, Christmas Eve, Christmas, and New Year's Eve. Admission is $8 for adults (13-59), $7 for seniors (60 and over), $5 for children (2-12), and free for children under 2 years of age. Discounted weekend passes are available.

Phone: www.borail.org; (410) 752-2490.

College Park Aviation Museum

The College Park Aviation Museum would get my vote for "best-in-show" in the small museum category. Though located in the Washington, D.C., suburbs, it's well worth the drive for families who fancy flight. The museum is modest in stature, but features a nice selection of historical aircraft and odd-looking planes. Iron birds hang from the ceiling and are parked about the display area. A red Monocoupe dating to 1932, a yellow Taylor J-1 Cub made in 1936, and the funky Berliner Helicopter dating to 1924, are but a few. Not to be missed is the reproduction of a 1910 rickety-looking, fabric-on-wood-frame plane employed by the Wright brothers. There are photos of planes, movies about historical flights, interpretive dioramas, and a wall of propellers. A special children's area features lots of books, puzzles, games, a virtual flight simulator, and a place to listen to actual radio correspondence from various airports. Also be sure to check out the re-creation of Wilbur Wright's hangar, which once stood on the grounds. Interactive displays weigh heavily in the children's enjoyment of this attraction. Children were obviously the main focus when architects gave the facility a multi-million-dollar facelift recently. Regular aviation-related programs and movies are held, and it's a great place to have a birthday party. The gift store is a requisite stop for fun toys.

The museum is justifiably located at the College Park Airport, the nation's oldest, continuously operating runway, which dates to 1909. In fact, the attention of museum visitors will frequently be diverted to passenger planes taking off and landing on the runway, which is viewable from inside the museum. The Wright brothers spent a good deal of time on these grounds training Army pilots. The airport was also the scene of the first U.S. Air Mail Service flight, the first controlled helicopter flight, the first mile-high flight, the first test of a machine gun from a plane, and the first flight with a woman passenger. Nearby is the 94th Aero Squadron Restaurant, a great place to grab a bite and end the day.

Location and Directions: At 1985 Cpl. Frank Scott Drive, in College Park. From the D.C. Beltway, take Exit 23, Kenilworth Avenue, inside the beltway. Proceed for three miles and turn right onto Paint Branch Parkway. Continue for one-half mile and turn right onto Cpl. Frank Scott Drive. Follow to museum parking.

Hours and Admission: Hours are daily from 10 a.m. to 5 p.m. Closed on major holidays. Admission is $4 for adults, $3 for seniors, and $2 for children and students. Kids under 2 are free.

Website and Phone: www.collegeparkaviationmuseum.com; (301) 864-6026.

Fire Museum of Maryland

If your child darts to the window with delight whenever a fire engine screams by, then he or she will turn cartwheels at a visit to the

▲ Enjoying the trucks at the Fire Museum of Maryland

Fire Museum of Maryland. The largest fire museum on the East Coast offers over 20,000 square feet of fire engines, equipment, and play space. Don't let the understated white shed building fool you; the interior glows from the sheen of 42 well-polished, antique fire-fighting vehicles. Visitors can trace the history of fire-fighting, from hand-drawn carts to horse-drawn carts to motorized trucks. Some of the units have an impressively gilded Victorian appearance. Other vintage fire-fighting equipment on display includes hoses, uniforms, helmets, and kerosene and whale-oil lanterns. One fascinating exhibit shows a collection of badges from various firehouses across Baltimore. A particularly fun display for the kiddies involves a generous collection of toy and model fire trucks.

Noise is in no short supply at the fire museum. A working fire-alarm telegraph system—the largest still operating in the country—stands ready for action in a life-size replica of a fire-station office. The telegraph alarm system is connected to a handful of antique alarm boxes scattered about the museum. Children can trigger the alarm system via any alarm box and trace the signal into the tele-graph alarm room. Expect to hear the alarm sounded again and again. On my visit, one friendly person offered an unsolicited but highly informative lesson on how the alarm telegraph system works.

Not to be missed is the Discovery Room, where kids can don authentic firefighter's garb and climb aboard an actual engine. A toy box is spilling over, and a bookshelf contains some informative reading. Space is ample for running around. The museum has a gift shop and sometimes shows short videos on fire-related topics.

Location and Directions: At 1301 York Road, in Lutherville. From the Interstate 695 beltway, take Exit 26, York Road, north and continue for one block. The museum is behind a business center to the right.

Hours and Admission: The museum is open on weekends from May through October. During June, July, and August, it's also open on Wednesdays, Thursdays, and Fridays. Hours are Wednesdays through Saturdays from 11:00 a.m. to 4 p.m. and Sundays from 1 p.m. to 5 p.m. Admission is $6 for adults; $4 for seniors, firefighters, and children 3–15; and free for children under 3.

Website and Phone: (410) 321-7500.

Great Blacks in Wax Museum

The unusual and educational Great Blacks in Wax Museum takes visitors on a stroll through African-American history, immersing them in such issues as slavery, civil rights, scientific discovery, and athletic achievement. Set inside a former firehouse, the museum features over 100 life-size wax figures, each with a story to tell. Madame Tussaud's it is not, but the exhibits are visually captivating and insightful. Typical African-American icons such as Martin Luther King, Malcolm X, and Jackie Robinson are well represented, but the museum shines in highlighting lesser-known African-

◀ Athletes on display at the Great Blacks in Wax Museum

◀ Great Scientists on display at the Great Blacks in Wax Museum

Americans who have played vital and consequential roles in our history. Look for exhibits featuring astronaut Ronald McNair, who was killed in the 1986 Challenger explosion; Booker T. Washington, who founded the Tuskegee Institute; Matthew Henson, who was on Robert Peary's expedition to locate the North Pole; and novelist James Baldwin, who penned *Go Tell It on the Mountain*.

The museum also features special exhibits. An elaborate replica slave ship, complete with holding cells, may prompt provocative questions from school-aged kids. A deeply disturbing lynching exhibit in the basement may be too graphic for children. A special room features wax figures of well-known Marylanders. When I last visited the museum, actual letters sent to Martin Luther King, Jr.—both complimentary and hateful—were displayed in an upstairs conference room. A gift shop is located on the premises.

Parents should note that the sparsely lit museum corridors, coupled with the static glare of life-size wax figures, may prove frightening to certain children. Children of all races, however, would benefit from the history lessons taught here. At the time of publication, plans were afoot to move this museum closer to downtown Baltimore.

Location and Directions: At 1601-03 East North Avenue, in East Baltimore. From downtown, take Charles Street north. Take North Avenue east and continue for about one mile to the museum on the right.

Hours and Admission: From January 15 to October 14, hours are 9 a.m. to 6 p.m. on Tuesdays through Saturdays, and noon to 6 p.m. on Sundays. From October 15 to January 14, hours are 9 a.m. to 5 p.m. on Tuesdays through Saturdays, and noon to 5 p.m. on Sundays. The museum is closed Mondays except for the months of February, July, August, and during certain holidays. Admission fees range from $3.75 to $6.00.

Website and Phone: www.greatblacksinwax.org; (410) 563-3404.

Maryland Science Center

(For a description, see Inner Harbor Attractions chapter.)

Port Discovery

(For a description, see Inner Harbor Attractions chapter.)

Walters Art Museum

Along with the Baltimore Museum of Art, this is the city's other national-class art museum. The Walters Art Museum hosts a breathtaking collection of art and statuary, but parents will be more interested in knowing that the museum has taken great strides in recent years to make the visiting experience more family-friendly. The Family Arts Center provides a refuge for kids who want to try their own hand at artistic creation. Classes and workshops are frequently given. The Artward Bound program runs on weekend afternoons, and caters to children and parents alike. There's a week-long summer camp for kids and frequent family festivals celebrating various occasions. And as with any art museum, kids will enjoy just strolling the aisles and marveling at the funky statues and paintings.

The Walters Art Museum is located just off Mt. Vernon Square, in downtown Baltimore. It began as one of the largest private art collections in the world, that of William Walters, who made his money in liquor and the railroad. Walters had a penchant for collecting the works of local artists, and amassed an impressive assemblage. During the Civil War, he fled to Europe, and there amplified his taste and acquisitions. Walters returned to his Mt. Vernon home in 1874 with a greatly expanded collection, and allowed visitors to view it for a fee, which he donated to charity. After Walters's death in 1894, his son Henry continued collecting and showcasing the family's pride, but needed more space. He opened what is now the main building of the

Walters Art Museum in 1909 for that purpose. Henry bequeathed the collection to the city.

Location and Directions: At 600 North Charles Street. From downtown, take Charles Street north to Mt. Vernon Square. The museum is on the left.

Hours and Admission: Tuesdays through Sundays from 10 a.m. to 5 p.m. Closed on New Year's Day, July 4th, Thanksgiving, Christmas Eve, and Christmas. Admission is $8 for adults, $6 for seniors, $5 for young adults 18-25, and free for anyone 17 and under.

Website and Phone: www.thewalters.org; (410) 547-9000.

Other Baltimore-Area Museums Children May Find Interesting

B&O Railroad Station Museum, Ellicott City
2711 Maryland Avenue, Ellicott City
(410) 461-1944

Baltimore American Indian Center
113 South Broadway, Baltimore
(410) 675-3535

Baltimore Civil War Museum
601 President Street, Baltimore
(410) 385-5188

Baltimore Streetcar Museum
1901 Falls Road, Baltimore
(410) 547-0264

Carroll County Farm Museum
500 South Center Street, Westminster
(800) 654-4645

Chesapeake Children's Museum
25 Silopanna Road, Annapolis
(410) 990-1993

Glenn L. Martin Aviation Museum
Martin State Airport, Middle River
(410) 682-6122

Havre de Grace Decoy Museum
215 Giles Street, Havre de Grace
(410) 939-3739

Jewish Museum of Maryland
15 Lloyd Street, Baltimore
(410) 732-6400

Maryland Historical Society
201 West Monument Street, Baltimore
(410) 685-3750

Museum of Incandescent Lighting, Mt. Vernon
717 Washington Place, Baltimore
(410) 752-8586

National Cryptologic Museum
Maryland Route 32 and Baltimore Washington Parkway
301-688-5849

National Museum of Civil War Medicine
48 East Patrick Street, Frederick
(301) 695-1864

National Museum of Dentistry
31 South Greene Street, Baltimore
(410) 706-0600

Ripken Museum
3 West Bel Air Avenue, Aberdeen
(410) 273-2525

Star-Spangled Banner Flag House
844 East Pratt Street, Baltimore
(410) 837-1793

U.S. Army Ordnance Museum
Aberdeen Proving Grounds, Aberdeen
(410) 279-3602

U.S. Lacrosse Museum and National Hall of Fame
113 West University Parkway
(410) 235-6882

U.S. Naval Academy Museum
Preble Hall, 118 Maryland Avenue, Annapolis
(410) 293-2108

War Memorial
101 North Gay Street, Baltimore
(410) 685-7530

Nature Centers

Nature centers are all the rage these days. They seem to be popping up everywhere. Many of the ones discussed here opened their doors in the past few years. Parents are figuring out that they are great places to spend quality family time together, commune with nature, and get a good dose of environmental education to boot. Here are Baltimore's favorite nature centers.

Anita C. Leight Estuary Center

This nature center has a slightly different slant from most others discussed in that it focuses primarily on water-based ecology. It's part of the 704-acre Chesapeake Bay National Estuarine Research Reserve, where various federal, state, and local environmental agencies conduct research and perform long-term monitoring on the surrounding water, wetlands, and woodland.

On weekends, the center offers programs for the general public—everything from water-based classes to basket-weaving to singing frog hikes. Those with a queasy stomach may want to pass on the edible insect seminar. Several programs involve birding, which is especially productive in the surrounding habitat; no fewer than 150 bird species have been identified here. There are also possibilities for volunteers to get involved in some of the research, which includes the planting of aquatic grasses and monitoring projects.

At the time of this writing, the estuary center had a turtle pond and some temporary displays inside the building. Plans were being made to develop a number of permanent exhibits, including ones on bay geology, the natural history of Otter Creek, and the research being conducted at the station. A relief model of the Chesapeake Bay will be displayed. The center owns a pontoon boat for research. Hiking opportunities are available around the surrounding grounds.

Location and Directions: At 700 Otter Point Road, in Abingdon. From Baltimore, take Interstate 95 north. Take Exit 77A, Route 24, south towards Edgewood. Continue for one mile and turn left at the light onto the access road to Route 40. At the T-intersection, turn left onto Route 40 east, and continue for one and a half miles. Turn right at the traffic light onto Otter Point Road and continue for one-half mile to the estuary center.

Hours and Admission: Saturdays from 10 a.m. to 5 p.m., and Sundays from noon to 5 p.m. Admission is free.

Website and Phone: www.otterpointcreek.org; (410) 612-1688.

Bear Branch Nature Center

The Bear Branch Nature Center has a lovely perch overlooking rolling hills and meadowland in northern Carroll County. The nature center is large and very active. It's part of the Hashawha Environmental Center, which is a camp offering cabins, tent camping, pavilions, a conference center, and lots of recreational activities. Environmental education plays an important role in Bear Branch's mission.

The main exhibition room has nice displays, the centerpiece being the model of a woodland ecosystem. There are insect mounts, an aquarium full of bass and panfish, and Nandi the bunny hopping around her cage. Other intriguing displays were under construction at the time of my visit. In an adjoining room are stacks of aquariums bearing snakes and toads and salamanders. A discovery box lets kids handle natural history artifacts, and a plastered hollow tree provides good crawling and climbing opportunities. Lots of mounted birds adorn the walls, and mounds of puzzles and books are available. A raptor cage out back harbors, among other birds, a bald eagle.

Several trails lead visitors throughout the 320 acres of meadow and woodland. The Vista and Stream Trails are user-friendly and ideal for young kids. The three-mile Wilderness Trail will prove a bit more challenging. Winding tight to the nature center is the wheelchair-accessible Bear Path, which leads to educational displays, a critter pond, a play area, a worm box, and a gazebo offering splendid countryside views.

The Bear Branch Nature Center has all the traditional ingredients of a regional nature center, but comes with a compelling twist: a 40-seat planetarium. Astronomy is a science that kids adore but rarely experience. Many of Bear Branch's programs deal with planetary sciences. Others involve hiking, native American skills, canoeing, crafts, and puppetry. An exhaustive class schedule can be found in its newsletter.

Location and Directions: At 300 John Owings Road, in Westminster. From Baltimore, take Interstate 795 to its terminus, and Route 140 west. In Westminster, veer right onto Route 97 and continue for about three miles. At the Carroll County Sports Complex, turn right onto John Owings Road. Entrance to the nature center and Hashawha Environmental Center is about one and a half miles up John Owings Road on the left.

Hours and Admission: Wednesdays through Saturdays from 10 a.m. to 5 p.m., and Sundays from noon to 5 p.m. Admission is free.

Phone: (410) 848-2517.

Blackwater National Wildlife Refuge

Blackwater National Wildlife Refuge spans about 26,000 acres of pristine wetland, waterways, and farmland in a remote section of Dorchester County, on the sun-baked Eastern Shore. The two-hour drive from Baltimore is very worthwhile for families who enjoy finding peace in nature, or who are looking for a real-world venue to teach their children about animals and ecology. The refuge sits smack on the Great Atlantic Flyway, a migratory bird route that extends from Canada to the Gulf of Mexico. The surrounding marshes and tidal areas make great resting and wintering spots for waterfowl and other birds. Tens of thousands of geese pass through here in late fall and winter, creating quite a spectacle.

The first stop at the refuge should be the Visitor Center. It's small, but one of the best I've seen. It's loaded with top-notch attractions, like the floor-to-ceiling hologram display showing how to identify butterflies. The stuffed and mounted animals seem less mildewy than most, and the reproduced eagle's nest should not be missed. An auditorium seats about 50 and shows a 20-minute documentary on the refuge. Other videos can be requested. The back wall of the Visitor Center is glass, and looks out over a field and marsh. A spotting scope is set up to observe wildlife, including a nearby osprey platform that in spring and summer holds a nest. Another spotting scope is set up outside the Visitor Center.

Birds are the forte at Blackwater. About 35 eagles nest year-round on the refuge—one of the greatest concentrations on the east coast. During our last visit, we counted 10 eagles—all soaring overhead above waterfront trees. Mature eagles are identifiable by their white heads and tails. From a distance, eagles can easily be differentiated from the ubiquitous turkey and black vultures that hover about; the vultures soar with their wings uplifted in a V shape, while the eagles cruise with their wings generally straight out. Eagles are more numerous in winter months, and more active in morning and dusk when out fishing. Herons, ducks, and songbirds can also be found in abundance. Over 250 bird species have been identified at the refuge. Bring a bird book and binoculars to maximize your enjoyment.

The most leisurely way to inspect the refuge is on the 6.5-mile Wildlife Drive, which loops through various marshes and woodland areas. You can pull over at interesting attractions, such as a duck blind that looks out over a heron rookery. Blue herons can also be observed in ditches along the road, and geese like to feed in the surrounding fields. Keep an eye peeled for woodpeckers and songbirds in the wooded tracts. A short spur on the drive leads to an observation point that reveals a stark and beautiful landscape (and one where eagles often fly over). A guide to the Wildlife Drive is available at the Visitor Center. Walking and biking are both popular along this drive. Two short trails can be accessed from the Wildlife Drive: the 0.3-mile paved Marsh Edge Trail, which weaves through the country's northernmost stand of loblolly pines to several waterfront viewing areas, and the half-mile Woods Trail, which explores another loblolly pine forest. Parking is available at both trailheads. One could hike both trails and the stretch of road between them in about 90 minutes (the total distance would be about three miles).

Keen observers at the refuge may also spot muskrat or nutria in the marshes. Look for the telltale V gliding across the water surface. Nutria are large, beaver-like rodents that were introduced a century ago from South America to supplement the local fur industry. A fur farm operated on this site until 1933. However, as with so many other introduced species, the nutria has few natural predators and has taken over the marshes, overwhelming the habitat and removing vital marsh grass. Their impact on the habitat is being studied. Also watch for the chubby Delmarva fox squirrels, which are endangered, working the woodland.

Parents should be aware that Blackwater is not a recreational area; it was established for the protection of wildlife. Do not expect to find playgrounds or ball fields. You will likely encounter serious birders, some of whom will not appreciate screaming children. All visitors are expected to act with a certain level of decorum. Bring a disposable camera, as Blackwater is an ideal place to introduce children to nature photography. Insect repellant is highly recommended in warm months.

At the time of this writing, plans were underway to carve six more miles of hiking trails through the refuge, and to designate a 20-mile ribbon of waterway as a canoe trail.

Location and Directions: At 2145 Key Wallace Drive, near Cambridge. From Baltimore, take Interstate 97 south to Annapolis and Route 50 east across the Chesapeake Bay Bridge. Continue on Route 50 to Cambridge. In Cambridge, turn right onto Route 16 (at the refuge sign), following it west. Go left onto Route 335 at Church Creek, following signs for the refuge. After about five miles, turn left onto Key Wallace Drive. The Visitor Center is about one mile to the right, and the entrance to Wildlife Drive is about 2.5 miles to the right.

Hours and Admission: Outdoor refuge facilities and Wildlife Drive are open daily from dawn to dusk, all year round. The Visitor Center hours are Mondays through Fridays from 8 a.m. to 4 p.m., and Saturdays and Sundays from 9 a.m. to 5 p.m. The Visitor Center is closed on Thanksgiving and Christmas. The cost to access the grounds is $3 for private vehicles, and $1 for each pedestrian or bicycle. Group rates are available. A yearly pass to Blackwater is $12. It also accepts Golden Eagle passes from other federal parks and monuments.

Website and Phone: www.friendsofblackwater.org; (410) 228-2677.

Carrie Murray Nature Center

Baltimore Orioles baseball fans may want to support the Carrie Murray Nature Center, established thanks to the generous donation by local favorite Eddie Murray. The center is, in fact, named after his mother. Eddie wanted to provide urban children with the opportunity to explore nature and the outdoors in an educational manner, and with its unusually fine collection of live species, this nature center serves its purpose well. It's located in West Baltimore, in Gwynns Falls/Leakin Park—the third largest urban park in the United States behind Fairmount Park in Philadelphia and Central Park in New York City. I have found, from personal experience, that the personnel here are particularly friendly and eager to share information.

The nature center includes a main classroom crammed full of cages and aquariums housing an impressive menagerie of snakes and mammals. My tots couldn't decide if the coolest was the iguana, the bearded dragon from Australia, or the eight-foot-long constrictor. In the end, the button-cute flying squirrel took top honors. Don't miss the colorful orange corn snakes—species that have been genetically altered to make decent house pets. Several stuffed and preserved animals dangle from the ceiling.

A favorite exhibit of kids is the Insect Zoo, which features hundreds of exotic and funky species including arachnids and crustaceans. Check out the Australian blue lobster and the whiptail scorpion. The giant African millipede was the size of a skinny cucumber, and the death's head cockroaches were as big as drink coasters. There are crayfish and stick insects and one wall of aquariums displaying every type of tarantula imaginable. Despite all the fetching critters, my kids were most enamored with a bucket full of noisy crickets which were used as spider food.

The Carrie Murray Nature Center also houses a rehabilitation center for injured raptors and other species. Owls and hawks convalesce in the shed building behind the main cluster of buildings. The center offers an array of nature-related programs and a reasonably priced summer day camp for kids.

Location and Directions: At 1901 Ridgetop Road. From the Interstate 695 beltway, take Exit 17, Security Boulevard, east toward the city. Continue on Security Boulevard for about two miles, and turn left onto Ingleside Avenue (Forest Park Avenue). Proceed for about one-half mile and turn right onto Windsor Mill Road. After another one-half mile, turn right onto Ridgetop Road, which is a tiny driveway road. There is a small white sign for the nature center at this turn. Continue on Ridgetop Road to the main parking lot.

Hours and Admission: Mondays through Fridays from 8:30 a.m. to 4:30 p.m., Saturdays from 10 a.m. to 4 p.m., and Sundays from 10 a.m. to 3 p.m. Admission is free.

Phone: (410) 396-0808.

Eden Mill Nature Center

The Eden Mill Nature Center is located in the far-flung reaches of Harford County, just minutes from the Pennsylvania border. The center was built in a 200-year-old grist mill, attractively restored through the hard labor of volunteers and the financial support of local businesses. The center educates visitors in the natural history of the Piedmont region through classes, mounted animals, and live displays. It includes the requisite aquariums full of snakes and frogs, but also has a nice turtle pond.

The mill has been restored to original condition and is open for inspection. Visitors will see the grain pits, grinding stones, power-generating equipment, and other mill paraphernalia. A nice power plant cross-section scale model hangs on the wall. The generating room is quite interesting and has windows overlooking the 18-foot-high dam. Water tumbling over the dam makes for soothing background music. Scattered about are bags of flour and cornmeal produced by the former mill.

The brunt of the nature center's outreach takes place outdoors. Canoe programs are among the most popular offered by Eden Mill, and are often held at twilight. Canoeing is done on the flat stretches of scenic Deer Creek. A naturalist accompanies the paddlers. The canoe launch area is handicapped-accessible. Eden Mill also offers lots of nature-based programs for families and kids, as well as a summer camp.

Five miles of easygoing hiking trails have been blazed across the 57-acre park. The Pollipot Trail leads through wetlands, while the Beaver Run Trail escorts visitors along Deer Creek. Some trails include steep climbs, so check with the nature center before setting off with toddlers. Eden Mill's website sets forth an impressive, 1.5-mile hike, laying out directions and interpretive information. Don't miss the stunning Stansbury Mansion located across the parking lot, which was home to the former miller.

Location and Directions: At 1617 Eden Mill Road, in Pylesville. From Baltimore, take Interstate 95 north. Take the Route 24 exit north and continue for about 12 miles past Bel Air. Turn left onto Route 165 and continue for about three miles. Turn right onto Fawn Grove Road and continue for about one mile. Turn left onto Eden Mill Road and proceed to the nature center.

Hours and Admission: Hours are intermittent, but the nature center is generally open on Sundays from April through October, from 1 p.m. to 5 p.m. Call first or check the website for details. Admission is free.

Website and Phone: www.edenmill.org; (410) 836-3050.

Irvine Natural Science Center

Situated in a lovely pastoral setting just north of Baltimore, the Irvine Natural Science Center is Baltimore's original environmental study center, dating to 1975. It's located on the campus at St. Timothy's School, and comprises a series of barns and outbuildings. There are interesting displays in the visitor center, a barn for group events, a pond lorded over by a gaggle of Canada geese, an art center, and a demonstration garden planted to provide food and shelter for animals.

The favorite exhibit in the visitors' center is the Kid's Korner, where children can handle and explore such natural artifacts as bones, sea shells, corals, animal furs, and tree slices. There are also puzzles and books to play with, and a table and chairs. Certain exhibits will also appeal to adults. A light-up display lets visitors match skeletons to animal pictures. Another showcases dozens of bird eggs, and still another shows why we must preserve our tropical forests (one critical reason: to save the cocoa beans that are used to make chocolate). Children will likely head straight to the reptile and amphibian wall, where live specimens are on display—everything from the eastern snapping turtle to the Chilean rosy-toed tarantula to a boa constrictor of hearty girth.

The heart of the Irvine Natural Science Center lies in its programs and camps. Covered are such far-reaching topics as birding, gardening, and astronomy. Week-long, summer-camp day programs immerse children in nature studies, with costs varying by age and program. The nature center sponsors stream-cleanings and an annual pumpkin festival. It also sponsors pricey, but fun-sounding, eco-tourism excursions to such exotic locales as Belize, Borneo, Costa Rica, and the Amazon Basin.

Irvine Natural Science Center offers an impressive nature shop. It includes not only the standard fare (T-shirts, hats, etc.), but also a substantial collection of nature and ecology books, and a wide assortment of bird feeders and houses. There are CDs, videos, binoculars, and all things ecological. Drinks are also available.

Visitors are encouraged to explore the nature center grounds on the short, interpretive White Oak Trail, which weaves through the nearby meadows and woodland. Access to the trail is only available when the nature center is open, and hikers must first register.

Be aware that at the time of this writing, consideration was being given to moving the nature center operations to the Caves Valley area of central Baltimore County, so call first before visiting.

Location and Directions: At 8400 Greenspring Avenue. From the Interstate 695 beltway, take Exit 22, Greenspring Avenue, north. Continue on Greenspring Avenue for about one mile, to the nature center, which is on the campus of St. Timothy's School.

Hours and Admission: Tuesdays through Saturdays from 9 a.m. to 4 p.m., and Sundays from noon to 4 p.m. Closed on Mondays. Admission is free.

Website and Phone: www.explorenature.org; (410) 484-2413.

▲ The spanking new Marshy Point Nature Center

Marshy Point Nature Center

Marshy Point Nature Center is the newest such facility in the Baltimore area. It was built in 2000 as part of Dundee and Saltpeter Creeks Park, a little-known and pristine, 492-acre waterfront preserve in southeastern Baltimore County, near Chase. The spanking new, 5,000-square-foot building is constructed of stone and wood to appear integral with the surrounding environment. Visitors can peek through the 100-foot ribbon of trees and see the Chesapeake Bay. The center's primary purpose is environmental education about the bay and surrounding wetlands and woodland.

Being so new, the nature center does not have the extensive dioramas and displays common to other such facilities. However, there is an exhibit room that shows handsome photographs of the bay and includes two aquariums (one featuring underwater bay plants and the other fish), and a few stuffed birds. A lovely tundra swan taking wing hangs from the ceiling. An impressive auditorium is used for lectures and events. The staff at the nature center was more than eager to share their knowledge, and very patient with kids running around.

Two trails begin at the nature center. One is a short bootleg that leads about 100 feet to the waterfront. The other, the Whitetail Trail, winds about one-half mile to another waterfront lookout area. This trail traces the course of an actual deer path. The bay in this area has exceptional water quality, and the ecosystem teems with life, particularly waterfowl. Nearby, at Poole's Island, is the bay's largest blue heron rookery. Three bald eagle nests are sprinkled about here, and one mature eagle did a nice flyover during my visit. I also saw many bluebirds flitting about the parking lot. Future plans for the nature center include blazing more trails, developing a canoe launch area, setting up wildlife observation areas, and possibly linking the grounds to nearby Gunpowder Falls State Park with a pedestrian bridge.

Kids and adults can take part in free outdoor-oriented programs offered by Marshy Point Nature Center. Representative topics include oysters, birds nests, wildflowers, trees, animal footprints, and waterfowl. Popular week-long summer day-camps are also available for $75 per session.

Location and Directions: At 7130 Marshy Point Road, in eastern Baltimore County. From Baltimore, take Eastern Avenue east. The center entrance is located just past the Glenn L. Martin State Airport, and is marked by a sign indicating Dundee and Saltpeter Creeks Park. Follow signs to the nature center. Alternately, take Route 40 to White Marsh. Take Ebenezer Road east, and turn right onto Earls Road, and continue on Earls Road until its terminus at Eastern Avenue. Turn left onto Eastern Avenue and proceed about one mile to the park's entrance.

Hours and Admission: Daily from 9 a.m. to 5 p.m. It may close early on Fridays. Admission is free.

Phone: (410) 887-2817.

National Wildlife Visitor Center

At 12,800 acres, the Patuxent Wildlife Research Center comprises what is reportedly the largest undeveloped tract of land on the East Coast between Boston and the Carolinas. It's the nation's premier spot for biological and ecological research, employing hundreds of scientists from around the world. Researchers here delve into such topics as bird migration, endangered species, and environmental contaminants. Rachel Carson's masterpiece *Silent Spring* was based on research here.

Most of the refuge grounds are off-limits to the public because of ongoing experiments. The few accessible areas are well worth a visit. I would recommend first stopping at the National Wildlife Visitor Center, which opened in 1994 as the Department of

▲ Entrance to the National Wildlife Visitor Center

the Interior's largest and most kid-friendly educational facility. Those expecting the turtles-in-aquarium decor of the more traditional nature centers will be shocked. Its high-tech gadgetry and hands-on approach make it more akin to facilities such as the Maryland Science Center or Port Discovery. The exhibits alone cost about $4 million and were designed by a team of 127 scientists.

The Visitor Center's main public area usually houses an art exhibit and displays various stuffed and mounted animals, including a ferocious-looking polar bear that appears to be having a bad day. An auditorium and movie theater have regular features on topics ranging from piping plovers to African wildlife to Rachel Carson. An information desk offers not only trail maps of the grounds and interpretive help, but also maps of all federal refuges. A nice gift shop sells way more than the usual T-shirts and books.

The displays that the kids will clamor for are in the Wisdom of Wildness hall. A pathway conducts you past each exhibit and deposits you back into the lobby. What becomes immediately apparent is that the exhibits do not have a local slant as most other nature centers do, but focus on global concerns. The first attractively illuminated exhibit introduces visitors to seven problems stressing the global environment, including ocean pollution, declining biodiversity, and population explosion. The next is about research taking place on four bird species: the bobolink, sanderling, wood thrush, and Swainson's hawk. "Habitats" is an especially impressive, hands-on exhibit edifying guests about the state of five distinct habitats:

the Chesapeake Bay, a Hawaiian rainforest, Dakota prairie potholes, the lower Mississippi Valley, and California's Central Valley. Kids get to push lots of buttons and turn levers to move exhibit parts

What follows is a chilling exhibit on endangered species. Realistic models of 14 species such as the Indiana bat, desert tortoise, California condor, red-cockaded woodpecker, and American crocodile are each shown in a vertical glass showcase. The showcase glass is etched with a shading so that the animals are barely visible, signifying that they are disappearing before us. A final exhibit shows the gray wolf, California sea otter, canvasback duck, and whooping crane in their natural habitat.

Outside, a 40-passenger, electric-powered tram takes folks on a 30-minute circuit through back reaches of the refuge, providing insight into the ongoing research projects and the local wildlife. The tram operates seasonally and is available on a first-come, first-served basis. Check with the information center for a schedule. Cost is $2 per adult, and $1 for children 12 and under and seniors 55 and older.

The Visitor Center can get crowded at times, but peace can always be found on the trail system outside. Six well-blazed trails lead to various lakes and woodland. The trails are gentle and easily navigable by children. Follow the Goose Pond Trail to the namesake pond and look for green and tree frogs along the shoreline. The Cash Lake Trail is particularly attractive, brushing up against a beaver lodge before reaching a fishing pier. Parts of the Cash Lake

▲ Learn about endangered species at the National Wildlife Visitor Center

Trail cross a fun floating bridge, but these sections may be closed because of waterfowl breeding. The information desk in the Visitor Center offers trail maps. A short ramble with commentary is delineated in the Hikes chapter.

Location and Directions: At 10901 Scarlet Tanager Loop, just off Route 197, between Laurel and Bowie. From Baltimore, take the Baltimore–Washington Parkway south. Take the Powder Mill Road exit and turn left onto Powder Mill Road, heading east. Continue for about two miles on Powder Mill Road and turn right onto Scarlet Tanager Loop. Continue about one and a half miles to the Visitor Center.

Hours and Admission: Daily from 10:30 a.m. to 5:30 p.m. Admission is free.

Website and Phone: patuxent/fws/gov/vcdefault.html; (301) 497-5760.

Oregon Ridge Nature Center

The Oregon Ridge Nature Center is an ideal place to school your children in many aspects of the Baltimore area's natural and cultural history. The center offers well-done and insightful exhibits on such topics as beekeeping (including a real bee colony), birds' eggs, wood-cutting, and archeology. A wall mural shows the effects of forest clear-cutting. Also scattered about are the usual complement of stuffed and mounted animals, such as a black bear, mountain lion, fox, and elk.

My kids were drawn to the stack of aquariums in an adjoining room. A fish tank houses a largemouth bass, bluegills, and dace. Other aquariums contain garter snakes, tree frogs, bullfrogs, a speckled king snake, a copperhead, and red-eared slider turtles. A separate greenhouse room includes lush flora and a tank swarming with various kinds of turtles. There is an extensive library of books and magazines on the premises.

The most fascinating exhibit here is a vertical glass-front cabinet displaying various artifacts found on Oregon Ridge, organized by time period. The bottom shelves show arrowheads and other artifacts dating to 500 B.C. Higher shelves display more recent items like bullets and ceramics from the Civil War era, and doorknobs, toys, and glassware from a later generation. The top shelf holds things found of late on the grounds, including litter and castaway toys.

Kids will enjoy climbing around on the enormous rock slabs piled near the nature center's entrance. They are examples of rocks found near Baltimore, including Cockeysville marble, Baltimore gneiss, and Loch Raven schist. Next door to the nature center is the Artifact Repository and Processing Laboratory, used by Baltimore County Public Schools to teach archeology. Beside that is the Tenant House, the last remnant of a mining and iron-smelting village located here a century ago, and now a museum. A booklet titled *The History of Oregon Ridge, 1720-2001*, for sale for $1 at the nature center, is a worthwhile purchase if you plan to spend time here.

Oregon Ridge Nature Center also hosts fun programs and classes for kids and adults alike, ranging from frog identification to canoeing to basket-weaving to Easter egg hunts. Organized hikes are also available, including full-moon hikes and a Mother's Day stroll identifying spring flowers. During my visit, a class was tapping sap from nearby maple and box elder trees and converting it to maple syrup; a pancake breakfast was in the plans.

Location and Directions: At 13401 Beaver Dam Road, in Cockeysville. From Baltimore, take Interstate 83 north. Take Exit 20-B, Shawan Road, heading west. At the first light, turn left onto Beaver Dam Road, and make a quick right, following signs to the nature center.

Hours and Admission: Tuesdays through Sundays from 9 a.m. to 5 p.m. The nature center is closed on Mondays. Admission is free.

Website and Phone: www.oregonridge.org; (410) 887-1815.

Piney Run Nature Center

The Piney Run Nature Center is a very homespun and hands-on facility that appears to have been developed with children in mind. The main room is bursting with informative displays and stuffed, mounted animals, including a wolf and bobcat. Through nice dioramas, visitors are taught about such topics as beavers, predators, animal footprints, and the lifeline of a tree. A special meeting room includes a generous library. A must-see children's room contains aquariums filled with icky things like a kingsnake, corn snake, garter snake, and teeny snapping turtle. A microscope is set up to show children close-up views of butterfly wings, snake skin, bugs, and other natural wonders.

Peek outside the nature center windows to see scores of birds jostling at the feeders. Titmouses and nuthatches were well represented during my visit. Behind the nature center is a high cage con-

taining various injured hawks and owls that are in physical rehab.
Nearby is a pier jutting into a reservoir inlet.

The nature center has a helpful and knowledgeable staff and
hosts a wide array of nature programs and summer camps. Many
programs are for children, including puppet shows and craft time.
A tiny gift shop offers reasonably priced items; I bought my daughter a purple gemstone ring for $1, and my son a bug magnifying box
for $1.25. Piney Run Park offers a full menu of activities, and is dis-
cussed in our County Parks chapter.

Location and Directions: At 30 Martz Road, near Sykesville. From
Baltimore, take Interstate 70 west, and then Route 32 north. In Eldersburg, turn left onto Route 26 and continue for 2.1 miles. Turn
left onto White Rock Road (at the park sign) and continue for 1.9
miles. Turn left onto Martz Road, and proceed to the park entrance,
following signs for the nature center.

Hours and Admission: The Nature Center is open year-round according to the following schedule: From November 1 to March 31,
on Tuesdays through Fridays from 10 a.m. to 4 p.m.; from April 1 to
October 3, on Tuesdays through Fridays from 10 a.m. to 4 p.m., and
on Saturdays and Sundays from 1 p.m. to 5 p.m. The Nature Center
is open on Memorial Day, July 4th, and Labor Day from 10 a.m. to 5
p.m. It is closed on Mondays. Admission to the park is $4 per car for
Carroll County residents and $5 per car for all other visitors. Se-
niors 62 and older are free.

Phone: (410) 795-6043.

Other Attractions

Some kid-friendly attractions are difficult to categorize, but deserve mention. Here are six.

BWI Observation Gallery

Airports are not usually considered destination spots, but Baltimore–Washington International Airport is trying to change that notion. Planners recently unveiled a $6.4 million observation gallery where children can play, watch airplanes take off and land, and learn in hands-on fashion about topics like aeronautics and weather. The gallery is worth a quick visit, even if you have no other business at the airport.

The gallery encompasses over 12,000 square feet of terminal space on two levels, between Concourses B and C. Younger kids will gravitate to the lower level, which is a play area loaded with climbing toys with a transportation theme. The truck and bus are fun, but my daughter's favorite is a sizable airplane with lots of passenger space and a cockpit where kids can pretend to fly.

A glass elevator hoists visitors to the second floor, which hosts an abundance of high-tech, hands-on gadgetry and a nice viewing area of the runways. Huge chunks of actual aircraft are on display, some hanging from the ceiling like avant-garde art. Check out the electronic intricacy found in the cockpit of the Boeing 737, as well as a cross-section of its fuselage and a right wing section. There's also the main launch mechanism of a Boeing 707, and a tail fin and stabilizer. The JT9D jet engine will intrigue mechanically minded kids.

In an adjoining room is an exceptionally compelling series of interactive dioramas providing insight into just about anything dealing with flight, including aerodynamics, meteorology, traffic control, and communications. On one computer, you can input the flight number of a plane en route, and in return get a map of the plane's location, its traveling height and speed, and its expected arrival. At another station, kids can pretend to pilot a simulated flight on a video screen. Visitors can also listen in on conversations between pilots and air-traffic controllers manning BWI's tower. The neatest attraction, however, is the simplest: a 150-foot-wide picture window that allows guests to view planes taking off, landing, and taxiing down the runways.

The observation gallery is bookended by nice, but not pricey, shops and a number of cafes in case you want to turn the visit into a luncheon. Don't let the usually onerous task of airport parking dissuade you from visiting the observation gallery, as parking at BWI Airport is cheap and easy for quick in-and-out visitors. A spacious parking garage located immediately in front of the terminal charges only $2 per half hour, with the first 30 minutes free. Just follow signs for hourly parking as you near the terminal.

Location and Directions: At BWI Airport, between the B and C concourses. From Baltimore, take Interstate 95 south. Take Interstate 195 east to BWI Airport, and follow signs for hourly parking.

Hours and Admission: Daily from 9 a.m. to 9 p.m. Admission is free.

Conowingo Hydroelectric Plant Tour

What child wouldn't be thrilled to venture deep into the bowels of one of our country's largest and most impressive dams? Conowingo Dam, part of the Conowingo Hydroelectric Plant, rises amidst the wooded hills and swanky horse farms of northeast Harford County. It's the Susquehanna River's final obstacle en route to the Chesapeake Bay. The Susquehanna Electric Company, owners of the facility, offers interesting and instructional public tours of its dam. Tours must be pre-arranged and are only offered in groups. Individuals and small families will likely be grouped with other visitors.

Conowingo Dam, completed in 1928, is 100 feet high, almost a mile wide, and generates enough power to illuminate 350,000 homes. It's called a gravity dam, since almost one million tons of concrete were poured directly onto the granite bedrock, pushing water back 14 miles into Pennsylvania. Tours begin with an informative video and chat session, using a scale model of the dam as reference. Visitors are then escorted through a tunnel onto a balcony overlooking a cavernous room

▲ Conowingo Dam on the Susquehanna River

housing six of the facility's eleven turbine-generator units. Each was embedded in a concrete pit about the size of a backyard swimming pool. The tremendous scale of everything is startling, and the room has an aesthetic Victorian feel, with a five-story wall of green-trimmed windows overlooking the river.

Visitors then climb to an outside patio along the dam crest and view the spillway area fanning out 100 feet below. The vantage offers inspiring views of the river as it pinches between two mountains. There are 125 species of fish inhabiting the tailrace waters, and 285 species of birds, including about 40 bald eagles, frequent the area.

The tour next swings by the most technologically advanced fish elevator in the world. A massive elevator bed is submerged in, and open to, the river. Target fish such as shad, herring, striped bass, and eel are attracted into the bed by artificially created water flows. Periodically, the elevator bed is hoisted 100 feet to the dam crest, where the fish are released upstream toward their ancestral spawning grounds. The success of the fish elevator is well-documented: In 1972, with just rudimentary fish passage available at the dam, 182 shad found their way upstream. Now, about 175,000 shad are lifted annually.

The tour ends after passing through several rooms filled with mechanical and electrical gear, some impressively vintage. Guests sneak through a low-ceilinged passage, where generators hum overhead and the mammoth turbines rumble below. The floor will shimmy from the stress of up to 38 million gallons of water passing beneath your feet each minute. Thick turbine shafts in this area whirl at about 80 revolutions per minute, by my estimate.

Fishing, hiking, and bird-watching are popular activities around the dam. Birders often have their spotting scopes trained on bald eagles, and probably wouldn't mind if you took a peek. The Shures Landing Wildflowers Viewing Area is beside the dam, and the Mason-Dixon hiking trail passes through the parking lot. Nearby is Susquehanna State Park, which features hiking, picnicking, biking, wildlife-viewing, a boat launch, the Rock Run historic mill area, and the Steppingstone Museum, a homage to rural arts and crafts.

Location and Direction: In Conowingo. From Baltimore, take Interstate 95 north. Take Exit 89, Havre de Grace, which is Route 155. Turn left onto Route 155, heading west. Continue on Route 155 for about three miles. Turn right onto Route 161 (Darlington Road). Continue on Route 161 for about five miles. In Darlington, turn right onto Shuresville Road, and continue for about one and a half miles. Turn right onto Shures Landing Road, following signs to the hydroelectric plant and Fisherman's Park.

Hours and Admission: Dam tours are offered Mondays through Saturdays. Tours are free, and available to anyone 12 years or older. Reservations are required, and should be made at least one month in advance. Call (410) 457-5011 for details.

General Motors Baltimore Assembly Plant Tour

The General Motors Baltimore Assembly Plant offers the most mind-bending plant tour in the Baltimore area. Visitors trace the course of the two-mile-long assembly line, and watch as sheets of metal, steel components, electrical instruments, windshield glass, and carpeting get molded into top-of-the-line minivans. You get to see first-hand the sweat and toil that go into putting a GMC Safari or Chevrolet Astro on the road.

The GM tour touches all phases of minivan assembly and inspection. The highlight of the tour will be watching 185 robots do their futuristic thing. At one point, a robot arm lifts a windshield into the air, and another arm applies a trail of caulk around its exterior edge. The windshield is then passed to another robot that hands it off to an assembly line employee for insertion into the van. Kids will marvel at such high-tech wizardry, and it may seed an interest in the sciences or engineering. Tour participants may get to chat with welders, machinists, and engineers.

The assembly plant is located on Broening Highway, in Dundalk, and has been operating since 1935. The plant is a behemoth, sprawling over three million square feet, generally under one roof. When running at full bore, it coughs up about 40 minivans per hour. A plant tour takes about two hours to complete, and requires a great deal of walking. Safety glasses are provided, but make sure to wear comfortable shoes with no open toes. Be warned that it may get loud and malodorous at times. Groups must have 10 participants to tour, but not more than 25. Children must be 10 or older to enter. Also be aware that, for safety purposes, there are restrictions on crutches, canes, and wheelchairs. Cameras are prohibited.

Location and Directions: At 2122 Broening Highway, in Dundalk. From Baltimore, take Interstate 95 north. Just past the Fort McHenry Tunnel, take Boston Street east. Turn right onto Broening Highway and continue to the General Motors plant.

Phone: For tours, call (410) 631-2111.

Ladew Topiary Gardens

Harvey Ladew lived a privileged and charmed life. He was born in 1886, the scion of a family of self-made millionaires who produced leather belts used to operate factory machinery. As a youth he rubbed elbows with other Manhattan socialites and took drawing lessons from the curator of the Metropolitan Museum of Art. Later he yachted, took lengthy romps through Europe, and immersed himself in fox-hunting. He hobnobbed with Cole Porter, Charlie Chaplin, Somerset Maugham, and T.E. Lawrence (of Arabia). In his 40s, Ladew bought the 200-acre Pleasant Valley Farm in Monkton, taught himself gardening, and turned his grounds into one of the country's loveliest and most famous gardens.

The Ladew Topiary Gardens are perhaps the most visually appealing and well-manicured tract of landscape in the Baltimore area. A visit to Ladew makes for a perfect family outing: parents can see the seasons change through the prism of gorgeous gardens, and children will have fun scudding about the open fields, fueled by fresh air and the perfume of flowers.

The Garden Club of America named Ladew the top topiary garden in the country. Topiary is the trimming and training of shrubbery into unnatural configurations. At Ladew, shrubs have been carved into animals and funky shapes. The swans drifting in a sea of waves are spectacular. Some shrubs molded into geometric peculiarities look as if they stepped out of a Dr. Seuss book. My personal favorite is a foxhunt scene, with a rider mounted on horseback following a pack of hounds in pursuit of a fox.

Topiary is the main attraction, but an abundance of fabulous flower gardens is interlaced throughout the grounds. The berry garden, water lily garden, rose garden, and cottage garden are all spectacular. The Victorian garden is particularly colorful and appealing. Statuary, fountains, and furniture of wrought iron and concrete are spread about. Ponds and a bubbling brook complete the idyllic landscape. If time permits, take the 1.5-mile, self-guided nature walk that meanders through pretty meadows and a nice patch of woodland.

Ladew's mansion is also open for tours. Built in the 18th century, it's crammed full of peculiar and stylish English antiques and unusual pieces of art. The oval library was listed as one of the 100 most beautiful rooms in the country.

Ladew Topiary Gardens offer an array of organized family activities. Special events are held on Mother's Day and around the Christmas holiday. A folk concert series is also held in summer. A café is open on the premises, but picnicking is another lunchtime option.

Location and Directions: At 3535 Jarrettsville Pike, in Monkton. From the Interstate 695 beltway, take Exit 27, Dulaney Valley Road (Route 146), north. Just past Loch Raven Reservoir, Route 146 veers left onto Jarrettsville Pike. Ladew Topiary Gardens are located on Route 146, about nine miles past Loch Raven Reservoir, and just before its intersection with Route 152 (Fallston Road).

Hours and Admission: The gardens are open from mid-April through the end of October. Hours are Mondays through Fridays from 10 a.m. to 4 p.m., and Saturdays and Sundays from 10:30 a.m. to 5 p.m. Admission to the gardens and nature walk is $8 per adult, $2 per child, and $7 for a senior or student. Admission to the house, gardens, and nature walk is $12 per adult, $4 per child, and $11 for a senior or student.

Website and Phone: www.ladewgardens.com; (410) 557-9466.

Lexington Market

Since the 18th century, municipal markets have been part of the city's social and economic fabric, providing gathering spots for locals and places to buy produce, meats, and baked goods. Many Baltimore municipal markets remain, having survived the passage of time and the changing urban canvas. They include Cross Street Market in Federal Hill, Hollins Market in Southwest Baltimore, Broadway Market in Fells Point, and BelAir Market in East Baltimore, all of which are worth a visit.

Lexington Market, however, is the patriarch. Located deep in downtown Baltimore, off the beaten tourist trail, it provides the truest glimpse into what city life was like in a previous generation. Vendors in hundreds of open-air stalls hawk everything from produce to peanuts to pork products to poultry to potato chips—as they have for decades. There are eight bakeries, a dozen delis, candy stands (try Rhebs for a real treat), and non-food merchandisers as well. The market bustles with vibrancy, and the crowds can be elbow-to-elbow at busy times, jockeying for counter space or a table. Having lunch and soaking up the atmosphere are great ways to pass an afternoon, and are eye-opening experiences for children. Frugal parents will love the affordable lunches, and epicureans will marvel at the international eateries that feature cuisine from such far-flung places as Greece, Singapore, Malaysia, and the Caribbean.

A fun time to visit is during a special event. The market hosts an annual chocolate festival, a crab derby during Preakness week, and on some Friday afternoons, live music. Each spring, while the circus is in town, watch for "Lunch with the Elephants," when the circus pachyderms march—trunk to tail—to the market for a meal consisting of thousands of apples, oranges, carrots, pears, and heads of lettuce—much to the delight of thousands of onlookers.

Lexington Market is the oldest operating open-air market in the United States. It opened at its present site in 1782 following a generous land donation from General John Eager Howard, who had just returned from the Battle of Lexington (hence the market's name). Farmers from surrounding regions brought their wares to the market in Conestoga wagons. The market has long been a showcase of ethnic foods, reflecting the waves of immigrants that have swept across the city. It's said that George Washington and Thomas Jefferson grabbed a bite here. Some visitors may find the neighborhood a tad intimidating, but a parking garage on the premises should alleviate any safety concerns.

Also worth a visit are the 32nd Street Farmers' Market in Charles Village, and, in summers, the Baltimore Farmers' Market, on Saratoga Street, located under the Interstate 83 viaduct.

Location and Directions: At 400 West Lexington Street. From downtown Baltimore, take Lombard Street west. Just past the Baltimore Arena, turn right onto Howard Street and continue three blocks to the market.

Hours: Mondays through Saturdays from 8:30 a.m. to 6 p.m.

Website and Phone: www.lexingtonmarket.com; (410) 685-6169.

U.S. Naval Academy

The U.S. Naval Academy is a stunning institution steeped in history and tradition, and supremely set on the sun-splashed waterfront in downtown Annapolis. The meticulously manicured grounds are strewn with fascinating memorials, plaques, and interesting relics like torpedoes and aircraft. Buildings on the academy grounds are nothing short of monumental. An entire day is necessary to do the academy justice, but a shorter excursion can be fun and rewarding.

Start your visit at the Armel-Leftwich Visitor Center, which is integral with the east side of the field house. The visitor center is a great place to pick up literature on the academy, and offers excellent views of the harbor of Annapolis and the Chesapeake Bay. You can explore the academy on your own, or take a guided tour. Tours leave hourly from the visitor center and cost $6 for adults, $5.50 for seniors 62 and over, $4.50 for students, and are free for pre-schoolers. I recommend the guided tour if you're interested in the historical minutiae of the academy. A short film shown regularly at the visitor center is decent, and there are also a snack bar and gift shop.

▲ Bancroft Hall, the world's largest dormitory, at the U.S. Naval Academy

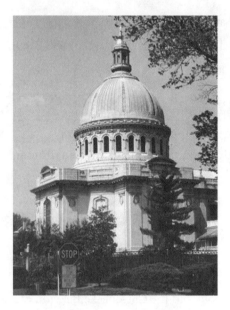

◀ The chapel at the U.S. Naval Academy

To explore on your own, I suggest walking down Turner Joy Road, which follows the waterfront, offering nice bayscapes and vantages of the Eastport community. It was off this seawall that the Peggy Stewart Tea Party—similar to the Boston Tea Party—occurred in the late 18th century. At the end of Turner Joy Road is the Santee Basin, where the naval training vessels are moored.

Stroll through Bancroft Hall, the world's largest dormitory and home to all 4,000 midshipmen; it has five miles of hallways. Pass through the spectacular foyer into Memorial Hall, with displays honoring academy graduates who have fallen in action. The Tecumseh statue stands sentry over the front of Bancroft Hall. Midshipmen toss pennies at Tecumseh before exams for good luck, and paint it before key football games. The Mexican War Monument, erected in 1848 on the quad outside Bancroft Hall, was the first monument built on campus, but the Herndon Monument, located nearby, is arguably the most famous. The 21-foot-tall obelisk is annually smeared with hundreds of pounds of lard, and midshipmen must ceremoniously climb it and replace a cup with a plebe cover.

Many other buildings, museums, monuments, and exhibits are worth exploring. The chapel, with its huge, sculpted iron doors and Tiffany-made, stained-glass windows, is a must-see. The remains of John Paul Jones are encrypted in the basement. Also check out the Naval Museum in Preble Hall, and the café in Dahlgren Hall. Sports-minded visitors should stop in at Lejune Hall to see, not only the swimming and wrestling facilities, but also the academy's sports hall of fame, located on the second floor. Look for paraphernalia honoring David Robinson, who went on to become one of the National Basketball Association's biggest stars.

Location and Directions: In Annapolis. From Baltimore, take Interstate 97 south. In Annapolis, take Route 50 east. From Exit 24, Rowe Boulevard, proceed into downtown Annapolis and find parking on-street or in a garage. Continue to the academy grounds on foot. Enter through Gate One, which is near the intersection of Randall and King George Streets, and continue straight to the Armel-Leftwich Visitor Center.

Hours: The tour schedule varies with the seasons. In summer, tours are offered on Mondays through Saturdays from 9:30 a.m. to 3 p.m., and on Sundays from 12:30 p.m. to 3 p.m., weather and academy activities permitting. Tour hours are cut back in off-seasons. No tours are given on New Year's Day, Thanksgiving, and Christmas.

Website and Phone: www.usna.edu; (410) 263-6933.

Railroads

If your child, like mine, eats, sleeps, and breathes trains, I offer this advice: dog-ear this page and refer to it often. This is where Baltimoreans go to get their train fix.

Light Rail

From Baltimore, access to the more touristy excursion railroad lines requires a lengthy drive and often a substantial financial commitment. For a close-by and affordable alternative, try Baltimore's Light Rail system. The Light Rail is a unique and easy-to-use train system that will not only make for a fun ride, but also reveal to riders some of Baltimore's most interesting city and suburban communities. The rail system began operating in 1995 primarily as a commuter route, but railroad recreationists enjoy it as well.

The Light Rail runs along 30 miles of track, the major stretch being a straight shot through the city between its northern terminus in Hunt Valley and its southern terminus in Glen Burnie. Riders will view sights ranging from scenic to gritty—seeing the city inside out. To the north, the Light Rail passes behind some industrial parks, bends around the lovely Lake Roland, and cuts through attractive residential communities. The most fun stretch is through midtown, where the train passes many former mill buildings perched along Jones Falls. Through downtown, it runs along Howard Street, which, a century ago, was among the elite shopping and theater districts in the nation, but is now the recipient of urban renewal proposals. The Light Rail next runs alongside Oriole Park at Camden Yards and Ravens Stadium, passes over the Middle Branch of the Patapsco River, and winds through desolate terrain before emerging into communities to the south of the city. Spurs of the Light Rail system lead to Penn Station in downtown Baltimore and BWI Airport. Riders will be privy to sights not seen from a car.

The Light Rail is reasonably priced. A one-way ticket costs $1.35 per person, the same as a ride on a city bus or subway. A $3 day pass is good for unlimited rides on the Light Rail, city buses, and subway system, and a week's pass is $14. Seniors and the disabled ride one way for 45 cents. Two children under the age of 6 can ride free with each paying adult. Ticketing is done through a self-service vending machine at individual stops, so bring change. Tickets may or may not be checked at any time aboard the train, so hang on to your ticket until the final stop. Trains run about every 17 minutes, and the schedule can be found on the website listed below. It takes about 75 minutes for a train to navigate between its two terminuses.

Your best bet for finding parking is at the outermost stops. To the north, the largest lot is in Timonium, along Deereco Road near Landstreet Road, which offers over 800 parking spots. Parking is also available at the Hunt Valley Mall on Warren Road, at the Timonium Business Park on Greenspring Avenue, at the Timonium Mall off Ridgely Road, and on Falls Road near Railroad Avenue. Best access points to the south are in Glen Burnie at Baltimore Annapolis Boulevard near Dorsey Road, in North Linthicum at Koch and Camp Meade Roads, and at Patapsco Avenue near Denham Circle. City dwellers with cars can get the Light Rail at the Mt. Washington stop, which offers 75 parking spaces. Parking is free at most stops. A fun day is to park at the North Linthicum stop, ride to the northern terminus at Hunt Valley Mall, partake in ice cream at the Friendly's restaurant near the stop, and return home.

Hours: Mondays through Fridays from 6 a.m. to 11 p.m., Saturdays from 8 a.m. to 11 p.m., and Sundays and holidays from 11 a.m. to 7 p.m.

Website: www.mtamaryland.com/schedules/lightrail/light_rail_schedule.cfm.

MARC Trains

MARC (Maryland Rail Commuter) is a commuter train system that links Baltimore and Washington, D.C. Much like the Light Rail, it's a fun and easy way to stave off a train craving. What makes the MARC system so enticing is that it terminates at Union Station in Washington, D.C., which offers lots of sit-down restaurants and shops, and an expansive food court in the basement. It's also within walking distance of the Capitol, the National Postal Museum, and a children's museum. Riding the MARC train to D.C. with the kids makes for an enjoyable day and is not done enough by Baltimore residents.

Now the downside. MARC is first and foremost a commuter train. During rush hours it may be packed, with standing room only. Parking may be a problem at certain stations. Also, it does not run on weekends and runs on an abbreviated schedule on holidays. Pleasure-riding on the MARC system can be enjoyable if you figure out where to park and when to go.

The MARC system includes two lines through Baltimore—the Camden Line and the Penn Line. The Camden Line starts at Camden Station, in front of Oriole Park at Camden Yards, and runs to Union Station. It passes through lots of industrial areas, runs by the Laurel Park racetrack, slices through downtown Laurel, and runs beside Route 1 for a good length. The Camden Line utilizes a cargo train rail, and runs less frequently than the Penn Line. An upside of the Camden Line is that parking is easy to find at several stations; 1,000 spots are available at its origin at Camden Station, though there is a fee. Your best bet may be to drive to the Dorsey Station, which is off Route 100 between Interstate 95 and the Baltimore–Washington Parkway, where there are 800 free parking spaces.

The Penn Line originates north of Baltimore, in Perryville, and runs through the city en route to Union Station. This line is faster and runs more frequently than the Camden Line. It operates on Amtrak tracks, so delays tend to be minimal. The Penn Line runs through nice scenery north of Baltimore, including pretty crossings of the Gunpowder and Bush Rivers. Between Baltimore and D.C., it passes through some industrialized zones, but also crosses natural areas, including the Patuxent Wildlife Research Center. Numerous wetland bogs line the tracks and several beaver dams can be seen. Parking for the Penn Line can be difficult. Space can usually be found at a large pay lot at the BWI Airport Amtrak Station, which may be your safest bet. There are lots of parking spaces at the Halethorpe Station off Route 1 and the West Baltimore Station in the city, but, depending on the day, they fill quickly with commuters' cars. Limited parking is available at Penn Station in Baltimore. A good time to ride is on Fridays in the summer, when parking is easier to come by at these stations (the commuting suits are on vacation).

MARC train cars are generally clean, comfortable, and roomy. Many trains include double-decker cars, which offer a nice elevated view. The MARC trains run regularly on Mondays through Fridays from 5 a.m. to midnight. Tickets can be purchased at any train station with a ticket counter. The cost of a round-trip ticket between

Baltimore and D.C. varies depending on the station, but most run in the neighborhood of $10. Tickets purchased on the train include a $3 surcharge. There are no discounts for children.

Specific ticket prices and detailed train schedules can be found at MARC's website: www.mtamaryland.com/schedules/marc/marc_schedule.cfm. It also includes maps to the various rail stops, as well as parking information.

Steam Trains at Leakin Park

The steam trains at Leakin Park are one of Baltimore's more curious and little-known attractions. The Chesapeake and Allegheny Live Steamers Club, a group of train enthusiasts who build and operate large-scale model trains, over a decade ago struck a symbiotic deal with the city. In exchange for the use of 10 acres of Leakin Park to lay track and run its miniature trains, members must regularly provide the public with free rides. What resulted was one of Baltimore's most fun, family-friendly activities, which are mostly advertised by word-of-mouth.

The live steamers of Leakin Park run a two-mile loop, mostly across open field, but also through some shady areas. The trains come up to about the knee, which makes them particularly delightful to children who tend to be enthralled by anything in scale. The conductor straddles the locomotive like a horse, and passengers sit on flat cars or in open box cars, two or three to each car. The trains lumber along at about six miles per hour, a jogger's pace; that's the scale speed of a full-size train moving at about 48 miles per hour. Each miniature locomotive pulls five to ten passenger cars, begging the question: How can such a small engine lug such a hefty payload? Prospective riders may be interested in the seven-minute video on the club's website that shows a steamer operating.

The miniature trains operate on the second Sunday of each month, from April through November, from 11 a.m. to 3:30 p.m. They also run during certain special events, such as the Leakin Park Herb Festival, and during All Aboard Day at the B&O Museum in Baltimore.

Members of the Chesapeake and Allegheny Live Steamers Club are part of an obscure but highly committed and talented subculture of rail enthusiasts. Participants craft each train model by hand down to the most minute details. Some spend days on end in a machine shop molding rods, valves, and pistons and assembling the boiler. Trains actually run on small chunks of coal. Each train

▲ Riding the pint-sized steam trains at Leakin Park

takes years, and even decades, to build. Each finished project is a sublime work of art. Club members enjoy showing their engines to the public when the trains are running through Leakin Park. Most replicate actual historical trains from such lines as the Southern Pacific, Baltimore and Ohio, and Potomac Valley. Observing such elaborate train models is as much fun as riding them.

Location and Directions: Off Windsor Mill Road in Leakin Park. From the Interstate 695 beltway, take Exit 17, Security Boulevard, east toward the city. Continue on Security Boulevard for about two miles, and turn left onto Ingleside (Forest Park) Avenue. Proceed for about one-half mile and turn right onto Windsor Mill Road. In about one-third of a mile, turn right into the park through the eagle-topped gates.

Hours and Admission: Trains operate on the second Sunday of each month from April through November. A specific schedule is posted on the club's website. There is no admission charge to ride the trains.

Website and Phone: calslivesteam.org; (410) 448-0730.

Stewartstown Railroad

Located just over the Mason-Dixon Line in Pennsylvania, the Stewartstown Railroad is a quintessential small-town rail line that continues to offer short but fun passenger excursions. The train cars and station lack the bells-and-whistles glamour of other tourist rail lines, but is generally free of the suffocating crowds. The passenger cars are steel hulks unchanged from decades of use, and the cute, wood-and-brick station retains its well-worn slate roof. The train schedule is still scrawled on a slate board in a tiny waiting room. Such genuine authenticity and lack of pretense will appeal to some. Volunteers weigh heavily in the operation of this line.

The railroad runs on an intermittent schedule, so call before making the trek. As a general rule, it operates most Sundays during nice weather. Countryside Excursions run on certain Sundays from May through August. Fall Foliage Specials run on Saturdays and Sundays in October, and Autumn Rail Rambles operate on Sundays in November.

Stewartstown Railroad also operates a revolving assortment of special events. Trains run on Mother's Day (half-price fare for mom), Father's Day (same deal for dad), and the Sunday of Memorial Day weekend. There's a Children's Day special that involves the state police and a local fire department, and a special fall run to New Freedom. The North Pole Express runs on weekends in December leading up to Christmas. The Easter Bunny train takes kids to a pretty wooded site for an egg hunt. Another popular special event is the Country Buffet Breakfast Trains, where passengers disembark at New Freedom for a morning meal. Reservations are recommended. Admission varies depending on the event, but mostly tickets are $8 for adults and $4 for children. Some special events may be more pricey.

▲ All aboard at the Stewartstown Railroad

The trains are steel and very authentic, down to the velour seats and utilitarian decor. Hung on each car is a sheet describing its history. Our car was #1351, which was used to ferry troops during World War II between Indiantown Gap in Pennsylvania and Fort Dix in New Jersey. The sheet tells how it's identifiable as a troop car by the two-foot-long yellow stripe placed just below the train's number. A "Spitting Is Prohibited" sign from that era remains. The engine is diesel, so don't expect the billowing steam.

Excursions on the Stewartstown Railroad vary in time and distance. The longest trips are about 15 miles, running to New Freedom and back. Most excursions turn around before that point. The rail passes through downtown Stewartstown, winds along Route 851 for a while, and finally breaks free into some pretty farm country. It passes over an iron bridge that is registered as a historical site. The ride is slow, and a rail volunteer jumps out at road crossings to ensure safe passage. The Stewartstown Railroad was chartered in 1884 as "The Farmer's Railroad," being used primarily to transport crops and other commodities to various markets.

Patrons of this railroad should consider eating at the Station House II restaurant, which is a brief walk from the station and features two model trains circling the dining area at ceiling level. The restaurant specializes in comfort dishes ranging from grilled cheese to crab cakes to liver and onions.

Location and Directions: On Route 851 in Stewartstown. From Baltimore, take Interstate 83 north into Pennsylvania. Take Exit 1, Route 851, in Shrewsbury, Pennsylvania, and head east for four miles. The train station is to the left, and parking to the right.

Phone: 1-888-345-2936 or (717) 993-2936.

Strasburg Rail Road

Strasburg is to excursion railroading as Macy's is to retail shopping: The layout is top-notch, the trains exquisitely restored, and the fares reasonably priced given the high quality of service. The hour-or-so drive from Baltimore is worthwhile for a trip on the restoration of America's first short-line railroad.

A round-trip journey on the Strasburg Rail Road lasts about 45 minutes and covers nine miles. It passes through rich Lancaster County farmland, on the fringe of lovely Amish farms. In spring it's fun to watch the horse teams plowing fields. The train passes by the

Red Caboose Motel, a string of 39 authentic cabooses that have been converted to rooms and are available for rent. It's supposedly the only place in the world where one can sleep in a caboose (see the Road Trips chapter). Along the journey is a turkey farm, a historical graveyard, and the Amazing Maize Maze, a labyrinth carved into a cornfield. At one point the train stops so that passengers can listen to the haunting bellow of Ghost Locomotive #5, an experience my daughter talked about for weeks. The entire trip is accompanied by commentary that is insightful, historical, and at times humorous.

Taking the family for a ride on the Strasburg Rail Road costs about the same as taking them to a movie. Coach fare is $9 for adults, $4.50 for children 3-11, and free for children under 3. I recommend upgrading to the very elegant and precisely restored Henry K. Long lounge car, which is adorned with jade-colored stained-glass transoms and well-lacquered maple woodwork. The cost is only slightly higher at $11 for adults, $5.50 for children 3-11, and $1 for toddlers. Fare on the open-air car and dining car is the same as that on the lounge car. If you want to ride as the upper crust once did, splurge for the parlor car, which is not only the most splendidly restored car, but also comes with sweets and beverages. The fare is $13 for adults, $9.50 for children 3-11, and $4 for the little ones. A one-day pass for unlimited rides in coach costs $18 per person, regardless of age.

A tiny, touristy village has sprung up around the railroad terminal. The Rail Road Toy Store has Thomas the Tank Engine paraphernalia oozing from the door. The Railroad Store next door hawks apparel and all sorts of train trinkets and toys. The Railroad Gift Shop offers much the same, and then some (train piñatas, train

▲ The Strasburg Rail Road ready to roll

▲ The Strasburg Rail Road rolls into the station

baking tins, train lamps). True rail enthusiasts will enjoy browsing the Second Floor Bookstore. A cafeteria-style restaurant is heavy on Pennsylvania Dutch cuisine, and a fudge shop also serves tasty lemonade. The Railroad Museum of Pennsylvania, one of the country's best, is located across the street, and the National Toy Train Museum is just down the road. If your choo-choo-centric child does not get a train fix here, seek help.

A fun dining option is to pack a lunch and get off at the railroad's picnic grove located along the route. Picnickers can then pick up another train back. Be sure not to miss the last train home, however. Strasburg Rail Road hosts an assortment of special events geared for kids, many of which involve Thomas the Tank Engine.

Location and Directions: On Route 741, about one and a half miles east of Strasburg, in Lancaster County, Pennsylvania. From Baltimore, take Interstate 95 north. In Perry Hall, take Route 222 north into Pennsylvania. Take Route 741 east and follow through Strasburg to the rail yard. The trip is about 90 minutes from downtown Baltimore.

Hours: The train schedule varies greatly depending on day of the week and month of the year. Check Strasburg's website for up-to-date information. In general, the train runs year-round in nice weather and on weekends through winter.

Website and Phone: www.strasburgrailroad.com; (717) 687-7522.

◀ Impeccably restored coach cars on the Strasburg Rail Road

Western Maryland Scenic Railroad

Most tourist trains in the Baltimore area take riders on short romps through bucolic countryside and farmland. If it's a lengthier mountain excursion you desire, head to Cumberland for the Western Maryland Scenic Railroad, or Mountain Thunder, as it is nicknamed. This attraction evokes an era when railroads were the primary mechanical means of travel and were called upon to scale steep hillsides, tunnel through mountains, and cross rivers on marvelous iron bridges. The scenery along this rail line is pleasing, if somewhat ornery, and the route bisects some of the state's most historical terrain. As its website proclaims, "More than three hundred years of American history are tied together by a ribbon of steel that thrills riders of all ages."

The Western Maryland Scenic Railroad traces a scribble between Cumberland and Frostburg. The 32-mile round trip lasts about three hours, including a stop-over in Frostburg. From Cumberland, the train slices through the Cumberland Narrows, a steep-walled, 1,000-foot-high mountain gap known as the "Gateway to the West." It then crosses Wills Creek over an iron truss bridge, and climbs steeply into the guts of the Allegheny Mountains. Keep an eye out for Cumberland Bone Cave, where fossils of the Pleistocene cave bear, saber-tooth cat, and extinct species of wolverines and elephants were found.

The train negotiates Helmstetter's Horseshoe Curve and passes through Brush Tunnel, which arcs for about one-quarter mile below Piney Mountain. Steep 2.8-percent grades through this area will get the children chanting "I think I can!" Riders will glimpse the Mt. Savage Mansion, once the grand residence of Scotsman Andrew Ramsay, an industrialist known for his production of ceramic glazed brick. Built in 1842, this lovely stone manor house replicates the Craig Castle in Scotland, and now operates as a bed and breakfast.

The train depot at Frostburg has been restored, and be sure to check out the Thrasher Carriage Museum, which displays a collection of over 50 horse-drawn carriages. There's also a restaurant in the depot complex. Don't let the kids miss the railroad turntable, which reverses the engine for the ride home.

Strings of trains on the Western Maryland Scenic Railroad are pulled by either diesel or steam engines. From May 1 to September 29, diesel engines run on Wednesdays and Thursdays, and steam engines on Fridays though Sundays. From October 2 to October 27, diesel engines work from Mondays to Wednesdays, and steam engines from Thursdays through Sundays. From November 2 to December 13, steam engines run on Saturdays and Sundays. The steam engine employed by the railroad was built in 1916 and was used to haul freight around Michigan's upper peninsula. The train schedule may unexpectedly change, so ascertain first by calling.

Generally, the Western Maryland Scenic Railroad operates from May through summer, and then intermittently through autumn and early winter. It's a great way to see fall foliage. The railway offers charter trips and many special events on holidays (see website for listing). Parents should look into the trips that include gourmet cooks aboard preparing treats for the riders. One particularly offbeat trip includes the re-enactment of a train robbery. There is a gift shop on the premises.

Location and Directions: At 13 Canal Street in Cumberland. From Baltimore, take Interstate 70 west, and continue on Interstate 68 west. Take Exit 43C into downtown Cumberland. At the stop sign, make a left and continue straight ahead, through a light, into the parking lot.

Hours and Admission: The trains operate on Wednesdays through Sundays from May 1 to September 9, daily from October 2 to October 27, and on Saturdays and Sundays from November 2 to December 13. Call ahead to determine whether scheduled trains have diesel or steam engines. Daily departure time is 11:30 a.m. Special trains may depart at other times. Standard fare is $19 per adult, $10 for children 12 and under, and $17 for seniors 60 or older. First-class fare is $35 per adult, $15 for children 12 and under, and $33 for seniors 60 or older. Children under 2 years of age ride free when not occupying a seat, except in the dining car. Fare is higher for certain special events.

Website and Phone: www.wmsr.com; 1-800-872-4650.

Fifteen Unique Places to Hold a Birthday Party.

1. Earth Treks Climbing Center, Columbia (410-872-0060)
2. Aboard the pontoon boat at Piney Run Reservoir (410-795-5165)
3. Babe Ruth Birthplace and Museum, Baltimore (410-727-1539)
4. Bear Branch Nature Center, Westminster (410-848-2517)
5. Barbie's Dress Up at Savage Mill, Savage (410-724-0060)
6. Northwest Ice Rink, Baltimore (410-433-4970)
7. B&O Railroad Museum, Baltimore (410-752-2490)
8. Heritage Tea Room, Havre de Grace (410-942-0290)
9. Stewartstown Railroad, Stewartstown, PA (1-888-345-2936)
10. Safari Party, Timonium (410-560-1094)
11. Carroll Gymnastics, Westminster (410-635-2322)
12. Cathy's Creative Kids Corner, Owings Mill (410-581-1607)
13. ExploraWorld, Columbia (410-772-1540)
14. Young Artists Theater, Scaggsville (301-604-2844)
15. Sports, Cockeysville (410-666-2227)

Restaurants

Whether a restaurant is child-friendly generally depends more on the temperament of the child than the atmosphere of the restaurant. My well-heeled five-year-old, for instance, would comfortably melt into the crowd at the most highfalutin steak house without raising an eyebrow, whereas my three-year-old, who makes more commotion than a caged spider monkey, can turn even lunch at McDonald's into a frustrating ordeal. That said, certain restaurants make a concerted effort to present themselves as being family-friendly, beyond merely setting out a bucket of crayons. And other local eateries are so quintessentially Baltimore, they deserve a visit just for the experience. Here are some recommended ones.

Ashland Café

The perennially jam-packed parking lot at Ashland Café should hint at what diners may find inside. The floor is energetic and rambunctious, the clientele friendly, and the food tasty. The aroma of chicken in the fryer will trick your salivary glands into a Pavlovian drool. It's a great place for families with rowdy kids to dine, as they will go practically unnoticed in the melee. A scale-model train that interminably circles a track hung from the ceiling will have a calming effect on the kids, and the train posters and pictures slung across the walls are fun to look at. The train motif derives from the café's is location near the southern terminus of the Northern Central Railroad, a former line connecting Baltimore with York, Pennsylvania. The rail line is now a popular rails-to-trails linear recreation park.

Ashland Café is open only for breakfasts and lunches. The menu is uncommonly extensive. The breakfast menu carries the usual complement of egg and pancake dishes, with omelets running from $4.05 to $5.85. Those eating lunch have a wide choice of sand-wiches, salads, pasta, or entrees. The pride of the café is its fried chicken, which can be had for $2.99 for a two-piece meal with fries and slaw, or $3.99 for a three-piece meal. A range of Greek special-ties is available including spinach pie, Greek-style pork chops, and a sampler plate. Children's entrees are available for $3.99 a pop. Chil-dren's meals are diner-style, with such entrees as meatloaf and spaghetti. The café does a healthy take-out business, with fried chicken being shipped out by the bucket.

Location and Directions: At 10810 York Road, in Cockeysville. From Baltimore, take Interstate 83 north from the beltway. Take Exit 18, Warren Road, and follow it east less than one mile to York Road. Turn left onto York Road and continue for about one-half mile. The café is on the left, at York Road's intersection with Cock-eysville Road.

Hours: Mondays from 5 a.m. to 4 p.m., Tuesdays through Satur-days from 4 a.m. to 4 p.m., and Sundays from 6 a.m. to 3 p.m.

Phone: (410) 666-3838.

Café Hon

Café Hon is an atmospheric diner tucked away in the up-and-com-ing neighborhood of Hampden, in North Baltimore. The café wears its infatuation for Baltimore on its sleeve, and the city reciprocates with a love affair that has been going on for over 10 years. Café Hon regularly garners "Best of Baltimore" awards, including Best Brunch, Best Breakfast, and Best Comfort Food. But what makes Café Hon so family-friendly is its low-key and retro air. Kids will experience how you dined as a child.

Food at Café Hon is homespun and tasty. Meatloaf, smoked ham, and roast beef are like Ma used to make. Unique fare, such as sour beef, hummus on pita, and Mexican salads, is available for more diverse palates. Dinner entrees run between $10 and $15, and a wide selection of salads is available in the $5 to $8 range. Don't miss a plate of fresh-cut french fries with homemade gravy for $4.25. Vege-tarians should find the black-bean burger and other specialties to their liking. Don't miss the glass-front, homemade pie display.

Café Hon offers a nice kids' menu that goes beyond the tired hot dog/chicken finger routine. A children's meatloaf platter with mashed potatoes and vegetable is available for $5.25, a pork chop platter for

$5.50, and pasta and salad for $4.95. These are only available after 4 p.m. Children's lunchtime platters include tuna or a cheese sandwich. Kids' breakfasts are also available. Just inside the entrance to the café is a table stacked high with children's books and other diversions.

When finished dining, take a moment to poke around in Hampden, an off-beat community difficult to categorize. Imagine a gritty, blue-collar mill town and chic urban neighborhood tussling to a draw. Café Hon is located on 36th Street, the main drag of town, amidst an eclectic array of pubs, galleries, and bric-a-brac shops. Among the notable are Fat Elvis, an antiques and collectibles shop, and Galvanize, a vintage clothing store (Julia Roberts purchased a few faux furs here).

Location and Directions: At 1002 West 36th Street, in Hampden. From downtown Baltimore, take Interstate 83 north. Take Exit 8A, Falls Road, and continue to the first traffic light. Turn right onto 36th Street and continue for about two blocks. Café Hon is on the left. On-street meter parking is available, or you can access a lot behind Café Hon via an alley beside Provident Bank.

Hours: Mondays through Thursdays from 7 a.m. to 9 p.m., Fridays from 7 a.m. to 10 p.m., Saturdays from 9 a.m. to 10 p.m., and Sundays from 9 a.m. to 8 p.m.

Website and Phone: www.cafehon.com; (410) 243-1230.

Chuck E. Cheese's

With a groan I mention Chuck E. Cheese's, as I've wasted many a sunny Saturday afternoon there at kids' parties. But face facts: tots and toddlers adore this place. Chuck E. Cheese's is a video arcade/playground/amusement center that also happens to serve food. Taking kids here on a rainy day will certainly put you in their good graces. Be forewarned, however, that the atmosphere is pure carnival. The floor reverberates from the collective stampede of dozens of teeny revelers, and the acoustical assault can be deafening.

Chuck E. Cheese's serves mostly pizza, with a large cheese setting you back $13.99 and a supreme $18.99. It also offers a few sandwiches in the $5 range. A $4.69 all-you-can-eat salad bar will appeal to those clamoring for healthy morsels. The food is decent, but will not make you forget that week in Tuscany.

But don't come for the food; visit for the games. They are numerous and, based on observations, as popular with parents as they are with children. Video games and bouncy rides dominate. Older kids and parents will gravitate to Skee-ball and the basketball shoot. Youngsters will be drawn to the rather large Habi-trail configuration of tubes and slides that stretches to the ceiling. Games operate on tokens, and some offer winners tickets that can be redeemed for prizes. Trying to win a Nerf hoops set (1,500 tickets) or a giant slinky (6,000 tickets), however, can be a wallet-draining experience. Remind your kids that Chuck E. Cheese's gives out free tokens for good report cards.

A stage full of electronic animatrons will occasionally activate and perform to the delight of the kids. Chuck E. Cheese himself has been known to make an appearance, though he once scared the bejesus out of my daughter when she was an infant.

Locations: Chuck E. Cheese's has several locations in the Baltimore area: 937 Fairlawn Avenue in Laurel (301-498-7100), 5 Bel Air South Parkway in Bel Air (410-515-0207), 6637 Ritchie Highway in Glen Burnie (410-761-3131), 5912 Baltimore National Pike in Catonsville (410-719-8850), 809 Goucher Boulevard in Towson (410-823-1756), 8354 Eastern Avenue in Dundalk (410-288-9393), and 2333 Forest Drive in Annapolis (410-266-1438). Call for directions and hours.

Website: www.chuckecheese.com

Crab Houses

Mention Baltimore cuisine and steamed blue crabs come immediately to mind. Eating at a crab house is a fun and unusual experience that will appeal to most kids. Tables are spread with thick, brown paper, and mallets and knives are placed alongside mountains of paper towels and napkins. Bibs are handed out, and then buckets of steamed blue crabs are disgorged onto the table. Then begins the commotion: hands reaching and ripping, mallets pounding. Children will probably enjoy bludgeoning the crustaceans with their mallets more than actually eating the tasty morsels of crab meat. Crab houses are often loud and festive, so kids should fit right into the fray. They will also love the side dishes, like corn on the cob and french fries.

Here is a sampling of recommended crab houses in and around Baltimore: Al's Seafood Restaurant, at 1551 Eastern Boulevard, in Essex; Bo Brooks Crab House, at 2701 Boston Street, in the Canton neighborhood; Bohager's, at 701 East Eden Street, in Fells Point; Carney Crab House, at 2014 East Joppa Road, in Parkville; Costa's

Inn, at 4100 North Point Boulevard, in Dundalk; Gunnings, at 3901 South Hanover Street, in the Brooklyn neighborhood; Mike's Restaurant and Crab House, at 3030 Old Riva Road, in Annapolis; and Obrycki's, at 1727 East Pratt Street, in Fells Point. A comprehensive list is provided at www.blue-crab.org/crabhouses. htm.

ESPN Zone

The ESPN Zone is categorized as a restaurant since it serves food, but I could easily have put it in the Fun and Games chapter. It's where both children and adults go for frivolous play, and perhaps to grab a bite. A vast array of electronic and virtual games is offered. In MoCap Boxing, you virtually fight against an opposing pugilist. There is a four-person NASCAR game, a basketball free-throw challenge, and a baseball-batting attraction. Other popular games include hockey, shooting, and bowling. Challenge a friend at the virtual climbing game. More traditional video games are numerous as well. While the kids play, parents can sneak over to the bank of lounge chairs and enjoy the wall of televisions, or just browse through the sports memorabilia.

The food at the ESPN Zone is decent, and the offerings extend well beyond "jock fare." There's an assortment of sandwiches and pasta entrees for about $10 each. Appetizers cost about $8. Try a plate of sliders, which are miniature burgers. The Maryland crab soup will

▲ ESPN Zone and Hard Rock Café at the Inner Harbor

only set you back $4.99. Vegetarians will appreciate their options, such as the tomato, mozzarella, and red onion salad, which costs $7.29. A pretty standard children's menu is also available. Diners should be aware that they will be besieged by more televisions than at Circuit City, with each playing, you guessed it, soap operas. I mean, sports.

It's fun to watch radio sports talk shows that often broadcast from the ESPN Zone, like WJFK's *Those Sports Guys* and ESPN radio's *Weekend Game Day* with Mel Kiper, Jr., and Andy Pollin.

Location: 601 East Pratt Street, in the north section of the Power Plant building.

Hours: Mondays through Thursdays from 11:30 a.m. to midnight, Fridays from 11:30 a.m. to 1 a.m., Saturdays from 11 a.m. to 1 a.m.; and Sundays from 11 a.m. to midnight.

Website and Phone: espn.go.com/espninc/zone; (410) 685-3776.

Friendly Farm Restaurant

Friendly Farm is the type of restaurant that comes to mind when one speaks of a "dining experience," and the experience is one well-suited for kids. First there's the location. The restaurant is situated on a picturesque farm in northern Baltimore County. The farmhouse and surrounding outbuildings are neatly maintained and enveloped by about 200 acres, many well manicured. Three ponds are strung together by a tiny brook. Bring a baseball or frisbee in case there is a wait or for post-dinner entertainment.

Kids will also enjoy the dining format. Food at Friendly Farm is served family-style. Patrons order a main entree at a booth in the restaurant's foyer and then sit in a cavernous dining room with picture windows offering sweeping views of the countryside. The main course is served to individual diners, but all side dishes are served in large bowls to be shared with all.

Food at Friendly Farm is grandma-caliber. Main dishes include fried chicken ($10.95), grilled ham ($13.50), broiled pork chops ($13.95), filet mignon ($16.50), fried oysters ($18.95), or a pair of huge crabcakes ($25.95). Side dishes include forgotten treats such as apple butter, cottage cheese, cole slaw, biscuits, and an assortment of vegetables and potatoes. Dessert and beverages are included in the meal cost. Children 3-10 years old have a choice of several entrees for $6.25, and those 1-2 years pay only $1.50. The place fills to the gills on Sundays, so plan on arriving before noon.

▲ Bucolic setting of Friendly Farm Restaurant

Baked goods like pecan pie and cinnamon bread are for sale in the lobby, and there is a craft-intensive gift ship on the premises.

Location and Directions: At 17434 Foreston Road, in Upperco. From Baltimore, take Interstate 83 north. In Hereford, take Exit 27, Route 137, and follow it west. Continue on Route 137 for about five miles. Turn right onto Foreston Road. Friendly Farm is on the left.

Hours: Daily from noon to 8 p.m., except over the Christmas holidays.

Phone: (410) 239-7400.

Hard Rock Café

The Hard Rock Café is the kind of place where even Elvis would have a "rockin' good time," so imagine what a blast it would be for your kids. Music memorabilia—on the walls, hanging from the rafters, squeezed into every nook and cranny—range from the interesting (Blondie's handwritten lyrics for her song "Rapture"), to the silly (Elvis's marching-band costume from the 1966 movie *Frankie and Johnny*), to the perverse (Madonna's brassiere), to the mundane (a ceramic plate painted by Pat Benatar), to the profound (Keith Richards's light-brown Gibson guitar). Hanging around are other guitars played by Joan Jett and members of Radiohead, the Sex Pistols, and the Red Hot Chili Peppers. Billy Idol fans will love his red suit with velcro closures that he wore on *The Tonight Show with Jay Leno*. Parents will especially enjoy the displays, since most are from their generation.

But enough about music; let's talk food. Appetizers at the café run from $5.99 (hickory-smoked chicken and spinach dip) to $13.99 (an artery-gagging combination of wings, onion rings, and potato skins). Burger prices vary according to ingredients, but all run about $8 with fries. Other sandwiches are also available. Grilled fajitas are popular here, and the famous barbeque ribs will set you back $14.99. Kiddies 10 and under can choose from a children's menu, where all items are a set price of $5.99. Entrees include standard kid's fare—cheeseburger, pizza, and macaroni and cheese.

Expect to be sweet-talked into buying your kids a Hard Rock Café T-shirt from the apparel store. Kids' shirts range from $12 to $18. Adult shirts start at $18.99. Other franchise apparel for sale includes hats, jackets, and fanny packs.

Guitar enthusiasts may notice that the 68-foot-tall, neon-red guitar atop the Power Plant, signaling the Hard Rock Café, is a McCarty model, and not the Fender or Gibson that graces most other Hard Rock Cafés.

Location: 601 East Pratt Street, in the south section of the Power Plant building.

Hours: Dining hours are daily from 11:30 a.m. to 1 a.m. Merchandise hours are daily from 10 a.m. to 11 p.m.

Website and Phone: www.hardrock.com; (410) 347-7625.

Matthew's Pizza

In this day and age when franchise pizzerias are blanketing America with pre-fabbed crusts and can-ripened tomato sauce, discovering an Old World pizzeria such as Matthew's Pizza is a find to take advantage of. Matthew's is a rowhouse-thin, hole-in-the-wall establishment on Eastern Avenue, in Highlandtown. It virtually goes unnoticed to the casual passerby. But ever since it opened in 1943 as the city's first pizzeria, locals have been flocking here in droves. Not only does Matthew's sling the best pizza pie in town, but it also offers quick and friendly service, and prices that are roll-back cheap.

The dining room is no-frills and very suitable to children. Spread about are a handful of tables, each topped with the requisite red-and-white-checked tablecloth. Walls are filled with "Best of" certificates and framed articles that mention the restaurant. An upright cooler offers Stewart's root beer, a special treat for kids. This is the type of restaurant that harks back to my childhood.

The food at Matthew's is first-rate. The pizzeria specializes in thick-crust pies. Basic no-cheese pies run $4.50 for a small and $4.95 for a large. Supremes cost $8.95 and $9.50, respectively. There are always pizza specials involving such tasty delicacies as portobello mushrooms and roasted peppers. The house salad is highly recommended and large enough for two. I find the spaghetti dinner as tasty as the pizza; it comes with a zesty marinara sauce ($4.95), meat sauce ($5.95), or shrimp ($6.95). Be decadent and wrap up the meal with an espresso or famous Vaccaro's cannoli. On the way out, grab a frozen Matthew's pizza to heat up later in the week. As an aside, Bob Dylan once bought $130 worth of pies from Matthew's for his band and crew.

Location and Directions: At 3131 Eastern Avenue, in the Highlandtown neighborhood of East Baltimore. From downtown, take Pratt Street east. Just past the Inner Harbor, go right onto President Street, and then left onto Eastern Avenue. Follow Eastern Avenue for one block past Patterson Park. Matthew's Pizza is on the right.

Hours: Mondays through Thursdays from 11 a.m. to 10 p.m., Saturdays from 11 a.m. to 11 p.m., and Sundays from noon to 8 p.m.

Phone: (410) 276-8755.

Papermoon Diner

The Papermoon Diner's website proclaims that its mission is to remind everyone how important it is to impulsively break out and giggle once in a while. From the minute you pull up to the curb of this Johns Hopkins University student hangout, the fun begins. The exterior is painted in a pleasing spectrum of bright hues. Offbeat statuary peek out at guests from behind shrubbery in whimsical fashion. Spread about are bathtubs, toilets, and sinks filled with plants and colorful aquarium gravel. A bronze torso emerges from a bathroom appliance.

The interior motif is equally funky. The main counter area has been invaded by literally thousands of toys. Action figures and Barbies cling to the walls and hang from the ceiling. Spider Man greets entering patrons, and Pez dispensers line several shelves. Tonka trucks hang from the ceiling and metal lunchboxes dangle from a light fixture. Naked mannequins, most armless, watch your every bite. A lava lamp injects that last iota of ambience. If you're eating at the counter, and you get this creepy feeling that Buzz Lightyear is breathing down your neck, you're probably right.

Besides the counter area, the Papermoon Diner has two adjoining rooms bearing more conservative, but equally interesting, decor. The food is tasty and the prices are reasonable. A basic grilled cheese with fries runs $5. The California Dream (avocado, basil, tomato, and cheese on tortilla) costs $9. Their garden veggie burger is referred to as the Weed Burger. Entrees run up to about $10, and include Nanner's spaghetti and vegetarian lasagna. The café also does a hefty breakfast business and offers interesting, non-traditional fare. A host of omelet options includes one filled with spinach, cheese, and portobello ($7), and another filled with grilled chicken breast, broccoli, and cheddar ($7).

Outdoor seating is available in nice weather, and on busy evenings expect a wait. The diner is a short walk from the Baltimore Museum of Art. Also, keep in mind that, despite all the alluring toys, this is not a children's diner per se, and toys are not to be played with. But, boy, will they tantalize.

Location and Directions: At 227 West 29th Street, southwest of the Johns Hopkins University campus. From downtown, take Charles Street north. Turn left onto 29th Street and continue for three blocks. The diner is just past Howard Street on the left.

Hours: Open 24 hours a day, seven days a week.

Website and Phone: www.charm.net/~diner; (410) 889-4444.

Rainforest Café

"Your adventure is about to begin," proclaims a mysterious voice over the loudspeaker calling a waiting party to its table. A khaki-garbed tour guide will greet and seat you, another khaki-garbed safari guide will take your order, a trailblazer will prepare your meal with help from a navigator assistant, and the safari assistant will clear your table. On your way out, a pathfinder will sell you apparel from the retail village.

Such is the modus operandi of one of Baltimore's most popular restaurants, where fun is treated as a requisite and not a personal choice. The Rainforest Café is an over-the-top, jungle-based theme restaurant that kids will certainly enjoy and parents may or may not, depending on how they feel about chain restaurants and crowds. The decor is lavishly faux Amazonian, with plastic plants cascading down the walls, piped-in sounds, and a very cool marine fishtank swarming with resplendent triggerfish, clownfish, bannerfish, and tang. A mechanical alligator lurks in a wishing pond, and a rainbow is projected on a leafy wall. If nothing else, the motif will surely captivate your kids.

The food at Rainforest Café is standard theme-restaurant fare. Appetizers range from about $7 to $13. Entrees are in the $10 to $18 neighborhood, with pasta dishes dominating the low end. There are lots of sandwiches and tasty desserts. They have a nice children's menu that offers a choice of pizza, burger, hot dog, or chicken fingers for $5.99, which includes drinks and fries. Kiddie desserts run $1.49 and yummy fruit smoothies are also available. The Magic Mushroom Bar offers alcoholic beverages and fresh-squeezed juices.

The Rainforest Café separates itself from other theme joints in one way: it's altruistic in both dollars and spirit. The corporation donates funds to rainforest preservation projects, and educates children in topics dealing with our natural environment. Menus have science lessons and the aquarium has interpretive signs. It also offers educational tours. That said, the Rainforest Café includes a massive retail store through which one must navigate to enter or leave the dining area. Besides the requisite apparel, you'll find mounds of toys, games, and other trinkets that are earth-themed.

Crowds prevail at the Rainforest Café and reservations are accepted and highly encouraged. One rainy Saturday afternoon I was looking down the barrel-end of a three-hour wait (no, I did not wait).

Location and Directions: In the Towson Town Center mall, at 825 Dulaney Valley Road. From the Interstate 695 beltway, take Exit 27A, Dulaney Valley Road, heading south. The mall is just ahead, on the left. The Rainforest Café is located on the second floor, near parking deck A. The restaurant is closed on Thanksgiving and Christmas.

Hours: Daily from 11 a.m. to 9 p.m.

Website and Phone: www.rainforestcafe.com; (410) 321-0300.

Snoasis

Summer in Baltimore unofficially commences when the ubiquitous snowball stands open for business. These treats of shaved ice and flavored syrup are catnip to the kids, not to mention a culinary respite from the oppressive heat. The most flavorful snowballs in the city are served at Snoasis, a tiny snack eatery in South Baltimore, near the Southside Marketplace. Snowballs here have ice shaved a bit finer, sweetness doused a bit thicker, and offbeat flavors not found elsewhere.

Snoasis offers an assortment of traditional flavors such as watermelon, root beer, orange, and scary-looking iridescent blue skylite. Prices for these flavors range from $1.10 for the small to $2.10 for the jumbo. Most patrons of Snoasis, however, splurge on a tasty premium flavor, which includes an injection of a special cream concoction. Crowd favorites are the cookie dough, dreamsicle, strawberry colada, almond joy, mocha cappuccino, and strawberry daiquiri flavors. My personal favorite is the tootsie roll, a mouthwatering combination of chocolate and lemon that tastes uncannily like the actual candy. Premium snowballs range from $1.50 to $2.50. Add a dollop of marshmallow for 40 cents, or a scoop of ice cream for 75 cents. Snoasis also offers gelati for those with more Italian taste buds. Outdoor deck seating is available, and next door is a nice Middle Eastern take-out restaurant.

The Snoasis in South Baltimore is not affiliated with the two Snoasis snowball stands located north of the city, which I also highly recommend (and which regularly garner "Best Snowball" honors in local publications). Those stands are at 30 East Padonia Road, in Timonium, and at the intersection of Joppa and Falls Roads, in Lutherville.

Location and Directions: At 1420 Lawrence Street, in South Baltimore. From downtown, take Light Street and turn left onto Key Highway just past the Inner Harbor. Follow Key Highway for about one mile, and turn right onto Lawrence Street. Snoasis is immediately to the left.

Hours: Daily, from noon to 10 p.m., when the weather is conducive to snowball-eating.

Phone: (410) 752-8588.

Sorrento's Main Street Station

Sorrento's in Ellicott City makes a nice lunchtime destination for train-crazed children. The facade is adorned with a large and attention-grabbing illuminated train. Walls of the restaurant are slung with train posters and murals of local scenery. But the real reasons children adore this place are the two scale-model trains that continually circle the dining area on tracks suspended from the ceiling. Even the rowdiest of children will be pleasantly distracted.

The food at Sorrento's is reasonable and affordable. The pizza is decent, with a large cheese pie setting you back only about $7. There's a wide selection of sandwiches and the ice cream desserts are a treat. Favorites are the real ice cream milk shakes and the root beer floats with whipped cream. The tabletops are marble, and the booths are extra spacious for restless kids to move around in.

Sorrento's is located on Main Street in Ellicott City, which is home to American railroading. Within walking distance is the B&O Railroad Station Museum, which occupies what was the first railroad station in the country. (This museum should not be confused with the much larger B&O Railroad Museum, located in downtown Baltimore.) Also near the restaurant are scads of antique shops and coffee shops. Don't miss stopping by Mumbles and Squeaks Toy Gallery, located nearby at 8133 Main Street, which offers a wide selection of unusual toys including lots of Thomas the Tank Engine paraphernalia.

Location and Directions: At 8167 Main Street (Frederick Road) in Ellicott City. From the Interstate 695 beltway, take Exit 13, Frederick Road, heading west (outside the beltway) . Continue for about five miles into Ellicott City. The restaurant is halfway through town on the left. On-street parking may be difficult to obtain, so I suggest parking in the lot on Oella Avenue just before town. Turn right onto Oella Avenue just before crossing over the Patapsco River, and the parking lot is about 100 yards on the right.

Hours: Sundays through Thursdays from 11 a.m. to 9 p.m. Fridays and Saturdays from 11 a.m. to 11 p.m.

Phone: (410) 465-1001.

Spoons Coffeehouse and Roastery

With their relaxed atmosphere and inexpensive menu items, coffee shops are great places to hang out with the kids. Spoons, tucked away in a Federal Hill alley, is on this list on behalf of all coffee shops across the city. But Spoons goes the extra distance to entice families. It offers a large bookshelf stacked high with books and games (including Battleship!), a shelf full of children's books, and even a special table for the kiddies. Families are a common sight at this low-key eatery.

Spoons is quintessentially Baltimore, set in a rowhouse in a charming, historic district. Its exposed brick walls are laden with avant-garde art, and the wood floors are well-trodden. There's a

◄ Spoons Coffeehouse and Roastery, hidden in the Federal Hill neighborhood

lounge area with couches and National Public Radio usually emanates from speakers.

The menu of drinks and food at Spoons is unusually varied. The typical roster of lattes, mochas, and café au laits is available, but things get more decadent. Try the Grande Milky Way, an exuberant mixture of espresso, chocolate, caramel, steamed milk, and whipped cream ($3.90). Kids will suck down the Smoothies with reckless abandon. I recommend the Berry Mango Freeze, a concoction of raspberry, strawberry, and mango ($3.20 for the small, and $3.50 for the large). The coffee of the day ($1.50 regular, $1.70 grande) usually comes from far-flung locales like Burundi, Costa Rica, or Papua New Guinea. Spoons offers an extensive breakfast menu, and has lite-fare sandwiches for lunch and dinner. Its tuna salad was voted best in the city. Spoons also does a healthy take-out business, and sells unusually flavored coffee beans in bulk.

Location and Directions: At 24 East Cross Street, adjacent to the Cross Street Market. From downtown, take Light Street south into the Federal Hill neighborhood. Just before Cross Street Market, turn right onto Cross Street. Spoons is on the right.

Hours: Sundays through Tuesdays from 7 a.m. to 5 p.m., Wednesdays and Thursdays from 7 a.m. to 10 p.m., and Fridays and Saturdays from 7 a.m. to 11 p.m.

Phone: (410) 539-6751.

Road Trips

Guidebooks such as *The Maryland One-Day Trip Book* by Jane Ockershausen and *Shifra Stein's Day Trips from Baltimore: Getaways Less Than Two Hours Away* by Gwyn Walcoff, Bob Willis, and Heidi Willis detail hundreds of deserving road trips Baltimore-area residents may want to consider. Here are eight that my kids particularly enjoy.

Antietam National Battlefield

Gettysburg offers a stunning battlefield with hundreds of monuments, well-developed tourist attractions, and a charming downtown shopping area. The downside to Gettysburg is the oppressive throngs of visiting scout troops, church groups, and school classes that leave little breathing room in facilities. Those seeking a less congested, but equally significant, Civil War battlefield should head to Sharpsburg, in Washington County, where the Antietam National Battlefield sprawls across a lovely tapestry of woods and pastureland.

Antietam was the site of the Civil War's bloodiest battle. On September 18, 1862, over 100,000 combined Union and Confederate soldiers clashed, with 23,000 left dead or wounded. By contrast, D-Day saw only one-ninth the number of casualties. Though the battle was officially fought to a draw, it greatly benefitted the Union side, which pushed Confederate soldiers back to Virginia. This landmark event also influenced Abraham Lincoln to issue his Emancipation Proclamation, which made freeing slaves a wartime mission for the Union.

Today the battlefield grounds are beautiful and pristine. First-time visitors will be surprised at how expansive the battleground is, and how tastefully it is preserved and remembered. Distributed

▲ Antietam National Battlefield

across 3,300 acres are 500 cannons, 300 military tablets, and 105 monuments. Begin your Antietam visit at the Visitor Center. Pamphlets and maps can be found at the information desk. Rangers here were particularly friendly and helpful. Downstairs is a small but tidy museum devoted to artifacts from the battle, such as rifles, sewing kits, and Bibles. Documentary films are shown regularly in a nice-sized theater. Some stately monuments are located within walking distance of the Visitor Center and are worth a visit.

There are several ways to explore the actual battleground. Most visitors drive the 8.5-mile circuit, stopping at 11 pull-offs for history lessons. On nice days, a swarm of bikers compete with cars for road space, and some intrepid folks even hike all or part of the route. An interpretive route map is available at the visitor center, and audiotapes can also be rented. Signage along the route may provide enough battle information for some. Along the circuit is a pretty stone observation tower with red terra-cotta roof, built in 1896 by the War Department, which puts visitors on eye-level with the hawks and vultures soaring about. Families planning to spend lots of time outdoors may want to bring butterfly nets or a Frisbee to take advantage of the supremely lovely surroundings.

A very appropriate time to visit Antietam National Battlefield is on the evening of the first Saturday in December. Volunteers light 23,000 luminary candles—one for each battle casualty—and disperse them across the battlefield. The ravages of the Civil War could not be put into a more moving perspective.

Location and Directions: Near Sharpsburg, in Washington County. From Baltimore, take Interstate 70 west. Take Exit 29, Route 65, south, and continue for about 10 miles. Follow signs to the Visitor Center.

Hours and Admission: The Visitor Center is open year-round from 8:30 a.m. to 5 p.m. (to 6 p.m. in summer months). It's closed on New Year's Day, Thanksgiving, and Christmas. Admission to the battlefield is $3 per person or $5 per family. Kids under 6 are free.

Website and Phone: www.nps.gov/anti; (301) 432-5124.

Assateague Island National Seashore

Sultry summer weather pushes crowds of Baltimoreans to Eastern Shore beach resorts, with Ocean City being the most popular. A select few, seeking a quieter and more nature-based retreat, will turn right onto Route 611 just before crossing into Ocean City, and complete their trek to Assateague Island, one the state's most beautiful settings. Assateague is a 37-mile-long, wind-swept barrier island stretching from across the inlet in Ocean City to Chincoteague, Virginia. The beach is wide and the sand very pure and white. It evokes images of the Outer Banks, in North Carolina, and attracts the same type of outdoor recreation-seeking crowd. It's the quintessential local antidote to the sometimes overbearing mass commercialism that is Ocean City.

▲ Hiking at Assateague Island National Seashore

▲ Exploring the beaches at Assateague Island National Seashore

Assateague Island once contained a smattering of private developments, but was wiped clean by a powerful hurricane in 1962. It now breathes second life as a public refuge, loaded with deer, over 300 species of birds, and a world-renowned herd of wild horses. Visitors to the Maryland side of the island, entering on Route 611, first encounter Assateague Island State Park. This is where many day-trippers from Ocean City end up. The usual beachy activities are found here, with lots of parking and bathhouses; 300 campsites are available in summer.

I recommend bypassing the state park and heading to the Assateague Island National Seashore, located another mile down the road. The beach here seems to be less crowded and there are more recreational opportunities available. Back roads lead to some quaint bay inlets that are fun to explore, and a bike trail caters to cycling and walking enthusiasts. Three short hiking trails, highly suited for children, pass through distinct ecosystems and are accompanied by interpretive signs. One weaves over sand dunes, another crosses a marsh on boardwalks, and a third threads through bird-populated woodland. Each offers great views and places to spy wildlife. Visitors to Assateague may be attracted to far-flung reaches of the beach, away from the congestion, but be forewarned that four-wheel-drive vehicles gravitate in that direction.

What puts Assateague Island on the national map is the herd of free-roaming, wild horses. About 150 graze the Maryland side of the island. Legend says the horses swam to the island in the 17th century from a Spanish galleon that sank off the coast. A more plausible explanation is that they were brought here in the 17th

▲ A member of the greeting committee at Assateague Island
  National Seashore

century by mainland farmers trying to avoid paying livestock taxes. Do not approach the horses, as they are aggressive and will bite. They readily rifle through campsites seeking anything edible, and will crush plastic coolers to get to food.

Assateague Island National Seashore offers some of the region's best camping. Sites are tucked just behind the front line of dunes shielding campers from the ocean. It's nice being lulled to sleep by breaking waves. I recommend checking out the walk-in sites, nice spots to which you have to carry equipment a short distance. From April 15 to October 15, campsites are $16 per night, and reservations are accepted and highly recommended. The rest of the year campsites are $12 per night on a first-come, first-served basis. Backpackers will want to take advantage of six dispersed backcountry sites—two ocean-front and four bayside—which are available on a first-come, first-served basis for a $5 backcountry permit fee. The experience is supreme. Backpackers trek up the littoral zone to the campsites, but may encounter trucks. Firewood is scarce at the campsites, so bring a stove. Mosquitos in warm weather are pernicious and numerous enough to carry off small children, so bring your most industrial-strength repellant.

Visitors to Assateague Island should make a point to stop at the Barrier Island Visitor Center, situated along Route 611, just before crossing the bridge onto the island. It's one of the best nature centers I've encountered. Included inside are a gargantuan aquarium with lots of funky marine wildlife, a touch tank where kids can pick up marine critters, and an adjacent room hosting a beachcombing exhibit where kids can handle an array of things found on a typical beach, like shells, antlers, animal bones, and corals. A small theater continually shows movies about Assateague Island. The Visitor Center is open daily from 9 a.m. to 5 p.m. (except Thanksgiving and Christmas), and can be reached at (410) 641-1441.

Location and Directions: Near Berlin, at the southern terminus of Route 611. From Baltimore, cross over the Bay Bridge in Annapolis and follow Route 50 toward Ocean City. Just before Ocean City, turn right onto Route 611 and continue to Assateague Island. Driving time is about three hours in light traffic, and probably longer in summer traffic.

Entrance Fee: $5 per vehicle, good for seven days.

Website and Phone: www.nps.gov/asis; (410) 641-3030.

Crystal Grottoes Caverns

Exploring a cave is a thrilling and offbeat adventure for a child of any age. Though Maryland boasts over 100 known caves, only Crystal Grottoes Caverns, near Boonsboro, are commercially available to the public. The cave system features about seven miles of narrow tunnels (one mile open to the public) with high ceilings and stunning formations. The caverns are said to have the greatest density of formations of any cave in the world.

What I personally like about Crystal Grottoes Caverns is their refreshing 1950s roadside-attraction feel. The cave's location along Route 34 is marked only by a simple sign. The sole intrusion to the surrounding environment, besides a picnic pavilion, is a tiny hut, where visitors pay and enter the caverns through a door to the rear. Calcium carbonate rock samples can be purchased there for anywhere from $1 to $10. Parents will appreciate the fact that the cave is especially kid-friendly. There are few steps and no steep grades to climb. Pathways are hardened dirt, typically flat and dry, and well lit. My 3-year-old was able to negotiate the entire tour with no problems.

Tours through the caverns are about 40 minutes long, and leave at set times. Visitors snake through very narrow and high-ceilinged passageways leading to plentiful and always unusual formations. The geology and history of the caverns were nicely explained to us in layman's terms by our enthusiastic tour guide, who went by the name of Spirit. He explained how the formations are

◀ Discovering a subterranean world at Crystal Grottoes Caverns

composed of calcium carbonate deposits, which were formed from rainwater leaking through rock fissures into the caverns and leaving their crystallized calling cards behind. He pointed out to us formations called Old Father Time and the King of His Throne. He showed us other formation structures called wedding cake flowstone, popcorn, cauliflower, and soda straws. He also enlightened us on how to remember the difference between stalactites and stalagmites: Stalactites cling "tight" to the ceiling, and stalagmites "might" grow up one day. At one point we squeezed past a well-camouflaged Pipistrellus bat clinging to a tunnel wall.

Crystal Grottoes Caverns have no immense, knock-your-socks-off cathedral rooms typical of other commercial caves, but the Crystal Palace chamber opens up to reveal some larger formations and gives claustrophobes a chance to catch their breath. Another small alcove contains a pool of water reflecting high-up formations that the observer cannot directly see. A highlight of the tour occurs when the guide cuts all lights, allowing visitors to experience total darkness, which is more eerie than one would expect. Heed warnings and resist urges to finger the formations, as they are fragile and you will be verbally reprimanded.

Crystal Grottoes Caverns were discovered in 1920 by a crew quarrying limestone for a road project. They are located near other attractions, including Antietam National Battlefield and Harper's Ferry National Historical Park. Do not discount winter as a time to visit, as the underground temperature remains constant at 54.6 degrees

Fahrenheit year-round. As a trivial aside, Route 34, which leads visitors to the cave, was the first road in the country to be blacktopped.

Location and Directions: Along Route 34 in Washington County, about a one-hour drive from Baltimore. Take Interstate 70 west to just before Hagerstown. Take Route 66 south to Boonsboro. Go left onto Alternate Route 40, and right onto Route 34. The caverns are located about 1.5 miles outside of Boonsboro.

Hours and Admission: Open daily from April 1 to October 31, from 9 a.m. to 6 p.m. Winter hours are weekends only from 11 a.m. to 4 p.m. Cost is $8.50 for adults and $4.50 for children under 12. Coupons are available on the website.

Website and Phone: www.goodearthgraphics.com/showcave/md/crystal.html; (310) 432-6336.

Knoebels Amusement Resort

Knoebels is a simple and homespun amusement park tucked between two lush mountains in central Pennsylvania, not far from Bloomsburg. You may call it the anti-amusement park, since it carries no theme and offers few bells and whistles or high-tech gadgetry. Knoebels is simple and inviting, and makes for a worthwhile drive for families with young kids.

Knoebels appeals to many tastes. Naturalists will appreciate the park's far-flung setting, so remote that black bears have been known to wander the park during off-hours. The 50-or-so rides, spread out across 200 leafy acres, are linked by shady walkways. Roaring Creek tumbles gin-clear through the park, and rainbow and brown trout can be seen feeding in the deep pools. A wild turkey once held up our train ride. And many of the rides are of the vintage kind, giving the park a nostalgic quality.

Knoebels also appeals to the budget-conscious. It's the largest free-admission park in the country. A fee is charged only for individual rides, and ranges from about 60 cents for most kiddie rides to $2 for the roller coasters. Our family bought a $20 book of tickets, and despite feverish efforts, couldn't use them all in a day. Parking, entertainment, and picnic facilities are also free.

Most of all, Knoebels appeals to the children. No less than 20 rides are designated as kiddie rides, and another 20 labeled family rides. Much of the fare is traditional: the Tilt-a-Whirl, Whipper, Antique Cars, and Tea Cups. Favorites of my daughter were the bouncy Kiddie Whip and the twirling Balloon Race. A unique and exceedingly fun attraction is the Hand Cars, where kids propel a sled-like cart down actual rail tracks by hand-pumping a wheel. The historic Grand Carousel, with its 63 exquisitely carved horses, remains pristine despite 90 years of use.

Kiddie rides may be the forte at Knoebels, but adrenaline-seeking parents will also leave satisfied. It features two world-class, wooden roller coasters and lots of other brain-scrambling rides. Despite being somewhat limited, Knoebels receives national-class accolades. The National Amusement Park Historical Association voted Knoebels best park in the country two years in a row. *Amusement Today* magazine named it tops in the nation for park food (don't miss the pickle-on-a-stick), and voted its historic Grand Carousel America's best. *USA Weekend* magazine selected its bumper cars best in America. And at 110 feet, the Giant Wheel is the tallest Ferris wheel in the state.

Knoebels also lays claim to the state's largest, and arguably most beautiful, swimming pool. At one million gallons, the Crystal Pool is a virtual lake, framed by diving boards, sliding boards, and two 400-foot-long water slides. From its center rises a stone volcano spilling water. The pool includes a new kiddie play area featuring spray fountains and other waterborne attractions. There is an admission charge to use the pool. Parents visiting Knoebels are reminded to pack a clothing change, as kids will get wet on certain rides. For overnight visitors, a campground is located on the premises.

Location and Directions: Knoebels Amusement Resort is located on Route 487, between Elysburg and Bloomsburg, Pennsylvania, about a three-hour drive north of Baltimore. Directions can be found at its website.

▲ All smiles at Knoebels Amusement Resort

Hours and Admission: Knoebels opens for the season in late April, and remains open through September. Hours and ticket prices vary, and are provided on its website. An unlimited-rides-for-one-price plan is available on certain weekdays.

Website and Phone: www.knoebels.com; (570) 672-2572.

Lewes, Delaware, and Cape Henlopen State Park

Beach resorts favored by Baltimore-area residents tend to be those extending from Rehoboth Beach southward to Ocean City. The quaint seaside village of Lewes, Delaware, located in the shadow of Rehoboth Beach, is often overlooked but worth a visit. The town was settled in the 1600s by Dutch settlers and has maintained its historical charm without succumbing to the heavy hand of tourism.

Lewes can be explored by foot or bike. Begin each visit with a trip to the Lighthouse Restaurant at Fisherman's Wharf, and enjoy a softball-sized sticky bun on the canal-side deck while watching the myriad fishing and pleasure boats embark on a day at sea. Then cross the canal and stroll the very tiny downtown shopping district (literally two blocks long) along Front and Second Streets, making a mandatory stop at Kids' Ketch for nice and unusual toys and apparel. Amidst all the antique shops is a good bakery, some small cafes, and a book shop. Then head northward to see the well-restored Victorian mansions and some smaller wood-frame historical homes. The foundation of the house located at 118 Front Street still contains a cannonball fired in the War of 1812. Bikers may want to head out on Pilottown Road a few miles to the University of Delaware's College of Marine Studies, which is idyllically situated on the water.

A visit to Lewes should include a trip to nearby Cape Henlopen State Park, which hosts possibly the region's most attractive beach. Bikers can easily do the three-mile trek, but walkers may want to make other transportation arrangements (bikes are available for rent in town). Much of the cape is a lip of sand separating the Atlantic Ocean from the Delaware Bay, creating an interesting and lightly developed marine ecosystem for kids to explore. There is a fine beachcombing and wading area in the back bay area, beside the fishing pier, which is usually swarming with kids.

Another fun thing to do is climb the cylindrical concrete lookout tower that was used in World War II to watch for German submarines entering the Delaware Bay. The tower offers sensational

▲ Beachcombing at Cape Henlopen State Park

views of this austere seascape. The state park has lots of bike trails and a good, sandy camping area where sites cost $21 per night for Delaware residents, and $25 for non-residents. Reservations are recommended and can be made by calling 1-877-987-2757. Hiking trails thread through sand dunes, cranberry bogs, and woodland, and lead to neat ponds and beaches. Don't miss the Great Dune, an 80-foot-tall mound of sand—the region's largest. Entrance to the park is $2.50 for in-state cars, and $5 for out-of-state.

Overnight visitors to Lewes should consider a day-trip excursion to Cape May, New Jersey. The one-way trip takes about 80 minutes and offers great bay and ocean vantages. Those making the trip early in the day will likely see lots of dolphins playfully following the boat. A shuttle leads from the Cape May ferry terminal into town, which is oozing with charm. A round-trip on the ferry costs $15 per person ($18 with the shuttle), and is free for kids under 6. Shuttle reservations should be made when purchasing tickets. Even if not sailing, kids will love watching the ferries come and go from the impressive terminal.

Location and Directions: Lewes is located off Route 1, north of Rehoboth Beach. From Baltimore, take Interstate 97 south to Annapolis and take Route 50 east across the Bay Bridge. In Wye Mills, take Route 404 east into Delaware. In Georgetown, take Route 9 east and follow to Lewes.

Website: The website for Cape Henlopen State Park is www. destateparks.com/chsp/chsp.htm.

Red Caboose Motel

In 1970, to win a dare, Donald Denlinger placed a bid on a string of 19 rusty railroad cabooses, each weighing about 25 tons, that were put up for auction. He bid an absurdly low amount—$100 less than the scrap-metal value of the rail cars—to assure he would not win. Much to his chagrin, Denlinger did and was given a matter of days to figure out what to do with the cabooses. With time running short, Denlinger made a life-altering choice: he decided to renovate the cars into sleeping quarters and turn them into a motel. What resulted is the Red Caboose Motel, billed as the only place in the world where one can sleep in an authentic caboose.

The Red Caboose Motel, located in Strasburg, Pennsylvania, has since grown to include about 40 caboose cars, and has been featured in *National Geographic, Readers Digest, Ripley's Believe It or Not*, and numerous other publications. It may be the country's best overnight destination for a train-loving youngster. My son experienced choo-choo nirvana there, unable to decide whether he wanted to be inside our caboose looking out the window at the others, or outside staring at our caboose.

The Red Caboose Motel sits on a rise and looks out over a mosaic of postcard-worthy Amish farms. In spring, it's fun to watch horse-teams plow the fields. Individual cabooses vary in sleeping arrangement, but most have a double bed in the fore area, and a pair of bunk beds in the rear. A bathroom with shower is in the mid-section. Each car comes with a television with cable, a heating unit, and air conditioning. Rooms are done in typical 1970s Penn-

▲ Rooms at the Red Caboose Motel

sylvania decor, with dark paneling and low lighting. They may seem cramped by today's standards, but what's sacrificed in luxury will be more than made up for in smiles.

On the premises is a restaurant where seating is in two Victorian dining rail cars. A farmhouse also features rooms for rent and animals for viewing and petting. The silo has been converted into a lookout tower and can be climbed for 50 cents. Buggy rides are offered from the motel's parking lot for $10 per person ($5 for kids). A gift shop and playground are also available. On nice weekends, mosey over to the barn for a country music hoedown. I recommend purchasing the *Red Caboose Lodge* pamphlet in the gift shop for $1 to read about how Denlinger painstakingly made the conversion from rail cars to motel. The motel is kitschy enough to make it fun for the kids, but lacks the heavy-handed dose of tourism felt in nearby Lancaster.

The area around the Red Caboose Motel is rife with possibilities for family fun, most centered on train themes. Adjacent to the motel is the National Toy Train Museum with lots of scale-model trains. One mile down the road, and within eyeshot, is the starting point for the Strasburg Rail Road excursion train and the very impressive Railroad Museum of Pennsylvania. A gigantic corn maze, open from late summer through fall, is a short hop away.

Location and Directions: Just east of Strasburg, Pennsylvania. From Baltimore, take Interstate 83 north. In York, take Route 30 east, and continue through Lancaster. Take Route 896 south into Strasburg. Make a left at the light onto Route 741, and continue outside of town, past the excursion railroad, to the motel, which is on the left at Paradise Road.

Rates: Rates vary depending on season and number in party, and range from $45 to $109 per night. A fall weekend family rate is $89.

Website and Phone: www.redcaboosemotel.com; (717) 687-5000.

Sideling Hill Road Cut

Parents of rock-hound children should consider an excursion to Sideling Hill, which is the state's—if not the East Coast's—most impressive road cut. Sideling Hill is a mountain running north and south in Washington County, near the border with Allegany County. Interstate 68 slices through the mountain about seven miles west of Hancock, opening up a 320-foot-high and 810-foot-long gaping wound, revealing multi-hued layers of rock and sediment, and providing a unique insight into the region's geologic history, which dates back 350 million years.

If I were a geologist, I would explain in lucid detail how the exposure reveals a perfect, tightly folded syncline, with rock layers curved in upward, concave fashion, like a bowl. I'd tell you all about how the colorful and clay-laden Rockwell formation underlies the Purslane formation, and about the marine fossils found in the silty shale layer. I'd chat about diamictite and graywacke and chert. But since I'm a layperson on such topics, I'll defer to the very informative discussion on Sideling Hill found at the Maryland Geological Survey's website: www.mgs.md.gov/esic/brochures/sideling.html.

The Sideling Hill Exhibit Center has been operating on the premises since 1991. It has a four-story display that interprets the exposed geology on the site, and also offers some regional wildlife exhibits. The center is staffed by personnel from the Maryland State Highway Administration, the Maryland Office of Tourism Development, and the Maryland State Forest and Park Service to answer questions. A walkway leads to the base of the cut, and picnic tables are available.

The Sideling Hill road cut was completed in 1984, and the highway was pushed through the following year. Over 5 million pounds of explosives were employed in the 16-month construction effort. Most of the 10 million tons of rock removed were crushed and used to construct the road leading to the cut. The cost of cleaving the mountain was about $20 million. Builders originally considered a tunnel, but deemed it too expensive and dangerous. A trip to Sideling Hill can easily be combined with a visit to Crystal Grottoes, the state's only commercial cave, located to the southeast. A fun time to visit Sideling Hill is in late fall, when millions of ladybugs pass through on their southward migration.

Location and Directions: At 3000 Sideling Hill, along Interstate 68, about seven miles west of Hancock.

Hours: The exhibit center is open daily from 9 a.m. to 5 p.m., except New Year's Day, Easter, Thanksgiving, and Christmas.

Phone: (301) 678-5442.

Thorn Run Inn

Finding a child-friendly bed and breakfast is no easy task. Finding one with a social conscience carries an added dash of appeal. Thorn

▲ Thorn Run Inn makes for a perfect, kid-friendly getaway weekend

Run Inn, located among waves of steel-blue mountains in the Potomac Highland section of northern West Virginia, offers both. With 20 acres of stomping grounds, a fishing pond, a modest nature center, and an in-ground swimming pool, the inn is a magnet for children. But it's also the first in the region to prominently tout itself as "eco-friendly," and use the term "ecotourism" in its marketing literature. Hosts Peter and Robin Mailles provide each guest with a bed and a meal—and a new way of thinking.

The Ecotourism Society defines the concept as "responsible travel to natural areas which conserves the environment and sustains the well-being of local people." The innkeepers at Thorn Run take great care to minimize their imprints on the environment. They prepare meals with organic foods, many grown on the premises. They line-dry the linens, and use biodegradable detergents. They perform extensive composting and recycling, and drive a gas-stingy car. They avoid the use of chemical fertilizers, pesticides, and herbicides. Each item used at Thorn Run Inn is scrutinized as to its origin, its material composition, and its possible impact on the environment. And a trio of domesticated sheep serve as groundskeepers, keeping the grass at a manageable height. What they can't get, a non-motorized reel mower does.

The inn is a Georgian-style brick farmhouse with a modest front portico and spacious windows. It rests neatly in a furrow of Knobley Mountain, where the trickle of water known as Thorn Run emerges and begins its search for the Potomac River. The inn has five guest rooms, three with private baths. A private cabin is also available. Its decor is simple and tasteful. Guest rooms are adorned with many antiques purchased locally, and there is a well-stocked library. A baby grand piano stands ready to entertain. The inn is an ideal haven for curious children, offering 20 acres of rolling woodland and pasture to explore, including several barns and other outbuildings. The setting is hopelessly bucolic. Sumptuous dinners at Thorn Inn are available at a reasonable extra charge, and usually include homemade bread, salad, local wine, and dessert.

Recreational opportunities abound near the inn. Greenland Gap Nature Preserve, just a few cow pastures away, offers a rugged hiking trail and a cool and inviting swimming hole. Within a comfortable drive are the rough-and-tumble Dolly Sods Wilderness Area, Seneca Rocks Natural Recreation Area, and Blackwater Falls State Park. Guests more enthralled by local culture—or less enthusiastic about mud and mountains—can ramble the countryside and small towns, and experience a region that has done little to impede its character and charm. A country auction located nearby usually coughs up some amazing bargains.

Location and Directions: In New Creek, in the Potomac Highland area of West Virginia. The inn is a little over three hours from Baltimore. Directions are on its website.

Room rates: Rooms range from $75 to $95 per night for double occupancy. The cabin rate starts at $85 per night. Room rates include breakfast and evening snacks. Dinner is available for a cost of $18 per person, and must be scheduled in advance.

Website and Phone: www.thornruninn.com; (304) 749-7733.

Spectator Sports

Baltimore area residents have the luxury of living in close proximity to a wide assortment of professional and semi-professional athletic teams. They provide great opportunities to view athletes playing sports at the highest level. Here are the teams.

Aberdeen Ironbirds

Cal Ripken is Baltimore's most celebrated sports personality, and his fans collectively wondered what he would do following his retirement from baseball in 2001. What Cal did, along with his brother Bill, was to purchase a minor league baseball team playing in Utica, New York, and move it to his hometown of Aberdeen. The Aberdeen Ironbirds, a Class A affiliate of the Baltimore Orioles, began play in June 2002 in the New York–Penn League.

The Ripken brothers also built for their team a spanking new brick stadium—one of the finest in minor league baseball. Appropriately named Ripken Stadium, it seats 6,000 fans and offers a generous scoreboard and lots of amenities. Getting to the ballpark is easy and parking is abundant. The only drawback to attending an Ironbirds game is that tickets may be hard to come by.

The team plays a 76-game schedule from mid-June through September, vying with such clubs as the Williamsport Woodcutters, Batavia Muckdogs, Mahoning Valley Scrappers, Oneonta Tigers, Tri-City Valley Cats, and Brooklyn Cyclones. Of their 38 home games in 2002, 20 featured some sort of promotion ranging from cap giveaways to fireworks to special guests. Most games are in the evening, starting at about 7 p.m., though certain weekend games are played in the afternoon. Tickets range from $6 to $11 per person. Nine-game plans cost $54, and season tickets range from $228 to $494. And Cal fans should rest assured that he is a regular at the games.

The Ripken Academy is planned for a lot next to the stadium. Included as part of the academy are six small playing fields modeled after iconic professional ballparks, like Fenway Park, Wrigley Field, and Memorial Stadium. The academy will also feature dormitories and a cafeteria, and will be used for baseball camps and tournaments.

On game day, head up early for a stop at the Ripken Museum. The museum is located in the former City Hall building in downtown Aberdeen. On display is a wide range of baseball paraphernalia donated mostly by various Ripken family members. Museum admission is $3 for adults, $2 for seniors 62 and over, $1 for children 6-12, and free for those under 6. Museum hours and directions can be found at www.ripkenmuseum.com.

Location and Directions: Ripken Stadium is located in Aberdeen, easily visible from Interstate 95. From Baltimore, take Interstate 95 north. Take Exit 85, Route 22, west toward Churchville. Take a quick right onto Gilbert Road and continue to stadium parking.

Website and Phone: www.ironbirdsbaseball.com; (410) 297-9292.

Baltimore Bayhawks

Lacrosse may have been invented by Native Americans, but you'd have a tough time convincing a Baltimore lacrosse fan that this city is not the sport's epicenter. Nowhere else in the world is the game as popular. Kids here grow up with lax sticks in hand; area high-school players funnel into the country's best collegiate programs; local colleges and universities enjoy perennial stays on the NCAA's top 20 list for the sport; and the U.S. Lacrosse Museum and National Hall of Fame is located on the main campus of Johns Hopkins University.

What makes lacrosse fun to watch is that the game is played at such a furious pace, yet requires impeccable technique and chesslike strategy. A Major League Lacrosse game is where lacrosse is played at the highest level. It's the only professional lacrosse league, and features the world's best post-collegiate players. Baltimore's entry into the MLL is the Bayhawks, a perennially competitive team.

The MLL season runs from early June to late August. The Bayhawks play 14 games during the course of the season against teams from Long Island; Rochester, New York; New Jersey; Boston; and Bridgeport, Connecticut. Seven of these games are at home, and are played at Ravens Stadium. This makes for a great way to see the inside of the stadium, since tickets for Baltimore Ravens games are difficult to come by. Games are typically played on Thursday and

Saturday evenings. Single-game tickets cost $15 to $20 per person, depending on seating location. Seven-game season tickets can be had for $91 to $126. Shorter game plans are also available. Call 1-866-994-2957 for ticket information.

Location and Directions: Ravens Stadium is located in downtown Baltimore, on Russell Street. From Interstate 95, take Exit 52, Russell Street, and continue to stadium parking. Parking is available in lots around the stadium.

Website and Phone: www.baltimorebayhawks.com; 1-866-994-2957.

Bowie Baysox

Attending a Baltimore Orioles game at Camden Yards is, by all means, a special summer treat that a child will cherish. Ticket prices have risen in recent years, however, and steep concession prices virtually suck the enjoyment out of munching a hot dog. Stadium parking is expensive and not easy to come by. A day at the park for a family of four now runs upwards of $100.

An excellent and affordable alternative is to attend a minor league baseball game. Baltimore has three minor league teams in its general vicinity. The highest class team is the Bowie Baysox, which plays at Prince George's Stadium, in Bowie. The Baysox are the Orioles' Class AA affiliate and should in theory offer a better brand of baseball than the local Class A affiliate teams in Frederick and Aberdeen. Further, Bowie is a great place to sneak a close-up peek at a major league player, since it's where some Orioles players go to recover from injuries or to get their curve ball back.

A Bowie game offers the same minor-league, user-friendly amenities discussed in the Frederick Keys section below. Event organizers craft a very family-friendly experience for the fans. Bowie's stadium is unusually large for a minor league park, with a capacity of over 10,000. For younger kids who can't sit still, there are lots of walkways and standing areas that offer pleasant views of the field. Most seats are benches, a bonus for rowdy children who feel the need to run up and down aisles. Along those lines, weekday evening games tend not to fill up, so the stands offer lots of elbow room.

At least once during the game try to visit the children's play area, located just off right field. Featured are a carousel and a large, inflatable sliding board resembling a sinking ship. Each ride costs $1. Other fun attractions like face-painting and a nice playground can also be found. Food at the stadium is affordable and tasty, with the soft ice cream being particularly good, according to my daughter.

Attending a Baysox game won't break the bank. Adult general admission tickets cost $8. Tickets are $5 for kids 6-12, and for seniors 60 or older. Kids 5 and under are admitted free, as are kids wearing an athletic uniform to games on Mondays through Thursdays. Reserved seat tickets run from $12 to $14.

Location and Directions: From Baltimore, take Interstate 97 south toward Annapolis. Take Exit 7, Route 3, south towards Bowie, and continue for about 11 miles. After passing beneath the Route 50 overpass (where Route 3 becomes Route 301), turn left at the second light onto Ballpark Drive. Continue to stadium parking.

Website and Phone: www.baysox.com; (301) 464-4865.

Baltimore Blast

The Baltimore Blast, the city's entry into the Major Indoor Soccer League, is a popular draw thanks to this city's burgeoning fascination with that sport. Games are played at the Baltimore Arena, where seating is close to the playing field, making for a fun place to watch such a fast-paced game. Seating capacity is over 11,000. (As an aside, this arena was the location of Baltimore's only Beatles concert.) The MISL season runs from late October through mid-March. The Blast plays 44 games over the course of the season against teams like the Philadelphia Kixx, Cleveland Crunch, and Harrisburg Heat.

Tickets for Blast games range from $11 to $17 per seat. Tickets can be purchased by calling the Blast box office at (410) 732-5278. Box office hours are weekdays from 10 a.m. to 5:30 p.m., and on game days from 10 a.m. to 9 p.m.

Location and Directions: The Baltimore Arena is located in downtown Baltimore, at the intersection of Howard and Baltimore Streets. From Interstate 95, take Exit 53, Interstate 395, and follow signs for downtown Baltimore. The arena is located just past Oriole Park at Camden Yards, near the end of the expressway. Nearby parking garages are well marked.

Website and Phone: www.baltimoreblast.com; (410) 732-5278.

Baltimore Orioles

Watching the Baltimore Orioles play in Oriole Park at Camden Yards is one of summer's greatest pleasures. The stadium is world-class and features a nostalgic ambiance. The setting is supreme, with fans getting to peer out over downtown Baltimore. It's at places like Oriole Park where childhood memories are cultivated.

Here are some tips to help make your visit to Oriole Park easier and cheaper. Professional baseball ticket prices seem to go up faster than an aging reliever's ERA. Single-game Orioles tickets range from $8 for standing room only to $40 for club box seats. To save a few bucks, keep an eye out for certain weekday games early in the season when tickets are discounted to as low as $5 per seat. Also, if you're bringing the kids, consider buying tickets at the box office instead of through the mail. This way, tickets for kids 12 and under are only $4 per seat when purchased with an adult ticket. In the 1990s, games sold out early and game-day tickets were a rarity, but now they're easier to come by.

Parking is widely available around the stadium, but not congregated in any one spot. In the Inner Harbor chapter, refer to the sidebar that details parking options around the harbor, most of which are also convenient to the stadium. My preference is to park on metered streets in the nearby Federal Hill neighborhood and do the 20-minute walk to the stadium. (Meters are only in effect until 6 p.m.) Do not park on non-metered streets in Federal Hill, as they

▲ The house that Cal built—Oriole Park at Camden Yards

◀ Bustling Eutaw Street at
Oriole Park at Camden Yards

have in effect two-hour limits on parking. Refrain from parking on poorly lit streets in run-down neighborhoods around the stadium.

Concessions inside the stadium are pricey. However, fans are allowed to bring in their own food and drinks (no glass containers) in plastic bags. Another alternative to purchasing stadium concessions is to check out the line of vendors along Conway Street—the three-block stretch of road connecting Oriole Park with the Inner Harbor. On game days they offer drinks, peanuts, and other snacks at a reasonable cost. Vendors along this stretch also sell hats, T-shirts, and jerseys at substantially lower prices than stadium vendors do.

Oriole Park does not offer the carousels and carnival games typical of minor-league ball parks, but if the kids need to burn energy, there are two good places to consider. At Gate E of the Eutaw Street entrance (near the park's southeast corner) is Kid's Corner at The Yard, which features a moon walk, a pitching game, and some photo opportunities. All attractions are free. Also, a spacious picnic pavilion just past the center-field wall is usually swarming with rowdy kids. From the picnic pavilion, pop your head over the standing-room-only fence to see players in the opposing team's bullpen. Kids will thrill at seeing a player so close.

It would be a sacrilege to catch a game at Oriole Park without experiencing the Eutaw Street vending area, which runs parallel to the right-field wall. Here is where gourmet vendors peddle their wares. Two popular eateries are Bambino's Ribs and Boog's Bar-B-

Que. Mom and dad will like the selection of microbrews. Watch for the Maryland Athletic Hall of Fame plaques on the brick wall near the restrooms. Also, check out the various metal baseball markers inlaid into the walkway. Each marks the landing spot for a notable home run hit here.

Oriole Park is anchored by the former B&O Warehouse, which runs just past right field parallel to the Eutaw Street corridor. At about one-fifth of a mile long, it's said to be the longest brick structure on the east coast. Babe Ruth was born in a rowhouse near the stadium, and his father ran a pub on the grounds where the stadium is situated.

Location and Directions: Oriole Park at Camden Yards is located in downtown Baltimore near the intersection of Hamburg and Russell Streets. From Interstate 95, take Exit 52, Russell Street, and follow signs to stadium parking. As an alternative, take Exit 53, Interstate 395, and follow signs to stadium parking.

Website and Phone: orioles.mlb.com; (410) 685-9800.

Baltimore Ravens

Baltimore is a football town and this city goes bonkers over its Ravens. Such does not bode well for fans who want to watch a Ravens game in person, however. Every game the team has ever played at Ravens Stadium has been sold out. Practically all seats belong to season-ticket holders who paid a hefty PSL (personal seat license) fee for the privilege of holding that seat. If you're dead set on scoring Ravens tickets, the best route is to either sweet-talk a season-ticket-holding friend, or peruse Internet auction sites. If you consider yourself a lucky person, try calling Ticketmaster when a limited number of single-game tickets go on sale in July. As a last resort, talk to drivers of charter buses that bring fans to the game; at times fans miss the bus or can't make the trip, freeing up tickets.

A word of warning for those parents who want to share the Ravens experience with their little ones: do not expect the same family-friendly atmosphere as that commonly found at Oriole Park at Camden Yards. This is not a wine-and-cheese crowd. Ravens games tend to be loud and raucous. Fans often curse, and fights have sometimes broken out uncomfortably near my seat. That said, there are few things in sports more exciting than watching your hometown professional football team play. Parents should carefully judge their child's readiness for such an experience.

Frederick Keys

The Frederick Keys are the Class AA affiliate of the Baltimore Orioles, and play out of Harry Grove Stadium, in Frederick. Attending a Frederick Keys game is to have the quintessential minor-league baseball experience. The park is cozy and very small-townish. The high outfield wall has three tiers of advertisements. Before the game, players percolate through the crowd, giving autographs to the young ones, and others fling Frisbees or T-shirts into the stands. Between-inning frolics include trike races and other fun contests. Local businessmen often throw out the first pitch. Toe-tapping music suffuses through the cheers, and the team's mascot works the crowd, offering photo-ops. It seems that the main reason minor league baseball exists is to make kids smile.

Harry Grove Stadium has a fine play area for kids. It features a carousel, a moon walk, a moon-walk sliding board, a baseball pitching game, and a few carnival activities. Each activity costs $1. Two playgrounds and many picnic tables are also scattered around. In addition, there are grassy hills to roll down or spread a blanket on.

Food at Harry Grove Stadium is tasty and reasonably priced. A decent-sized slice of pizza runs $3 and a funnel cake is $3.50. You can get your fries in a tiny plastic batter's helmet. Note that outside food is not allowed in the stadium. Before leaving, consider a visit to the souvenir stand, where a children's Keys cap can be had for $9 and a baseball for $6.

▲ Minor league baseball with the Frederick Keys

The prices of tickets to a Keys game are reasonable. Adult general admission tickets are $8 and children 6-12 pay $5, as do seniors 60 or over. Children 5 or under are free, as are kids wearing an athletic uniform to games on Mondays through Thursdays. Reserved seat tickets are also available for $9 to $11.

Location and Directions: From Baltimore, take Interstate 70 west. In Frederick, take Exit 54, Market Street. After the exit ramp, turn left onto Market Street, also called Route 355, toward downtown Frederick. Proceed for about one-quarter mile. Turn left onto New Design Road and proceed one block to the stadium parking lot.

Website and Phone: www.frederickkeys.com; (301) 662-0013.

Stadium Tours

Camden Yards is generally regarded among the best professional sports complexes in the world. The two stadiums that comprise the complex—Oriole Park at Camden Yards, where the Baltimore Orioles play, and Ravens Stadium, where the Baltimore Ravens play—were both designed in retro fashion. Oriole Park, in particular, was among the first such stadiums, and its design has been replicated in new stadiums across the country. Though hundreds of thousands of fans attend Ravens and Orioles games each year, it's surprising how few ever go beneath the bleachers for a behind-the-scenes perspective of these two teams and their stadiums. Tours of these two venues are easy to arrange, inexpensive, and fascinating for the true fans.

Hard-core baseball fans will appreciate delving deep into Oriole Park. Tours last about 75 minutes and pass through such facilities as the press box, the scoreboard control room, and the dugout. Tour guides are very knowledgeable about Oriole trivia and lore, and will point out arcane facts, like where Eddie Murray's 500th career home run landed.

Tour times and hours vary depending on what's going on at the stadium, but in general tours are given daily except on days of afternoon games. Tours generally begin in the late morning and run every half hour through the afternoon. The cost of a tour is $5 for adults, $4 for kids 12 and under, and $4 for seniors 55 and over. Tickets must be purchased the day of the tour at the stadium's ticket office, which is located at the north end of the warehouse, near Gate H. Plan to arrive about 30 minutes before the tour starts. For specific tour dates and times, call (410) 547-6234.

Tours of Ravens Stadium are only offered to groups of 20 or more. They last one hour and take visitors into the locker room area, the press box, and onto the field. To arrange a tour, call the Ravens ticket office at (410) 261-7283.

College Athletics

College playing fields are where kids can see new talent in a close-by and affordable setting. Here are websites for the athletic departments of some local colleges and universities. These sites provide links to schedules and other relevant information for spectators.

Community College of Baltimore County (CCBC), Catonsville:
www.ccbc.cc.md.us/cat/home.html

CCBC Dundalk:
www.ccbc.cc.md.us/dundalk/home.html

CCBC Essex:
www.ccbc.cc.md.us/essex/home.html

College of Notre Dame:
www.ndm.edu/activities/athletics/index.cfm

Coppin State University:
www.coppin.edu/athletics

Johns Hopkins University:
hopkinssports.ocsn.com

Loyola College:
www.loyola.edu/athletics

Morgan State University:
www.morgan.edu/athletics

University of Maryland at Baltimore County:
www.umbcretrievers.com

Swimming Holes

Baltimore has its fair share of community swimming pools. But swimming day in and day out within the confines of concrete, in four feet of water and surrounded by "no diving" signs, can become mundane. Here are some options for adding zest to your summertime swim routine.

Beaver Dam Swimming Club

Beaver Dam Swimming Club makes for a unique swimming experience; it's one of the few places around Baltimore where one can (legally) swim in a quarry. Guests here swim in a former marble quarry, surrounded by high rock walls with lush greenery spilling over. The water is deep and cool, with depths averaging about 40 feet. Zip lines, rafts, diving boards, and other water games add to the fun. And don't miss the cliff dive, which lets you know what belly-flopping out of a second-story window feels like. For the teeny tots, a shallow wading area is cordoned off from the deeper water. It should go without saying that those swimming in the quarry should possess outstanding aquatic skills, and parents should keep a wary eye on their brood.

If the thought of swimming in a deep-water quarry gives you the creeps, try one of the two swimming pools on the grounds. One comes with a fun water slide. The swim club also has a concession stand, as well as places to play beach volleyball and basketball. There's no shortage of shaded areas for picnicking.

Location and Directions: At 10820 Beaver Dam Road. From Baltimore, take Interstate 83 north. Take Exit 18, Warren Road, which heads east. At the first light, turn left onto Beaver Dam Road. Continue for about one-quarter mile to the swimming club, which is on the left.

Hours and Admission: The swimming club is open daily from early June through late August or early September. Hours are 11 a.m. to 7 p.m. Single-day admission is $10.50 for adults ($12.50 on Sundays and holidays) and $7 for children. Season passes range from $60 to $175 per person, depending on the plan.

Website and Phone: www.beaverdamswimmingclub.com; (410) 785-2323.

Cascade Lake

Cascade Lake is a privately owned, off-the-beaten-path swimming lake located in a secluded patch of Carroll County, near Hampstead. Parents will appreciate the quiet, wooded setting, and kids will love the wide range of dives, slides, and piers. Though the swimming area appeals to all children, Cascade Lake is especially accommodating to the younger set. Its gently sloping sand beach provides ideal wading opportunities and makes for a safe place to introduce children to water. Swimmers may use inner tubes, beach balls, and swim aids. A fun, toddler-friendly frog water slide is icing on the cake.

Older kids will want to take advantage of more exciting water attractions. A favorite is the 150-foot, twisting-and-turning water slide that discharges riders into a deep pocket of the lake. Two smaller water slides also see lots of action. There are piers to walk on, floating rafts for resting and playing, and a rickety high-dive platform for showing off. The swimming area is roped off and tended to by lifeguards. A thin strand of sand fringes the swimming area, though there is limited grassy space on which to toss a blanket. Consider bringing an umbrella, since shady areas around the waterfront are at a premium.

Swimming may be the focus at Cascade Lake, but other water- and land-based activities add to the fun. Kids will enjoy wetting a line in the six-acre lake for stocked and native largemouth bass, bluegill, catfish, and crappie. Fishing is included in the general admission price, and since the lake is private, no state fishing license is required (the lake does not rent gear, however). Paddle boats are also available for $5 per hour on weekdays and $6 per hour on weekends. A goat-intensive petting zoo provides a nice diversion from swimming. The $1 admission includes a bag of animal food.

▲ Beating the summer swelter at Cascade Lake

Hiking trails, horseshoe pits, playgrounds, picnic pavilions, and a water volleyball court add to the enjoyment. There is a concession stand and store selling toys and candy.

Location and Directions: At 3000 Snydersburg Road, near Hampstead. From Baltimore, take Interstate 83 north. Take Exit 27, Mt. Carmel Road, west and continue into Hampstead. Take Route 30 north, and just outside of town turn left onto Route 482. Continue for about two miles and turn right onto Snydersburg Road. Cascade Lake is located about one mile up the road on the right.

Hours and Admission: Cascade Lake is open on weekends from Memorial Day through Labor Day, and daily from early June through late August. Hours are 10 a.m. to 7 p.m. Weekday admission is $6 for adults and children over 5, $5 for children 2-5 and seniors 62 and over, and free for children under 2. Weekend and holiday admission is $9 for adults and children over 5, $5 for children 2-5 and seniors 62 and over, and free for children under 2.

Website and Phone: www.cascadelake.com; (410) 374-9111.

Gunpowder Falls State Park— Hammerman Area

The Hammerman Area of Gunpowder Falls State Park offers the finest sand swimming and wading beach in the immediate Baltimore area. Swimmers immerse themselves in the choppy waters of the Gunpowder River, a wide and scenic tributary of the Chesapeake Bay. Legend has it that the river got its name around 1600 when Native Americans living here tried to plant an unknown substance called gunpowder, hoping it would reap food. Hammerman's beach is almost one-third of a mile long, and the clean sand is very friendly to the feet. The scenery is pretty and the atmosphere very festive. Lifeguards are on duty at the Hammerman beach from Memorial Day to Labor Day, and swimming at other times is at your own risk.

This area is well developed and can get crowded, but it is also spread out enough to prevent unruly congestion. There are a large bathhouse and concession stand for swimmers. Parking is plentiful and an array of other activities is available. Lots of picnic tables dot the area. The park also has three picnic pavilions available for rent ($200 per day with a 100-person capacity), and four playgrounds scattered about. One is a tire park, which is a particularly fun and environment-friendly play area that incorporates lots of recycled tires. Three cabins are available for overnight stays from April through October, each renting for $35 per night. A canoe launch is located nearby.

Swimmers here may want to check out the boat rental shack, run by Ultimate Watersports. Sea kayaks, sit-atop kayaks, windsurfers, and Hobie Cat catamarans can be rented by the hour or day. For the inexperienced, Ultimate Watersports offers lessons on each craft. Kayak tours are also given. More details can be found in the Boat Rentals chapter.

Location and Directions: The Hammerman Area of Gunpowder Falls State Park is located in Chase. From downtown Baltimore, take Interstate 95 north. Take Exit 67-A, Route 43, and follow it east to Route 40. Take 40 east, and continue to the first light. Turn right onto Ebenezer Road and continue for about 4.5 miles, to the park entrance. Follow the park access road to the waterfront, where parking is available.

Hours and Admission: The Hammerman Area is open year-round. Summer hours are 8 a.m. to sunset. At other times, hours are 10 a.m. to sunset. Entry is $2 per person, though seniors 62 or older and children in car seats are free.

Website and Phone: www.dnr.state.md.us/publiclands/central/gunpowder.html; (410) 592-2897.

Hunting Creek Lake

Hunting Creek Lake is a generous-sized body of cool, clear water situated deep in the Catoctin Mountains, in the Houck Area of Cunningham Falls State Park. The lake is popular with boaters and swimmers, and has three designated areas for swimming, all fringed by thin, white sand beaches. The numerous shallow wading areas are popular with tots. The lake area is very clean and there are lots of picnic tables and facilities around, including restrooms and a concession stand. Lifeguards are on duty during posted hours between Memorial Day and Labor Day. A dip here is nothing short of invigorating.

There is much to do around Hunting Creek Lake besides swimming. A decent playground has many slides and some climbing apparatus. Lots of large boulders nearby also beckon more adventurous kids to climb. A boat launch offers canoes and rowboats for rent, and a fishing pier is perfect for wetting a line. The surrounding countryside is breathtaking, making Hunting Creek Lake an ideal place to pass the afternoon.

A short distance from the lake is Cunningham Falls, the region's highest at 78 feet. It's a cascading waterfall that has lots of pockets of water in which to relax and soothe yourself. A large pool at the bottom of the falls is also popular with swimmers. Be forewarned that swimming and wading around the falls may be dangerous and are generally unsuited for young kids. The one-half-mile, red-blazed Lower Trail links the lake to the falls, and has benches and interpretive information along the route. More intrepid explorers may opt for the slightly longer, yellow-blazed Cliff Trail, which also connects the two features, but follows a rougher and more challenging path.

Location and Directions: Hunting Creek Lake is located in the Houck Area of Cunningham Falls State Park, near Thurmont. From Baltimore, take Interstate 70 west. In Frederick, take Route 15 north. In Thurmont, take Route 77 west and continue for just over three miles. Turn left into the main entrance of the Houck Area of Cunningham Falls State Park, and follow signs to the beach.

Hours and Admission: Swimming at Cunningham Falls State Park runs from Memorial Day through Labor Day. Admission is $3 per person on weekends and holidays, and $2 per person on non-holiday weekdays.

Website and Phone: www.dnr.state.md.us/publiclands/western/cunninghamfalls.html; (310) 271-7574.

Miami Beach

No, not *that* Miami Beach. You'd be hard-pressed to find a string bikini or merengue-spewing boom box at this Baltimore County park. This Miami Beach is more amenable to families, and at a diminutive 59 acres, a wee bit smaller. Despite its size, the beach is refreshing and offers lovely views of the Chesapeake Bay waters.

Miami Beach is narrow and sandy, with several rock structures set up to stop sand from washing away. The grounds include picnic tables and a large pavilion available for rent. A fun playground and a set of swings sit next to a thicket of 10-foot-high phragmite reeds. A sign on the playground says that it's designated for children aged five through twelve, but my three-year-old had a ball there. Included in the park is a bathhouse and concession stand. Be aware that Miami Beach has many restrictions in place, including no inner tubes, inflatable toys, swimming aids, or large beach balls. From Miami Beach, Hart-Miller Island is visible across the water and to the right. Now in part a state park accessible only by boat, this is where sediment dredged from Baltimore Harbor is being pumped.

At the time of this writing, swimming was not permitted at Miami Beach, supposedly because of pollution caused by an over-abundance of geese inhabiting the nearby waters. Before you venture here, ring the Baltimore County Department of Recreation and Parks to get an update on its status.

Location and Directions: Near the town of Chase. From Baltimore, take Eastern Avenue east. Just past the Glenn L. Martin State Airport, turn right onto Carroll Island Road, and make a quick right onto Bowleys Quarters Road (this is near where the F-117A stealth fighter crashed during an airshow in 1997). Continue on Bowleys Quarters Road for just over two miles, and turn left onto Goose Harbor Road. Follow signs for Miami Beach.

Hours and Admission: The park is open daily from 10 a.m. to 7 p.m. The hours of swimming, when allowed, are daily from 10 a.m. to 6:15 p.m. No admission is charged unless swimming is allowed.

Phone: (410) 887-3780.

Milford Mill Swim Club

Milford Mill Swim Club is another converted quarry. The setting is supreme, with the swimming area set against a backdrop of sheer, golden rock, with trees and vines hanging down. The water is deep (18 feet) and cool. Entering the water is the most enjoyable part about swimming here. Option one is to plunge into the depths from a zip line that originates on a high platform. Option two is to cartwheel off another platform from a rope swing. Less intrepid swimmers can simply walk out onto a pier and dive in. Once in, exploring the sheer cliff walls and some hidden areas is fun and exciting.

Younger kids will likely hang out at the Baby Quarry, which is a large, shallow, concrete wading area built into one side of the rock pit. A fun sprinkle toy and high slide are located there. Behind the wading area is a large, sandy area for digging around or pitching a blanket. The swim club also has a swimming pool on the premises if the quarry is not to your liking.

Because of the uniqueness of this swim club, stringent rules are posted and must be strictly adhered to. The club is well guarded and has three patrol boats docked near the zip lines. Parents should keep in mind that swimming in the quarry's deep end may sound exhilarating, but kids may find it scary not to be able to touch or see bottom. Those using the deep quarry must first pass a swim test before entering. Spread about the swim club grounds are lots of picnic tables, a few picnic pavilions, and a large, well-shaded concession stand that sells snacks like ice cream, snowballs, drinks, and even little funnel cakes with powdered sugar. Milford Mill Swim Club prides itself on being a friendly, family-oriented park, and based on my experience, that is certainly the case.

Location and Directions: At 3900 Milford Mill Road, near Randallstown. From the Interstate 695 beltway, take Exit 18, Liberty Road, west. At the first light, turn right onto Washington Avenue. Continue on Washington Avenue for about one mile, until it dead-ends at Milford Mill Road. Continue straight across Milford Mill Road into the swim club's parking lot.

▲ Taking the plunge at Milford Mill Swim Club

Hours and Admission: The swim club is open daily from Memorial Day through Labor Day. Weekday hours are 11:30 a.m. to 7:30 p.m., and weekend hours are 10:30 a.m. to 7:30 p.m. Weekday admission is $9 for those 12 and older, $5 for kids 3-11, and $2 for those under 2. Weekend admission is $11 for those 12 and older, $6 for kids 3-11, and $2 for those under 2.

Phone: (410) 655-4818.

North East Beach

This beach, on a wide stretch of the North East River, in Elk Neck State Park, carries no more appeal than many closer sand beaches, but is still well worth a visit if you are venturing through Cecil County. The beach is situated in the North East River Area of the state park, in close proximity to lots of hiking trails and boating opportunities, and just a stone's throw from one of the state's most popular campgrounds. When I've been there, the water has been turbid, and it can also get choppy on windy days. The beach offers distant and pleasant views of Havre de Grace.

The sand at North East Beach is coarse, but there is lots of room on the adjoining hillside to spread your blanket. A snack bar on the premises also sells sundries, and there is a restroom for changing. Parents will appreciate the extensive tire park playground situated just off the beach, with lots of slides, swings, and unusual climbing apparatus. Environmentally friendly playgrounds are becoming a hit in the state. Parents should be forewarned that lifeguards are not present at this beach.

Location and Directions: In the North East River Area of Elk Neck State Park. From Baltimore, take Interstate 95 north. Take Exit 100, Route 272, south. Continue for about 10 miles, past the town of North East, to Elk Neck State Park. Follow signs for the North East River Area.

Hours and Admission: Beach facilities operate from Memorial Day through Labor Day. Use of the beach and facilities costs $2 per person on weekends and holidays, and $2 per carload on non-holiday weekdays.

Website and Phone: www.dnr.state.md.us/publiclands/central/elkneck.html; (410) 287-5333.

Oregon Ridge Lake

Oregon Ridge Lake is a refreshing, spring-fed swimming hole formed in the early 19th century when iron ore was excavated from a hillside in what is now Oregon Ridge Park. The lake is tiny, and the setting is pleasantly shaded. It's more serene than many public beaches. The water is cool and clear, and the beach sandy. It offers both deep-water swimming for the brave, and shallow-water wading for the kiddies. If boredom sets in, hiking trails circle the lake, inviting exploration.

Oregon Ridge Lake is administered by the Baltimore County Department of Recreation and Parks, and offers many modern facilities, including a bathhouse and concession stand. A playground, horseshoe pit, and volleyball court are also available. Picnic tables and grills can be used for lunches. The beach is well staffed with certified lifeguards. For special occasions, interested parties can rent a 50-person pavilion or the Lake Overlook Room, in the lodge above the bathhouse. The beach is open from Memorial Day through Labor Day. A trip to Oregon Ridge Lake can be part of an afternoon that also includes a hike, a visit to the park's spectacular nature center, or a fun foray to the purple playground, each of which is discussed in the respective chapters of this book.

Location and Directions: Off Beaver Dam Road, in Oregon Ridge Park. From Baltimore, take Interstate 83 north. Take Exit 20-B, Shawan Road, heading west. At the first light, turn left onto Beaver Dam Road, and follow signs to the lake. It is located just before the nature center.

Hours and Admission: The beach operates daily from Memorial Day weekend through Labor Day weekend (though it's not open on weekdays when local schools are in session). Admission is $6 for adults on weekends and holidays ($5 on weekdays), $2 for children 11 and under, and $3 for seniors 62 and older. Unlimited season passes cost $85 for adults, $35 for children 11 and under, $50 for seniors 62 and older, and $50 for students with valid identification. Unlimited family passes are available for $165.

Phone: (410) 887-1817.

Rocky Point Beach

Big-water swimmers will relish a dip in Maryland's biggest pond—the Chesapeake Bay. The Rocky Point peninsula pushes out into the bay near the mouth of the Back River. In 1969, Baltimore County opened at the tip of the peninsula a park that includes a 300-foot-long sand beach, which has since been a favorite summer, take-a-dip spot for residents of communities east of Baltimore. The beach offers fetching views of the Chesapeake Bay and Craighill Light. Ospreys and blue herons frequent the beach area, and an occasional bald eagle glides by. Note that since the beach opens to the Chesapeake Bay, it is also exposed to its temperamental weather.

Swimming may be the favorite activity at Rocky Point Park, but it's not the only one. Two playgrounds and a sand volleyball court stand ready for break time. Folks also come to fish from the two piers, launch boats, or play golf at the nearby Rocky Point Golf Course. There are restrooms, a bathhouse, a first-aid station, and about 20 picnic areas. Shade tents and a pavilion are available for group rental. Children under 12 years of age must be accompanied by an adult.

The water at Rocky Point Beach may be big, but it's relatively calm thanks to the protection afforded by Hart-Miller Island, the landmass situated about one mile off the beach. Hart-Miller Island is a state park accessible only by boat. The island attracts campers, swimmers, hikers, and naturalists observing waterfowl and other birds. Hart-Miller Island was built from sediment dredged from Baltimore's harbor.

Location and Directions: In Essex, in eastern Baltimore County. From the Interstate 695 beltway, take Exit 36, Route 702, south. Continue on Route 702 south until it merges with Back River Neck Road. Continue on Back River Neck Road for 2.3 miles, and turn left onto Barrison Point Road. Take the first right onto Rocky Point Road and proceed to the beach.

Hours and Admission: Swimming at Rocky Point Beach is allowed daily from Memorial Day weekend through Labor Day weekend, from 10 a.m. to 6 p.m. Daily weekend and holiday admission is $6 for adults, $3 for seniors 62 and over, and $2 for children 11 and under. Weekday daily rates and twilight daily rates (arrival after 4 p.m.) are discounted. Unlimited season passes cost $85 for adults, $35 for children 11 and under, $50 for seniors 62 and older, and $50 for students with valid identification. Unlimited family passes are available for $165.

Website and Phone: www.co.ba.md.us/agencies/recreation/rockypoint; (410) 887-3780.

Sandy Point State Park

Sandy Point State Park is Baltimore's and Washington's "in-a-pinch" beach. It's where sun and beach worshipers go who don't want to brave the three-hour drive to Ocean City or Rehoboth Beach. Sandy Point's beach is the area's closest approximation to an Atlantic coast shoreline. Fine waves roll in off the Chesapeake Bay, and the sandy area stretches for almost a mile. Much like a coastal resort, Sandy Point plays host to throngs on nice summer days.

Sandy Point is a multi-use state park, but swimming, sunbathing, and wading are the favorite activities there. A number of comfort stations are scattered about, and there's a large food concession area. The beaches along Sandy Point are agreeable for wading and beachcombing. It's a popular spot for children, with a playground available for swimming breaks. The beach also offers outstanding views of both spans of the Chesapeake Bay Bridge, which links Anne Arundel County with Maryland's Eastern Shore. Another favorite activity of swimmers is watching the boats ply up and down the bay—everything from pleasure craft to tankers to the venerable wooden skipjacks, which are our country's sole remaining wind-powered work boats. A perennial stiff breeze coming off the bay makes for exciting kite-flying. Parents should take note that sea nettles (jellyfish) appear when the waters are warm, usually around midsummer.

Sandy Point offers a host of other activities. There are 22 boat launches and a place to rent motor boats and rowboats. One pier is dedicated to fishing and another to crabbing (crabbing equipment is available for rent). Fishing is also popular off the various stone jetties that jut into the bay. Naturalists will be pleased to know that Sandy Point is situated along the eastern flyway, so waterfowl may be numerous. Though Sandy Point is a well-developed park, two trails snake through unspoiled sections. The Symbi Trail traverses a pine forest and some marshland, while the East Beach Trail passes through deciduous forest en route to a scenic lookout point.

Location and Directions: At 1100 East College Parkway, in Anne Arundel County, just east of Annapolis. From Baltimore, take Interstate 97 south. Just before Annapolis, take Route 50 east towards the Chesapeake Bay Bridge. Pass the Annapolis exits and cross over the Severn River. Continue for about five more miles. As you approach the Chesapeake Bay Bridge, just before the toll plaza, take Exit 32, and follow signs to the park.

Hours and Admission: Hours vary; call for details. Admission from April through October is $3 per person on weekdays, and $4 per person on weekends and holidays. From November through March, admission per vehicle is $1, which is deposited into an automatic toll gate (requiring exact change). Season passes can be bought at the park entrance during the summer season, and at the park headquarters year-round.

Website and Phone: www.dnr.state.md.us/publiclands/southern/ sandypoint.html; (410) 974-2149.

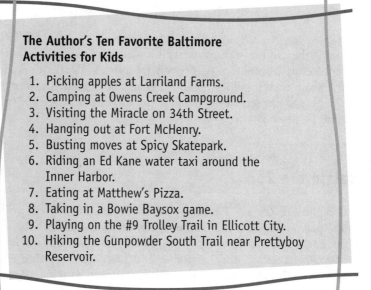

The Author's Ten Favorite Baltimore Activities for Kids

1. Picking apples at Larriland Farms.
2. Camping at Owens Creek Campground.
3. Visiting the Miracle on 34th Street.
4. Hanging out at Fort McHenry.
5. Busting moves at Spicy Skatepark.
6. Riding an Ed Kane water taxi around the Inner Harbor.
7. Eating at Matthew's Pizza.
8. Taking in a Bowie Baysox game.
9. Playing on the #9 Trolley Trail in Ellicott City.
10. Hiking the Gunpowder South Trail near Prettyboy Reservoir.

Zoos

Bridging the gap between fun and education is not an easy task for parents. Zoos represent a surefire way to grab a kid's attention and at the same time provide valuable lessons about nature, the environment, and conservation. Here are the three zoos located in and around Baltimore.

Baltimore Zoo

The Baltimore Zoo is a national-class facility and takes great pride in its spacious displays that authentically replicate natural habitats. Over 2,000 species, many rare and endangered, are housed here across 200 acres of leafy grounds. The pathways are wide and stroller-friendly, and the animals are spread out enough to keep crowds thin. The zoo is located in Druid Hill Park, in West Baltimore. It was founded in 1876, making it the third oldest in the country, but it is maintained as one of the most modern.

Visitors to the zoo are immediately greeted by a smattering of bears, tigers, foxes, and colorful birds. Just beyond is a spacious dirt display overrun with scores of hyperkinetic prairie dogs that will thrill young kids. Magnet, the water-loving polar bear, lives next door with his lady-friend. Also look for the stunning snow leopards and fanciful flamingoes.

In the Africa exhibit, among the zoo's best, animals dwell in a realistic-looking ecosystem. Antelope, zebras, rhinos, and ostriches can be seen lazing around the water hole, and cheetahs and leopards prowl about. Two adorable warthogs, Niles and Frasier, are not to be missed. You'll have to pry the kids away from watching monkeys cartwheel around the Chimpanzee Forest. Lucky visitors will see the elephants being fed (ask at the ticket booth for the feeding schedule).

The Children's Zoo is rated among the country's finest. It has the usual assortment of domesticated animals to pet and feed, but offers lots of perks, including a carousel and short train ride for a nominal extra charge. Kids will love jumping from lily pad to lily pad in the frog pond and wrestling around in huge tortoise shells. A beaver display lets kids climb around in a replica dam while actual beavers ply the waters above them. There is an educational bog display and a make-believe tree trunk to climb through. Lots of slides and play apparatus are spread around. Youngsters also get to handle everything from tiny bugs to robust pythons.

Food at the zoo is standard concession fare. As an alternative, bring a cooler, keep it in a rented locker, and use the picnic area. A shop at the zoo sells fun toys and apparel as remembrances. Frequent visitors should consider purchasing an annual membership which runs about $65. If you can bear the cold, winter is a good time to drop in at the zoo; crowds are sparse, animals are active, and seasonal events are regularly held. Also, don't forget to visit the Reptile House, which is located a short walk from the main zoo grounds.

Location and Directions: In Druid Hill Park, in West Baltimore. From downtown, take Interstate 83 north. Take Exit 7, Druid Hill Lake Drive, west, and follow directions to the zoo.

Hours and Admission: Daily year-round from 10 a.m. to 4 p.m., with extended hours from May through October. Closed on Thanksgiving, Christmas, and one Friday in June for the Zoomerang fundraising gala. Admission is $10 for ages 12-64, $8 for ages 65 and up, and $6 for children 2-11. Children under 2 are free. There is a $1 charge to enter the Reptile House, located in Druid Hill Park outside the zoo grounds. On the first Thursday of every month, children under 12 are admitted free with a paying adult from 10 a.m. to noon. Zoo parking is free.

Website and Phone: www.baltimorezoo.org; (410) 396-7102.

Catoctin Wildlife Preserve and Zoo

Catoctin Zoo, located at the foot of the Catoctin Mountains, near Thurmont, began as a somewhat kitschy roadside attraction in the 1960s, but has since matured into a full-fledged and well-maintained zoo. The grounds are peaceful and pretty, and the 35 acres of exhibits and walkways are well landscaped. The zoo makes for a worthwhile day-trip from Baltimore.

Catoctin Zoo offers the usual assortment of species ranging from the domesticated to the exotic. The lions, monkeys, tigers, and bears are well represented, as are more unusual species like lemurs, marmosets, and tamarins. Tank, a burly, 600-pound Aldabra tortoise, calls this zoo home. Catoctin Zoo prides itself on providing a rather intimate zoo-going experience for its visitors. It offers "encounters," where guests can actually handle certain species (in a safe and controlled environment), and considers education a central focus of its mission. Its Meet the Keeper series allows guests to interact with the animals' caretakers, and get further insight into the various species. Other hands-on activities such as camel rides are offered in the summer.

The Jungle Nights program allows groups of children to sleep overnight at the zoo and have an added level of interaction with the animals after the gates close. Its Family Zoo-fari Sleepover allows families to do the same, and includes a twilight zoo tour, campfire, and live music. Certain Wednesdays in summer are dubbed Wild Wednesdays, when kids go beyond being just visitors, and actually get involved in the zoo's operations. They learn animal care, what the critters eat, and how zoo exhibits are designed. They also get a needed lesson in the conservation of endangered species. Catoctin Zoo is a great and unusual place to host a birthday party.

A visit to Catoctin Zoo can be followed up with a trip to the Cozy Inn, in Thurmont, which offers a reputable buffet. Catoctin Mountain Park and Cunningham Falls State Park, both of which feature lots of hiking trails, fishing, and other recreational opportunities, are located nearby.

Location and Directions: At 13019 Catoctin Furnace Road, just south of Thurmont. From Baltimore, take Interstate 70 west. In Frederick, take Route 15 north and continue for about 13 miles. The zoo is visible from Route 15 to the right, across from the Manor Area of Cunningham Falls State Park. You will have to take a cut-off road to get to Catoctin Furnace Road.

Hours and Admission: In March, hours are daily from 10 a.m. to 4 p.m.; in April, daily from 10 a.m. to 5 p.m.; in May, daily from 9 a.m. to 5 p.m.; from Memorial Day to Labor Day, daily from 9 a.m. to 6 p.m.; in September daily from 9 a.m. to 5 p.m.; and in October, daily from 10 a.m. to 5 p.m. Admission is $9.95 plus tax for adults 13-59, $7.95 plus tax for seniors 60 and up, and $5.95 plus tax for children 2-11. Children under 2 are free. Season passes are available with costs ranging from $17 to $21.

Website and Phone: www.cwpzoo.com; (301) 271-3180.

Plumpton Park Zoo

Plumpton Park is a low-key zoo located in a rural setting, in northern Cecil County, near Rising Sun. It succeeds in creating a small-town, neighborly feel, while offering a nice selection of exotic and unusual species. For instance, not far from a pen full of cute bunnies is a cage harboring a regal Siberian tiger. And it's not every day you get to see the family cat prowling around in a cage amidst a herd of white fallow deer. The zoo has giraffes, kangaroos, various types of monkeys, and lots of unusual birds and smaller mammals. Seeing zebra, camels, and bison roam around an eastern deciduous forest landscape, totally out of their element, takes you by surprise.

Kids will particularly enjoy the Reptile House with its lineup of snakes, skinks, caimans, tortoises the size of sofa cushions, and even a few tropical birds. The aggressive and funky-looking bearded dragon freaked me out a bit. A nice side-touch is the squadron of peacocks that patrol the zoo grounds, occasionally opening up their resplendent and geometrically pleasing tail feathers for passers-by.

Plumpton Park Zoo is built around an historical mill that dates to 1711, and is now used as administrative offices. Lots of hand-washing stations are spread about, and there is a modest concession stand and store. A large picnic area with playground is usually packed with kids, though many favor playing in the nearby stream. The zoo offers an adopt-an-animal program that may interest some families.

▲ Resplendent symmetry at the Plumpton Park Zoo

Location and Directions: At 1416 Telegraph Road, in Rising Sun. From Baltimore, take Interstate 95 north. Take Exit 100, Route 272, north. At the second traffic light, turn left onto Route 273. The zoo is one mile on the left.

Hours and Admission: From March 1 to September 30, hours are daily from 10 a.m. to 5 p.m., with last admittance at 4 p.m. From October 1 to February 28, hours are daily from 10 a.m. to 4 p.m. (weather permitting); closed Tuesdays and Wednesdays. The zoo is also closed on Thanksgiving and Christmas. Admission is $3.50 for kids 3-12, $6.75 for teenagers and adults 13-59, and $5.75 for seniors 60 or over. Kids under 2 are free. Parking is free.

Website and Phone: www.plumptonparkzoo.org; (410) 658-6850.

▲ Another curious face at the Plumpton Park Zoo

Corrections

Things change. Restaurants open and close. Parks get new playgrounds and museums shut their doors. Inaccuracies creep into literature. So that future editions of *Baltimore with Children* are as accurate as possible, please send any corrections for this edition to:

Camino Books, Inc.
P.O. Box 59026
Philadelphia, PA 19102
camino@caminobooks.com

Or e-mail the author directly at gramzili@bcpl.net

About the Author

Mike Strzelecki is a technical writer by trade, a travel writer by avocation, a husband to Kelly, and an exhausted father of two hyperkinetic kids: Zi Li (6) and Graham (4). He's author of *Urban Hikes in and around Baltimore* and a contributor to *Running through the Wall: Personal Encounters with the Ultramarathon*. Other publication credits include *The* [(Baltimore)] *Sun*, *Baltimore's Child*, *Blue Ridge Country*, *Running Times*, *Pennsylvania*, *Central PA*, and *Trail Runner*. He currently writes the "Focus on Fathers" column in *Baltimore's Child* magazine. When the kids aren't looking, he likes to sneak off and skateboard, surf, or hike. He resides in Catonsville, Maryland.

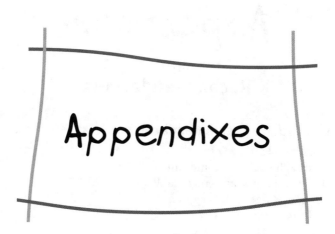

Appendixes

Appendix A

Expert Recommendations

Zi Li's Top 15 Recommendations

1. Larriland Farm
2. Biking the Baltimore and Annapolis Trail
3. Renting a canoe at Centennial Park
4. Oregon Ridge Park Playground
5. Baltimore Museum of Art
6. Oregon Ridge Nature Center
7. Baltimore Zoo
8. Federal Hill Park
9. Arundel Mills
10. Lighted boat parade
11. National Aquarium in Baltimore
12. Fort McHenry National Monument
13. Camping at Owens Creek Campground
14. Hiking at Patuxent Wildlife Research Center
15. Cascade Lake

Graham's Top 15 Recommendations

1. Train gardens
2. Patapsco Valley State Park—Tire Park
3. Fire Museum of Maryland
4. College Park Aviation Museum
5. B&O Railroad Museum
6. Bowie Baysox game
7. Kinder Farm Park
8. Thomas A. Dixon Aircraft Observation Area
9. Spicy Skatepark
10. Carousel at Inner Harbor
11. Miracle on 34th Street
12. Strasburg Rail Road
13. Light Rail
14. Red Caboose Motel
15. Thorn Run Inn

Appendix B

Activities with Birthday Party Facilities

American Visionary Art Museum
Arundel Mills (Crayola Store and Muvico theater)

B&O Railroad Museum
Babe Ruth Birthplace and Museum
Baltimore Museum of Industry
Baltimore Zoo
Bear Branch Nature Center
Bowie Baysox

Catoctin Wildlife Preserve and Zoo
Chuck E. Cheese's
Clark's Elioak Farm
College Park Aviation Museum

Earth Treks Climbing Center
ESPN Zone
ExploraWorld

Frederick Keys

Hard Rock Café

National Aquarium in Baltimore
Northwest Ice Rink

Piney Run Park (pontoon boat)
Port Discovery

Shadowland Laser Adventure Center
Sharp's at Waterford Farm
Sports
Stewartstown Railroad

Appendix C
Free Activities

Anita C. Leight Estuary Center
Annapolis historical walk
Anne Arundel County Public Library
Arundel Mills

Baltimore and Annapolis Trail
Baltimore County Public Library
Barnes & Noble
Bear Branch Nature Center
Benjamin Banneker Historical Park and Museum
BWI Observation Gallery
BWI Trail

Canton Waterfront Park
Carrie Murray Nature Center
Carroll County Public Library
Catoctin Mountain Park
Cecil County Public Library
Centennial Park
Chesapeake and Ohio Canal Towpath
Columbia trail system
Conowingo Hydroelectric Plant Tour
Cromwell Valley Park
Cylburn Arboretum

Druid Hill Park

Eden Mill Nature Center
Ellicott City #9 Trolley Trail
Ellicott City historical walk
Enoch Pratt Free Library

Federal Hill Park
Fort McHenry National Monument grounds

Frederick County Public Libraries
Frederick historical walk
General Motors Baltimore Assembly Plant Tour
Gunpowder Falls State Park— Falls Road
Gunpowder Falls State Park— Hereford Area
Gwynns Falls Trail

Hannah More Park
Harford County Public Library
Howard County Library

Irvine Natural Science Center

Ken Zo's Yogi Magic Mart

Lake Montebello
Lake Waterford Park
Leakin Park
Lexington Market
Light Street Pavilion
Lighted boat parade
Loch Raven Reservoir
Lyn Stacie Getz Creative Playground

Marshy Point Nature Center
Miracle on 34th Street
Mt. Vernon historical walk

National Postal Museum
National Wildlife Visitor Center
Northern Central Railroad Trail and York County Heritage Trail

Oregon Ridge Nature Center
Oregon Ridge Park

Appendix D
Rainy Day Outings

American Visionary Art Museum
Anita C. Leight Estuary Center
Anne Arundel County Public Library
Arundel Mills
Ashland Café

B&O Railroad Museum
Babe Ruth Birthplace and Museum
Baltimore Blast
Baltimore Children's Theatre
Baltimore County Public Library
Baltimore Museum of Art
Baltimore Museum of Industry
Baltimore Public Works Museum
Barnes & Noble
Bear Branch Nature Center
Benjamin Banneker Historical Park and Museum
BWI Observation Gallery

Café Hon
Carrie Murray Nature Center
Carroll County Public Library
Cecil County Public Library
Chuck E. Cheese's
College Park Aviation Museum
Conowingo Hydroelectric Plant Tour
Crab houses
Crystal Grottoes Caverns

Earth Treks Climbing Center
Eden Mill Nature Center

Enoch Pratt Free Library
ESPN Zone
ExploraWorld

Fire Museum of Maryland
Frederick County Public Libraries
Friendly Farm Restaurant

General Motors Baltimore Assembly Plant Tour
Great Blacks in Wax Museum

Hard Rock Café
Harford County Public Library
Howard County Library

Irvine Natural Science Center

Ken Zo's Yogi Magic Mart

Lexington Market
Light Street Pavilion

Marshy Point Nature Center
Maryland Science Center
Matthew's Pizza

National Aquarium in Baltimore
National Postal Museum
National Wildlife Visitor Center
Northwest Ice Rink

Oregon Ridge Nature Center

Papermoon Diner
Piney Run Nature Center
Port Discovery

Rainforest Café
Red Caboose Motel

Appendix E
Activities for School Groups

American Visionary Art Museum

Anita C. Leight Estuary Center

Antietam National Battlefield

B&O Railroad Museum

Babe Ruth Birthplace and Museum

Baltimore Maritime Museum

Baltimore Museum of Art

Baltimore Museum of Industry

Baltimore Public Works Museum

Baltimore Zoo

Baughers

Bear Branch Nature Center

Benjamin Banneker Historical Park and Museum

Blackwater National Wildlife Refuge

BWI Observation Gallery

C&O Canal National Historical Park

Carrie Murray Nature Center

Catoctin Wildlife Preserve and Zoo

Clark's Elioak Farm

College Park Aviation Museum

Conowingo Hydroelectric Plant Tour

Cromwell Valley Park

Crystal Grottoes Caverns

Cylburn Arboretum

Eden Mill Nature Center

Fire Museum of Maryland

Fort McHenry National Monument

General Motors Baltimore Assembly Plant Tour

Great Blacks in Wax Museum

Horizon Organic Farm and Education Center

Irvine Natural Science Center

Kinder Farm Park

Larriland Farm

Marshy Point Nature Center

Maryland Science Center

Mason Neck Peninsula

National Aquarium in Baltimore

National Postal Museum

National Wildlife Visitor Center

Oregon Ridge Nature Center

Oregon Ridge Park

Piney Run Nature Center

Piney Run Park

Plumpton Park Zoo

Port Discovery

Sharp's at Waterford Farm

Sideling Hill Road Cut

Smithsonian's National Museum of Natural History

Susquehanna State Park

Thorn Run Inn

Top of the World Observation
    Level and Museum

U.S. Naval Observatory

U.S.S. *Constellation*

Walters Art Museum

Watkins Regional Park

Weber's Farm

Appendix F
Activities Grouped by County

Allegany County
Western Maryland Scenic
    Railroad

Anne Arundel County
Annapolis historical walk
Anne Arundel County Public
    Library
Arundel Mills
Baltimore and Annapolis Trail
BWI Observation Gallery
BWI Trail
Chesapeake Children's Museum
Downs Memorial Park
Horizon Organic Farm and
    Education Center
Kinder Farm Park
Lake Waterford Park
Light Rail
MARC trains
National Cryptologic Museum
Quiet Waters Park
Riviera Beach Volunteer Fire
    Department train garden
Sandy Point State Park
Thomas A. Dixon Aircraft
    Observation Area
U.S. Naval Academy
U.S. Naval Academy Museum
Wincopin Trail and Quarry
    Trail

Baltimore City
American Visionary Art
    Museum
B&O Railroad Museum
Babe Ruth Birthplace and
    Museum
Baltimore American Indian
    Center
Baltimore Bayhawks
Baltimore Blast
Baltimore Children's Theatre
Baltimore Civil War Museum
Baltimore Maritime Museum
Baltimore Museum of Art
Baltimore Museum of Industry
Baltimore on Ice Skating Rink
Baltimore Orioles
Baltimore Public Works
    Museum
Baltimore Ravens
Baltimore Rowing Club
Baltimore Streetcar Museum
Baltimore Zoo
Barnes & Noble
Café Hon
Canton Waterfront Park
Carrie Murray Nature Center
Cylburn Arboretum
Druid Hill Park
Ed Kane's Water Taxis
Engine House No. 45 train
    garden
Enoch Pratt Free Library
ESPN Zone
Federal Hill Park
Fort McHenry National
    Monument
General Motors Assembly
    Plant Tour
Great Blacks in Wax Museum
Gwynns Falls Trail

Gwynns Falls/Leakin Park
Hard Rock Café
HiFlyer
Inner Harbor carousel
Inner Harbor paddle boats
Jewish Museum of Maryland
Ken Zo's Yogi Magic Mart
Lake Montebello
Lexington Market
Light Rail
Light Street Pavilion
Lighted boat parade
MARC trains
Maryland Historical Society
Maryland Science Center
Matthew's Pizza
Miracle on 34th Street
Mt. Vernon historical walk
Mt. Vernon Museum of
    Incandescent Lighting
National Aquarium in
    Baltimore
National Museum of Dentistry
Northwest Ice Rink
Papermoon Diner
Patterson Park
Port Discovery
Senator Theatre
Sherwood Gardens
Snoasis
Spoons Coffeehouse and
    Roastery
Star-Spangled Banner Flag
    House
Steam Trains at Leakin Park
Top of the World Observation
    Level and Museum
U.S. Lacrosse Museum and
    National Hall of Fame
U.S.S. *Constellation*
Vaccaros
Walters Art Museum
War Memorial

Washington Monument
    lighting

Baltimore County

All Timber Hill Farm
Arbutus Volunteer Fire
    Company train garden
Ashland Café
Baltimore County Public
    Library
Beaver Dam Swimming Club
Bengies Drive-In Theatre
Benjamin Banneker Historical
    Park and Museum
Cromwell Valley Park
Ellicott City #9 Trolley Trail
Elliott's Ventura Farm
Fire Museum of Maryland
Freezer's Farm
Friendly Farm Restaurant
Frostee Tree Farm
Glenn L. Martin Aviation
    Museum
Green Hill Farm
Grist Mill Trail
Gunpowder Falls State Park—
    Falls Road
Gunpowder Falls State Park—
    Hammerman Area
Gunpowder Falls State Park—
    Hereford Area
Gunpowder Falls tubing
Hannah More Park
Hart-Miller Island State Park
Irvine Natural Science Center
Ladew Topiary Gardens
Light Rail
Loch Raven Fishing Center
Loch Raven Reservoir
Long Green Volunteer Fire
    Department train garden
MARC trains
Marshy Point Nature Center

Applewood Farm
Conowingo Hydroelectric
    Plant Tour
Deer Creek Valley Tree Farm
Eden Mill Nature Center
Environmental Evergreens
    Tree Farm
Harford County Public Library
Havre de Grace Decoy
    Museum
Lyn Stacie Getz Creative
    Playground
MARC trains
Ripken Museum
Rocks State Park
Sewell's Farm
Silver Meadow Farm
Susquehanna State Park
Thomas Tree Farm
U.S. Army Ordnance Museum

Howard County

B&O Railroad Station Museum
Baltimore Children's Theatre
Centennial Lake
Centennial Park
Clark's Elioak Farm
Columbia trail system
Earth Treks Climbing Center
Ellicott City Fire Department
    No. 2 train garden
Ellicott City historical walk
ExploraWorld
Greenway Farms
Howard County Library
Larriland Farm
MARC trains
Patapsco Valley State Park—
    Hollofield Area
Shadowland Laser Adventure
    Center
Sharp's at Waterford Farm
Sorrento's Main Street Station
Symphony of Lights

TLV Farm
Yoga Center of Columbia

Lancaster County, Pennsylvania

Red Caboose Motel
Strasburg Rail Road

Montgomery County

C&O Canal National Historical
    Park

Northumberland County, Pennsylvania

Knoebels Amusement Resort

Prince George's County

Bowie Baysox
College Park Aviation Museum
National Wildlife Visitor
    Center
Patuxent Wildlife Research
    Center
Watkins Regional Park

Sussex County, Delaware

Lewes and Cape Henlopen
    State Park

Washington County

Antietam National Battlefield
Crystal Grottoes Caverns
Greenbrier State Park
Maple Tree Campground
Sideling Hill Road Cut

Worcester County

Assateague Island National
    Seashore

York County, Pennsylvania

Stewartstown Railroad

Index